THE SPIRIT AND THE FLESH:

Sex in Utopian Communities

by **Robert H. Lauer**
and **Jeanette C. Lauer**

The Scarecrow Press, Inc.
Metuchen, N.J., & London 1983

Library of Congress Cataloging in Publication Data

Lauer, Robert H.
   The spirit and the flesh.

   Includes index.
   1. Sex customs.   2.   Utopias.   I. Lauer, Jeanette C.
II. Title
HQ16. L38   1983   306. 7   83-7444
ISBN 0-8108-1635-0

Copyright © 1983 by Robert H. Lauer and Jeanette C. Lauer

Manufactured in the United States of America

To Jon, Julie, Jeff, and Erica

CONTENTS

v

PREFACE

Throughout their history, many Americans have been dissatisfied with existing social arrangements, including those for sexual relations, and have striven either to alter them or to establish a society with different and, to them, better arrangements. The utopian communities of the 19th and 20th centuries fall into the latter category. In this book, we examine these sexual arrangements in order to answer a number of questions. First, what were the various arrangements that the different groups considered ideal? Second, how were these varied arrangements maintained-- what kinds of ideology and other mechanisms of social control sustained them? Third, what were the experiences of the people in the different communities--to what extent were the various experiences satisfying? And finally, what do the experiences of the utopians teach us about the nature of sexuality?

To answer these questions we have gathered material from the libraries of universities and state historical societies throughout the nation. We have also used the collections at the Library of Congress. Both primary and secondary materials were useful, but a substantial part of our evidence comes from published and unpublished primary materials produced by members of the various groups.

In the course of the research, we discovered once again that librarians are a special breed. Time and again, librarians went out of their way to be helpful, in many cases identifying communities in their areas whose existence was unknown to us. We are grateful to the librarians at the following institutions: the Library of Congress; Baylor University; Southern Methodist University (DeGolyer Library); University of Texas; University of Missouri; University of Iowa; University of Nebraska at Omaha; University of Wisconsin; University of Minnesota; Ohio State University; University of Indiana (Lilly Library); University of Illinois; Syracuse University; University of Michigan; Temple University; University of California at San Diego, Riverside, Los Angeles, and Berkeley; University of Southern California; University of Nevada at Reno; University of Utah; and the state historical societies of Missouri, Illinois, Ohio, Indiana, Iowa, Wisconsin, Minnesota, Western Reserve, Michigan, Pennsylvania, New York, New Mexico, California, Nevada, Colorado, and Kansas. We owe a special debt of gratitude to Joyce Giardina of the interlibrary loan department of Southern Illinois University at Edwardsville. She did yeoman's service for us. Finally, we are grateful to the National Endowment for the Humanities for a summer stipend that enabled us to complete the research.

Robert H. Lauer
Jeanette C. Lauer

Part I

Human Sexuality

From the murky beginnings of humankind to the present age of scientific wonders, people have struggled to better their lives and their societies. Some have dreamed of a golden future and have set down their dreams in utopian novels. Others have set about to build the good life in small communities. Both the dreamers and the builders reflect the common aspiration of people for a life that surpasses in quality their present existence.

Whether the utopian venture is literary or real, there are certain questions that must be answered. Every society, including the utopians, confronts certain problems, certain tasks, certain arrangements that must be worked out. For example, how shall we survive economically? What kind of education must be provided for our children? Who shall be admitted, and under what circumstances shall people be admitted? How will we maintain order? What will relationships between males and females be like and what roles will each play? What kind of a family structure will we have? What kind of rules will we have about sexual relationships?

This book is concerned with the last question. All utopians have addressed the crucial question of the kind of sexual arrangements necessary for an ideal society. If a society is to survive, and if it is to achieve its goal of a more fulfilling life for all members, the sexual question can no more be ignored than can the question of economics. In other words, it is not only the utopians, but all human societies that must address the question of sexual arrangements. And all have. In this first section, therefore, we will pave the way for a fuller understanding of the utopian effort--as well as for our interpretation of the meaning of that effort--by providing an overview of the practice and theory of sexuality, including cross-cultural and historical variations.

1. SEX IN PRACTICE AND THEORY

According to an old story, one of the shortest lectures on sex ever given was that of an after-dinner speaker who rose and said: "Ladies and gentlemen. Sex. It gives me great pleasure." The speaker then sat down. His experience with sex has undoubtedly been shared by many people. But if some find sex pleasurable, others have found it painful in some sense. As an Englishman once put it: "I could be content that we might procreate like trees, without conjunction, or that there were any way to perpetuate the world without this trivial and vulgar way of union." [1]

In this chapter, we will see many examples of diverse attitudes and behavior in the area of sexual relationships. We will see variety both over time and across different societies. We will also look at the way in which people have tried to understand and explain human sexuality. Our coverage of these materials is necessarily brief, but it is important for understanding and interpreting the utopian experience.

SEX IN CROSS-CULTURAL PERSPECTIVE

Both the meaning of sex and the pattern of sexual behavior change as we move from one society to another. Our purpose here is not to give an exhaustive account of the variations, but to illustrate the diversity by looking at a few of the important aspects of human sexuality.

Sex As Good and Pleasurable

Is sex good? Is it pleasurable? Most Americans would undoubtedly say "yes" to the two questions, especially if we put them in the context of marriage. But not all people regard sex as good and pleasurable, even within the confines of marriage. Margaret Mead reported that the Manus,

3

an island people in the South Pacific, have little pleasure in sexual intercourse. Among them, sexual relations seem to be fraught with hostility. The women typically resist sex. The men seem to express their anger in sexual relationships, and complain of women who reject them but who also insist on having sex to prove that the men have not been unfaithful. Things have changed among the Manus since the earlier part of the century, but sex "is still associated with anger, with rights, with expression of or response to various sorts of resistance, and love is defined as a relationship in which sex can be ignored in favour of affection." [2]

If the Manus find little pleasure in sex because of the hostility and competition that surrounds the act, the people of Inis Beag seem to have little pleasure in sex because of their extremely negative views about it. Inis Beag is an Irish island community, and is, according to John Messenger, "one of the most sexually naïve of the world's societies." [3] Sex is never discussed around children; many parents never have anything to say to their children on the subject. The onset of menstruation is frequently a traumatic experience because there is no explanation for it. Men are considered more sexually motivated than women, though even the men believe that intercourse diminishes their vigor (and therefore they may not have sexual relations on the night before a particularly hard day's work). Marriage occurs relatively late (age 36 for males and 25 for females, on the average). Some people remain celibate. Those who marry tend to have large families. But they do not develop what Americans would call a meaningful sexual relationship. There is little foreplay in sex, and the underclothes are not removed during the act. The female orgasm seems to be unknown, "or at least doubted, or considered a deviant response." [4]

The people of Inis Beag do not even have a tradition of "dirty" jokes. Sexual repression is rife, and is maintained by a combination of religious beliefs and gossip about anyone who deviates. Sex may yield some pleasure for some people, but it is an illicit pleasure, a pleasure that reflects the baser nature of people.

Sex As Basic and Powerful

Most people, even those not influenced by Freudian ideas, take it for granted that sex is a basic and powerful part of human life. And, among most people, a good deal of energy is expended in either sexual expression or sexual repression. The Grand Valley Dani of Indonesia are an exception to the general experience. They force us to reconsider the questions of the fundamental nature of sexuality and of the overwhelming power of the sex drive.

Among other things, the Grand Valley Dani do not begin to have sexual relations until a particular ceremony is held, a ceremony which occurs two years after the couple has been married and living together. And the weddings take place only at a major feast which is held every four to six years. Once sexual relations begin, they seem to occur only barely enough to maintain the population at a stable level. After the birth of a child, there is a four- to six-year period of abstinence. This period of abstinence seems to be observed by nearly all of the people. There is very little extramarital sex, and no system of social control seems necessary to enforce the abstinence. Furthermore, according to Karl Heider, the anthropologist who studied the Dani, there is no evidence of masturbation, homosexuality, or bestiality among the people. Yet "no one shows any signs of unhappiness or stress during the period of abstinence." [5]

Heider considered a variety of explanations for the exceptionally low level of sexual activity among the Dani. Are there hormonal or dietary deficiencies? Or do the people channel their sexual energies into creative activities in accord with the Freudian principle of sublimation? The answer to both questions is "no." The Dani are a healthy people with no evidence of physical deficiencies. But they also lack interest in creative activities like art. Furthermore, they are generally a "low-energy" people in the sense that they do not show strong emotions or much in the way of intellectual interests. They even seem incapable of developing strong hatred for an enemy. They live comfortably. They are a pragmatic people. They do what is necessary to maintain their comfort and their health. Beyond that, they have little interest in anything that involves intense emotions.

The Frequency of Sex

How often do people desire sex? How often are sexual relationships possible? The Dani represent the extreme of indifference. Surveys of Americans indicate that the average couple has intercourse two or three times per week during their twenties; the frequency declines to about once a week for those over 45 years of age. [6] Studies of people in other societies show that, apart from the first weeks of marriage, marital intercourse averages from two to five times per week. [7]

Do such studies suggest certain inherent limitations to human sexual desire? There may be such limitations, but we do not yet know what they are. When a group of Bala men from the Congo were asked how often they had had intercourse during the previous 24 hours, a question repeated for ten successive days, the average even for those in their fifties and sixties was more than once per day. [8]

Another group with a high rate of sexual activity is the Mangaians of the South Pacific. Sex is a principal concern for the Mangaians. Virtually all of them have extensive sexual experience prior to marriage. This sexual experience is not based on affection. On the contrary, each individual is likely to have a considerable variety of sexual partners. If affection does occur, it is the result of the sexual relationship rather than the basis for such a relationship.

Mangaians, incidentally, lay great emphasis on the pleasure of sex. Males take pride in helping females reach multiple orgasms. Both unmarried and married men say that the most important facet of sex is to give pleasure to the female; in fact, a substantial part of the male pleasure in intercourse is making the experience pleasurable for the female. How often can males do this? According to the Mangaians themselves, an 18-year-old male will, on the average, have three orgasms per night each night of the week. A 28-year-old male will average two orgasms per night from five to six times per week. And a 48-year-old male will have one orgasm per night from two to three times per week. [9]

There is one other aspect of Mangaian sexuality that we should note in terms of what it has to say about the frequency of sexual desire and relationships. The Mangaian male may "pay a biological penalty" for his sexual activity, for he is "probably far more subject to impotency and sterility in later years than is the American male." [10] Obviously, impotence would be harder for the Mangaian than for some others to accept because of the centrality of vigorous sexual activity in Mangaian culture.

The Techniques of Sex

Americans have a great many manuals available that provide information on every conceivable technique of sex. There is little, if anything, that is new in the manuals. Throughout human history, people have experimented with all kinds of sexual techniques. But different people tend to develop preferred techniques, which then become the typical pattern in a society. As a result, what is defined as erotic in one society may be considered asexual in another society. Or what is defined as good and pleasurable in one society may be considered evil and undesirable in another society.

Consider, for example, the practice of kissing on the mouth. The practice is universal in Western society, but is missing in many non-Western groups. The Mangaians, who engage in quite a variety of different techniques, did not regard kissing on the mouth as an erotic activity prior to Western influence on the island. Even after the younger people began to kiss as part of their erotic activity, the older Mangaians did not find the practice appealing.

Americans learn from their sex manuals that the period of foreplay is a crucial part of the overall sexual experience. In particular, a female is likely to remain unsatisfied and perhaps unable to reach orgasm if the male proceeds too quickly and ignores the foreplay. In other societies, people have a variety of notions about the importance of foreplay, some of which contradict the American advice and some of which carry it to an extreme. In their survey of nearly 200 different societies, Ford and Beach note some of the variations in the practice of foreplay:

> There are several societies in our sample in which couples indulge in a minimum of sexual foreplay. The general pattern among the Lepcha, for example, is for a man and woman to proceed immediately to copulation, although the man may fondle the woman's breasts just prior to intromission. Similarly, the Kwoma engage in very few preliminaries and almost no embracing occurs before coitus. On Popape, by way of contrast, precopulatory stimulation is quite extended, and hours may be consumed in working up to actual intercourse. [11]

Finally, we may illustrate the diversity in techniques by noting that the typical position for intercourse varies from one society to another. The preferred American pattern involves the woman lying on her back with the man lying above her and facing her. In other societies, the typical position is a side-by-side or a sitting position, or one in which the man squats and draws the woman toward him until her legs rest on his hips or his elbows. The Trobriand Islanders use the latter technique and consider the Western pattern to be unpractical and ineffective. They speak with some contempt about the so-called "missionary" position: "The man overlies heavily the woman; he presses her heavily downwards, she cannot respond." [12] They believe the squatting position to be far superior because the man has considerable freedom of movement and the woman is not hampered in her movements of response. When the woman is ready for orgasm, the man "presses his face to the woman's, embraces her body and raises it towards him, she putting her arms round him at the same time and, as a rule, digging her nails into his skin." [13] The technique, the natives say, requires more time and energy than white men give to sex but is far more effective and satisfying.

Male vs. Female Sexuality

The resurgence of the women's movement in the late 1960s spawned a wealth of research and writing about the nature of men and women, including male and female sexuality. A number of women reacted angrily to the Freudian interpretation (to be discussed in the last section of this chapter) and its manifestation in the popular consciousness. The work of Masters and Johnson supported the rejection of certain Freudian notions. The work of anthropologists could also be used for combatting some of Freud's erroneous notions.

For example, one difference that Freud postulated with respect to male vs. female sexuality was the greater passivity of the female. Males are by nature, he argued, more aggressive in sexual matters. But this is not true in all societies. There are a number in which the female is more sexually aggressive than the male:

> ... among the Cubeo of northwest Amazonia, the men complain that the women are too ardent. Among the upper-class Tuareg, the female courtiers and troubadours are the sexual aggressors and the males the guardians of decorum. An upper-

class Tuareg warrior would blush deeply in the
love court of the lady troubadours if his veil
slipped down (for men wear the veils here, not
women). [14]

The Mangaians also despise passivity in the female;
both males and females expect themselves and their partners
to be very active during intercourse: "The principal require-
ment of the female (and the reason that the Mangaian male
dislikes coitus with a European female) is that the woman
'must move'--there must be plenty of pelvic action to satisfy her lover." [15] Even Americans began to have different
ideas about any innate female passivity in the 1970s when
reports appeared in the news media about male impotence
that resulted from the sexual aggressiveness of females.

There are, of course, societies where the females
are passive and seldom experience orgasm--Inis Beag is
one example. But when we look at the whole range of human societies, we cannot conclude that there are fundamental differences, biologically based differences, between male
and female sexuality.

Deviant vs. Normal Sex

What is deviant and what is normal in the realm of
sexual behavior? Again, one society's deviance is another
society's norm. Julia Brown studied over 100 preindustrial
societies and found considerable differences in the kinds of
sexual behavior tolerated and the kinds punished in some
way. [16] All of those societies for which she had data
punished incest and the abduction of a married woman. But
for other kinds of sexual behavior the norms varied. Ninety-
five percent of the societies punished people for having relations during the postpartum period. Eighty-five percent
imposed punishment for the seduction by one man of another
man's fiancée. Sixty-seven percent punished sex during
pregnancy. Forty-four percent punished the woman and 41
percent punished the man for having premarital relations.
And 10 percent had punishment for intercourse with one's
betrothed.

A rather striking illustration of cross-cultural differences is provided by child sexuality among the Pilagá Indians
of South America. In spite of Freud's writings about infant
sexuality, Americans have preferred to think of childhood as

a time of "innocence." The views of the Pilagá Indians are virtually the reverse of ours: "While we demand and achieve children who are relatively celibate, and adults who are less so, the Pilagá expect children to be exuberantly sexual and expect that adults will be much more restrained." [17] Sexual experiences among American children tend to be covert; among the Indian children, they are open and frequent, and include both homosexual and heterosexual experiences. Their heterosexual play includes various sexual games, handling one's own or a playmate's genitals, and attempts at intercourse. In other words, the children do precisely the kinds of things for which American children would be reprimanded. Among the Pilagá, such behavior is normal.

Sexual Norms in Perspective

One might conclude from the cross-cultural studies that "anything goes" in the realm of sexual behavior, that no society should impose sanctions for any kind of sexual behavior since that behavior is likely to be approved somewhere else. Such a conclusion would not be correct. It is true that, apart from incest, virtually any kind of sexual behavior is approved and typical somewhere. But each society also has norms about what is deviant. Every society sets up rules and punishes those who break the rules. Moreover, it is important to have rules. Humans do not function well in a normless situation. Normlessness, as a great many studies tell us, is psychologically stressful as well as socially disruptive and destructive.

On the other hand, there is no particular set of rules that is demanded by the inherent nature of sexuality. As the societies we have discussed illustrate, various kinds of sexual arrangements can work. Indeed, as we shall see in the communitarian groups, anything from celibacy to a kind of group marriage can be successful over a long period of time. Norms are necessary for a viable social order. But no particular sexual norms are inherently more necessary or more appropriate than others.

SEX IN AMERICA

We need to look more closely now at American attitudes and behavior, for the American way has varied considerably over time. As we move from Colonial days to the

19th century and finally into the 20th century, it is almost as if we were looking at totally different peoples.

Sexuality in Colonial America

The Puritans have been wronged. Later generations talked about prudishness and sexual repression as "puritanical." But the Puritans were quite open about sexual matters. And they certainly did not view sex as something innately "dirty" or evil. They did, of course, insist on marriage as the only appropriate context for sexual relations. Those who engaged in relations outside of marriage had sinned; but they were to confess their sin openly in church and, in fact, confessions of fornication were rather common.

Within marriage, sex was a good and desirable form of behavior. If an individual felt "dirtied" by sex, the individual was being tempted by Satan, not led by God. [18] In fact, unless a marriage was consummated by sexual union, it was not valid. The refusal to engage in sexual relations by one of the mates was one of the few reasons a divorce could be granted. As Edmund Morgan has pointed out, the Puritans were "a much earthier lot" than later generations realized. They never regarded marriage as a purely spiritual relationship. Morgan quotes from a wedding sermon of John Cotton, in which the Puritan divine recalled the case of a couple who had agreed to remain together but to live a celibate life. The arrangement, Cotton said, was "an effort of blind zeal, for they are the dictates of a blind mind they follow therein, and not of that Holy Spirit, which saith, It is not good that man should be alone." [19]

In some ways, relationships between the sexes were more open among Americans than they were among Europeans. A French traveler in America in the 1780s was surprised to see a young man and woman holding hands and kissing even though they were not betrothed. He concluded that Americans reached puberty at an early age, were "warm" by nature, had few restraints, and lost "no time in completing the great object, the population of the country. [20]

In general, colonial American men and women both were fairly frank and open about sexual relationships. [21] Sex outside of marriage was not approved, but it was also not uncommon. Benjamin Franklin was probably one of the more amorous of the founding fathers. He openly acknowledged his own sexual exploits in his autobiography. Because of his circumstances and his trade as a printer, he noted, it was some time before he could find a suitable wife.

> In the mean time, that hard-to-be-governed passion of youth hurried me frequently into intrigues with low women that fell in my way, which were attended with some expense and great inconvenience, besides a continual risque to my health by a distemper which of all things I dreaded, though by great good luck I escaped it. [22]

Other founding fathers tended to marry somewhat late also, but they were more conventional than Franklin in their sexual behavior. John Adams pointed out in his autobiography that he was very fond of females from an early age; nevertheless, his children could be sure that they had no illegitimate brothers or sisters. For Adams accepted the moral principles of his parents: "... my natural temperament was always overawed by my Principles and Sense of decorum. " [23] If Adams and Franklin differed in their behavior, they shared an attitude of openness about sexuality that typified 18th-century Americans. They saw nothing inherently evil about sex. On the contrary, they considered sexuality a part of human nature. Sexual relations help people to be fulfilled. As Adams put it, love is a "divine Passion" implanted in us "for the Renovation of the species, and the greatest solace of our Lives, " and meant by God to be "the greatest source of our Bliss. " [24]

Sexuality in 19th-Century America

By the second quarter of the 19th century, a totally different perspective on sexuality from that described above existed in America. In general, sexual matters were characterized by ignorance, prudery, a depreciation of sexuality, and a sense of moral alarm.

Ignorance was evident at both the professional and the popular levels. We shall see a number of examples of professional ignorance when we discuss the way in which sex was depreciated. Perhaps the nadir of popular ignorance was illustrated by a physician, Dr. Joseph Howe, who wrote about one of his male patients. The patient was married at age

25. Both he and his new wife were completely ignorant of sexual matters. Neither had the slightest notion of how to proceed with a sexual relationship. After a few nights of frustration, the man somehow learned that

> the male organ should be introduced into the "water passage" of the female. The gentleman essayed the experiment on several different occasions without success, and was then compelled to the ludicrous necessity of searching for the place with a candle. Even then it was some days before he succeeded in effecting a natural intercourse, and that too after other consultations with friends.... [25]

Dr. Howe went on to note that such ignorance was more common among women than men, but that there were a surprising number of men who were as ignorant as his patient.

Such ignorance is less surprising when one considers the amount of prudery among 19th-century Americans. The prudery extended to art, literature, and language as well as to behavior. Many historians have quoted or referred to Captain Marryat, the British writer who visited America in the early part of the 19th century. According to Marryat, some American women were embarrassed or offended by the use of the word "leg" in mixed company; "limb" was the proper word. He also reported seeing a piano at a school that had small trousers with frills on each of its "limbs." The latter incident may have been a practical joke played on Marryat. Nevertheless, the extent of prudery in America was remarkable.

Nineteenth-century prudery resulted in a minimal acknowledgement of the existence of sexual love. Anything that might suggest such love or that might generate any kind of sexual thoughts or feelings could be suppressed. Consider a number of illustrations of this point:

(1) Males and females were required to visit the Philadelphia art gallery in separate groups so that a mixed group would not have to look at a nude statue;

(2) Some nude statues were draped out of deference to female morality;

(3) Books like Mark Twain's The Adventures of

Huckleberry Finn were banned in some libraries because they were considered obscene or immoral;

(4) Nineteenth-century novels typically portray young
men as lacking any strong sexual interest in women;

(5) A book of advice for young women warned "that
certain parts of the body are not to be touched except for purposes of cleanliness, and that the most
dreadful suffering comes from disobeying these com-
mands." [26]

There were also efforts to cleanse the language of
suggestive or erotically stimulating terms. Parts of the
body that were covered by clothes would be avoided in conversation, if possible, and if not would be referred to by
some euphemism. Some women spoke of the "bosom" of
the chicken. Rugoff sums up some of the other changes
that occurred:

Banished were pregnant, virgin, whore, seduce,
rape, castration, and abortion; the names of gar-
ments such as trousers, breeches, shirt, corset,
and women's stockings; and the names of such
animals as ass and cockroach. Syphilis became
the social disease, masturbation the solitary vice,
adultery turned into criminal conversation, and
whores were fallen women.... High on the scale
of affectation was enceinte for pregnant, statutory
offense or criminal assault for rape, house of ill
repute for brothel, linen for shirt, lingerie ... for
women's underclothes, lower extremities for legs,
be confined for give birth and, sickening in their
coyness, unmentionables and inexpressibles for
trousers, breeches, and underdrawers and ...
pants. [27]

This ignorance and prudery flourished in the context
of various beliefs that depreciated and to some extent even
denigrated sex. Three of these beliefs capture the essence
of the dominant 19th-century perspective on sexuality--the
doctrine of female sexuality, the doctrine of spermatic
economy, and the law of frequency, as we label them.
These beliefs, incidentally, are also important for our understanding of the sexual ideologies and practices of the
communitarian societies.

First, the doctrine of female sexuality asserted that women had minimal sexual needs. This doctrine, which was a shift of opinion from past beliefs, became particularly prominent in books written after 1840. [28] Dr. William Acton summed up the doctrine when he said that most women were not "very much troubled with sexual feelings of any kind. What men are habitually, women are only exceptionally." [29] Dr. William Sanger made a study of prostitution and was startled to find that a considerable number of the women he interviewed said that they entered the life voluntarily. In trying to reconcile such findings with his notion of female sexuality, he argued that sexual desire "in the bosoms of most females" remains "in a slumbering state until aroused by some outside influences." The outside influence might be close relationships with males or with other females who have yielded to the desire. Or a state of intoxication might lead to an awakening of the desire. At any rate, "without these or some other equally stimulating cause, the full force of sexual desire is seldom known to a virtuous woman." [30]

To the extent that a virtuous woman did have sexual desire, it was linked up with her maternal instincts. Dr. John Cowan, one of the more popular authors of the 19th century on this subject, noted that there are some women who are strongly passionate, but they are also "often diseased" and are likely to reduce a husband to a state lower than "the brute." There are fewer such women than men, of course. And the normal state is for a woman to have sexual desire when she is ready to conceive:

> The highest enjoyable season at which a healthy woman desires sexual congress is immediately following the cessation of her monthly menses, and this is the season in which the reproductive element is most intensified, and when her whole organism is ready to take on the loving and holy duties of reproduction--the originating and developing of a new life. [31]

Obviously, Dr. Cowan was in error about the fertility cycle as well as about female sexuality.

This lack of strong sexual needs was not to be lamented. Happily for her, the sex manuals agreed, a woman's sexual drive was minimal. They maintained that frequent sex is debilitating to both males and females. We

shall further discuss this notion when we deal below with
the law of frequency.   Here we want to stress the point
that the doctrine of female sexuality was not developed on
a theme of sadness.   There was no mourning of the loss
of pleasure as women's lack of sexual drive was discussed.
On the contrary, the doctrine of female sexuality comple-
mented the male part of the 19th-century perspective--the
doctrine of spermatic economy.

G. J. Barker-Benfield, who coined the term "spermatic economy," points out that the doctrine applied an economic principle to the expenditure of sperm. [32] In essence,
the doctrine said that man's mental and physical energy was
inextricably linked up with his sperm, so that loss of sperm
also meant loss of mental and physical energy.   An ounce
of semen was said to be the equivalent of 40 ounces of
blood.   Every time a man ejaculated, therefore, whether
from masturbation, "wet dreams," or sexual intercourse,
he "lowered his life force and thereby exposed his system
to diseases and premature death." [33]   As Dio Lewis put
it in his manual of advice, a healthy man may discharge
semen occasionally without great loss.   But if that same
man should choose, like many great men in history, to be
celibate, nature knows what to do with those "precious
atoms of blood" that are part of the semen: "She finds use
for them all in building up a keener brain and more vital
and enduring nerves and muscles." [34]

In other words, a man's body was viewed as a
bounded system of energy.   The loss of sperm represented
a drain of energy out of man.   The body could replenish
the loss, but too frequent loss would overtax the body's
capacity and result in both mental and physical problems.

The law of frequency is therefore a logical part of
the doctrines of female sexuality and spermatic economy.
There were two parts to the law--a catalog of the consequences of sexual overindulgence, and a statement of the
frequency of sexual intercourse consistent with good health
and morality.   The consequences of overindulgence included
virtually any known affliction of the mind or body, including
throat diseases, nervous exhaustion, respiratory diseases,
dizziness, loss of memory, invalidism, insanity, dyspepsia,
and ultimately even death.   One physician said that he had
had a number of patients who had indulged in sexual relations
as often as once a day.   The result was invariably "premature decay, and often permanent invalidism." [35]   Dr.

Cowan, after providing a long list of ailments related to overindulgence, summed up the matter for his readers by pointing out that his list was only a partial one:

> for in the abnormal exercise of amativeness, the great drain of the nervous fluid and the loss of semen ... so lowers the life-force as to form the foundation for, and lay open the system to, all manner of contagious, acute and chronic diseases, and in this way--though sexual excesses may not be the immediate cause of sickness and premature death--it in thousands of cases is the remote cause. [36]

Of course, these consequences could be avoided by control of frequency. Unfortunately, there was no consensus on how frequently one could have sexual relations and remain healthy. Some physicians advised people to engage in sex from one to three times a month when young, noting, as one said, that when women reach the age of 45 and men reach the age of 55 the sexual passions "are but rarely awakened and seldom solicitied." [37] Sylvester Graham, for whom the cracker is named, said that a precise rule was impossible. But while one could not say what was appropriate for every individual, one could say, in general, that a "healthy and robust" young man should not exceed once a month, while once a week would surely be mentally and physically debilitating. [38]

Dr. Cowan, as we noted above, suggested that sexual relations should take place immediately after the woman's menstrual period. At that time, hopefully, the woman will conceive. From that time until the woman has menstruated after the weaning of the child that has been conceived, there should be no sex. That would mean at least 21 months, but Dr. Cowan said a three-year period of abstinence would be ideal in order to insure the health of the mother. [39]

Though there was no consensus it is clear that 19th-century advisers on sexual matters were indicating a much lower frequency of sexual congress than previous or subsequent writers. The advice was consistent with the doctrines of female sexuality and spermatic economy. Furthermore, the advice was apparently heeded by a considerable number of couples, for the fertility rate of American women declined dramatically throughout the 19th century in spite of the fact that contraceptives were not readily available. [40]

Not everyone believed or listened to the advisers, of course. There was consequently a sense of moral alarm in many of the writings about sexual matters. Masturbation was not merely an activity that would physically and mentally ruin an individual; it was a "vice" as well. Dr. Cowan noted that in spite of all warnings masturbation was probably as common in his day as it was earlier. Not only would the practice bring physical and mental harm, he argued, but it would also wreak moral havoc on those who indulged. A young man, for example, who masturbates "lays down his nobleness, dignity, honor and manhood, and is no longer bold, resolute, determined, aspiring, dignified, but becomes depreciated, irresolute, undermined, undetermined, tamed, and conscious of his degradation." [41] Other writers warned that masturbation almost inevitably led a young person further down the road of moral degeneracy into other forms of sexual perversion, including homosexuality. [42]

Even overindulgence in marital sex took on moral implications, and a wife with strong sexual needs was viewed as particularly dangerous. Barker-Benfield points out that female castration was practiced in order to deal with the immoral rebellion or sexual promiscuity of women. Any woman who did not fit the stereotype of the dependent, passive, virtuous, and more or less asexual creature, would be viewed by some men as a fit subject for castration, for

> any attempt by women to break out of their circumscription signified to men that such disorderly women wanted to become men. Female castration was designed to take care of such a threat.... An 1893 proponent of female castration claimed that "patients are improved, some of them cured; the moral sense of the patient is elevated ... she becomes tractable, orderly, industrious, and cleanly." Doctors claimed success for castration when it returned woman to her normal role. [43]

The "normal role" included minimal sexual desire. Even those who opposed large-scale castration of women were willing to use the technique when a woman evidenced intense sexual desire.

If we take the 19th-century view to its logical extreme, we would advocate celibacy for everyone. Just short of this extreme, Dr. Cowan advocated sex only for procreation. He argued for the "law of continence," defining a continent man as one who is able to reproduce the species and who, "through a true life and firm will, exercises his reproductive element only at the right seasons, and only for the purpose of reproduction." [44] Dr. Cowan told his readers that one way to achieve continence was for husband and wife to sleep in separate beds, a rather fitting image with which to sum up the 19th-century perspective.

Sexuality in 20th-Century America

The 20th century has been a time of sexual revolution, particularly when we compare American sexuality in this century with that of the 19th. Both professional and popular attitudes have changed dramatically. A sexual "revolution" occurred after World War I. During the 1920s, Americans developed a near obsession with sex. Freud was popularized (and sometimes misinterpreted). Novelists pursued the topic; heroes were no longer portrayed as sexless beings. In Hollywood, the "vamp" appeared in films. Men and women once again talked with each other about sex, and even began to tell each other off-color jokes. Women spoke openly about their sexual desires and needs. Parental control over dating behavior, including the presence of chaperones at dances, became far less restrictive. Premarital sex increased considerably (Kinsey found a significant difference between the amount of premarital sex of women born before 1900 and those born after 1900).

Some observers said that yet another revolution occurred in the 1960s. The "pill" made contraception far easier (since females continued to be held primarily responsible). Motion pictures, novels, and magazines became extremely explicit about sexual behavior. Various people openly advocated what was once called "free love." Premarital sex became ever more common. Movements to legitimate such things as homosexuality gathered momentum. As a national news magazine expressed it: "The U.S. seems to be undergoing a revolution of mores and an erosion of morals that is turning it into what Reich called a 'sex-affirming culture.'" [45]

In the last quarter of the 20th century, Americans view and practice sex in ways that are strikingly different from those of the 19th century. Sexual matters are openly discussed. Women are acknowledged to have sexual desires and needs just as men do. Sex is not evil or debilitating;

on the contrary, it is an important aspect of human fulfillment. Even religious leaders discuss sex in terms of our fulfillment as sexual beings. And physicians and scientists, who furthered the cause of sexual repression in the 19th century, now speak out in behalf of sexual freedom.

Yet, we have not reached utopia. In broadest terms, we have proceeded from a decorous enjoyment to a morbid suppression to an uneasy liberation. We say "uneasy" because many observers agree that Americans have not yet made their peace with themselves as sexual beings. The news magazine noted above concluded its discussion of the sexual revolution of the 1960s by pointing out that the Victorians talked a good deal about love but knew very little about sex. "Perhaps it is time that modern Americans, who know a great deal about sex, once again start talking about love." [46] Similarly, historian Arthur Schlesinger wrote in 1967 that our "Age of Love" has not become an age of fulfillment. The sexual repression of the 19th century may not have brought us happiness, he insists, but neither has the sexual liberation of the 20th century. [47] There is some evidence to support this conclusion. Among other things, a University of Michigan survey of well-being which was first taken in 1957 and repeated in 1976 (a period that included the "second" sexual revolution) reported somewhat more anxiety and pessimism at the latter date. And a 1978 Gallup poll about social values reported that 62% of the respondents would not welcome more acceptance of sexual freedom. Such findings, combined with the proliferation of advice columns on sexual matters and the increase in the number of sex therapists, suggest that Americans have reached an uneasy liberation at best. The search for sexual utopia continues.

Themes and Subthemes

What we have discussed thus far has been the dominant perspective in America at various points in time. But sexual attitudes and behavior vary within a society at a particular time as well as over time. Not all colonials viewed sex as good. Not all Victorians were prudes. And not all 20th-century Americans take a liberated stand on sex. To illustrate the latter point, a study of a small Missouri town around 1940 reported a degree of prudery reminiscent of the 19th century. [48] Most married couples believed it improper to undress totally before each other in the light; some of the people reportedly had never seen their spouses nude. Sex was not discussed with children; sex organs were given no names. The children of an expectant woman would be sent to a neighbor's house when the new baby was due. If they raised questions when they returned and saw their new sibling, they might be told that the doctor had brought it in his satchel, or the stork brought it, or even that the father had found it in the orchard!

What is the basis for such differences at various points in time? For one thing, there are generally differing views among scientists and physicians. The various physicians we quoted in our discussion of 19th-century views represented the dominant theme. There were others who disputed the debilitating consequences of sexual activity (though none, so far as we know, who doubted the untoward results of masturbation). There are also differing views among lay people. In the 19th century a number of writers, including some feminists, free thinkers, and others, scoffed at the prevailing ideas and advocated free love.

Apart from the divergent opinions of professionals and intellectuals, people tend to hold differing views of sex on the basis of either religion or socioeconomic status. For instance, in 1965, in the midst of rapid change in America's sexual attitudes and behavior, a reader of a Christian magazine reacted to an article on the "new morality" by pointing out that whether married or not "the flesh is abomination in God's sight." [49] Unlike most Americans, the reader could not accept sexual activity as a good thing under any circumstances and used religion to justify the notion of sex as evil.

Similarly, Philip Greven divided colonial Americans into the evangelicals, the moderates, and the genteel and pointed out that the three groups had quite different views of sex. In contrast to the idea that sex within marriage is one of the good gifts of God, some "evangelical men found themselves profoundly uncomfortable not only with masculinity but also with sexuality in general, and with the parts of the body that were most closely connected to sexuality." [50] Like the reader noted above, they viewed sex even within marriage as repugnant to their God.

Even more important than religion for different attitudes and behavior is socioeconomic status. The Kinsey studies established, and later studies support the fact that

American sexual attitudes and practices vary from one so-cial class to another. [51] For example, those in the lower strata are likely to have sexual experiences at an earlier age than those in the upper strata. Males in the lower strata tend to have more sexual partners than do males in middle and upper strata. Females in the lower strata are less likely than females in higher strata to react positively to their first sexual experience. And so on. Such social class differences must be kept in mind when we evaluate the Mosher survey, an examination of female sexual atti-tudes and behavior conducted between 1892 and 1920. [52] The survey has been used to argue that Victorian women were much sexier creatures than we have thought. [53] But the survey only included 45 women and they were all middle to upper class in status. At best, therefore, they repre-sented a small minority of all women. There have always been differences between the working and lower classes on the one hand and the middle and upper classes on the other. The kind of sexual attitudes and behavior that are dominant will depend upon the numbers of people in the various social classes. The dominant theme of Victorian America was sexual repression. As Mosher helps us recognize however, there was also a counter-theme of sexual expression and enjoyment.

THEORIES OF SEXUALITY

Given the great diversity in attitudes and practices, how can we understand human sexual behavior? The most important, best-developed, and influential of all theories of sexuality is that of Freud. We will outline Freud's theory, then look briefly at some other explanations of sexuality.

Freud

Sexuality is central to the thought of Freud, who ar-gued that the sex instinct is innate and extremely powerful. Freud said that all individuals have two sets of instincts, the life and death instincts. He called the life instinct (which includes both the sex drive and aggression) "eros," which is the Greek word for sexual love. He illustrated the innate nature of the sex drive by pointing out that children can be seduced into all kinds of sexual "irregularities," which shows that the aptitude for them is innately "present in their dis-position." [54]

The capacity for perversion, according to Freud, also illustrates the power of the sex drive. In fact, the sex drive is so strong that it can lead to pathological behavior such as intercourse with a dead body. Such behavior shows the "astonishing lengths" to which the sex drive can go "in successfully overriding the resistances of shame, disgust, horror or pain." [55]

Although it is innate and powerful, the sex drive is not changeless. Rather, there is a development of sexuality in the human, a development that begins in infancy. We should keep in mind that Freud used the term "sexuality" in a broader sense than others have. Just as he expanded the concept of "mental" to include unconscious as well as conscious processes, he expanded the term "sexuality" to include things that "are not 'genital' and have nothing to do with reproduction." [56] Sexuality refers to the seeking of pleasure through the erogenous zones of the body. Thus, the first "sexual" excitement for the infant is feeding at its mother's breast and "as it sinks asleep at the breast, utterly satisfied, it bears a look of perfect content which will come back again later in life after the experience of sexual orgasm." [57] The experience is so pleasurable that the infant may repeat it (such as by sucking its thumb) even when it is not hungry.

This oral stage of development is succeeded by the anal stage. The infant discovers pleasure through the fulfillment of a need in another erogenous zone--elimination through the anus. The elimination reduces the tension built up by the accumulation of fecal material. In the third stage, the phallic, the infant is preoccupied with his or her genitals, and discovers the pleasure of manipulating them.

Around the age of five a latency period begins, and sexual impulses are subdued. At puberty, the individual's sexuality is revived and a new phase begins, one that hopefully leads to mature sexual development. In this genital phase, the individual's sexuality develops in a way that fulfills the biological aim of reproduction. That is, the individual becomes heterosexual. In contrast to the pregenital phase, when the sex drive mainly involved pleasure-seeking through the erogenous zones, the genital phase leads to heterosexual attraction and, eventually, sexual union.

Furthermore, Freud claimed that sexual union provides people with more satisfaction than anything else. Sex-

ual love "has given us our most intense experience of an
overwhelming sensation of pleasure and has thus furnished
us with a pattern for our search for happiness." [58] It is
only natural that we would continue to seek our happiness
through sexual union. But sexual love, Freud argued,
comes into opposition with the interests of civilization.
For one thing, civilization attempts to weld people together
into a larger family, so that there is a conflict between
family unity and civilizational unity. Secondly, women
represent the interests of family and sexual life, while the
work of civilization is the business of men. But a man
doesn't have an unlimited amount of energy, and "What he
employs for cultural aims he to a great extent withdraws
from women and sexual life." [59] Women find themselves
forced into the background by civilization. They resent this,
and tend to be restraining influences on the further development of civilization.

Civilization also imposes restrictions on man's aggressive tendencies. Since both sexuality and aggressivity
are inhibited by the demands of civilization, it is difficult
to be both civilized and happy. In effect, "civilized man
has exchanged a portion of his possibilities of happiness for
a portion of security." [60]

In sum, Freud portrays human sexuality as innate,
powerful, and leading ultimately to heterosexual union. Such
union not only perpetuates the race but affords people with
their most intense experience of pleasure. But the demands
of building civilization require men to sacrifice some of this
pleasure for other pursuits. People cannot have the full
measure of both the security of civilization and the pleasure
of sexual union. In Freud's view, that would be having your
cake and eating it too. Freud saw human life as a trade-
off among the various things which are desired and important
for fulfillment. Utopians would disagree with that somewhat
depressing conclusion. We shall see in succeeding chapters
how they attacked the Freudian dilemma.

Non-Freudian Theories

Some aspects of Freud's theory are almost beyond
dispute. Few people would disagree, for example, with
Freud's argument that sex is a powerful drive and a fundamental part of human life. But Freud's emphasis on the
instinctual nature of the sex drive does not seem to account

for the enormous variation in sexual behavior. Non-Freudian theorists have attempted to explain the diversity as well as the ubiquity of human sexuality.

One way to account for the diversity is to give greater stress to social and cognitive factors. Social psychologists acknowledge the biological basis for sex, but also emphasize such things as social norms, past experience, situational factors, and the meaning of sexual behavior to individuals. [61] As Jeffrey Victor points out in his discussion of sexual arousal, the meaning of any sexual stimulus is not to be found in the nature of the stimulus itself, but in the way the stimulus is perceived and understood. Humans can be aroused by a far greater number of stimuli than other animals, a result of our "ability to attribute erotic meanings to all sorts of stimuli. Erotic meanings may be attributed by some people, for example, to articles of clothing, particular body parts, special words, artistic creations, and even certain foods." [62]

Another way to explain diversity is to point out its evolutionary value, as the sociobiologists have done. For example, Edward Wilson notes two ways in which sexual diversity has survival value. [63] First, cultures vary in their normative sexual pattern because they have developed customs in accord with the exigencies of their environments. Second, humans "are connoisseurs of sexual pleasure," engaging in all sorts of sexual behavior that have nothing to do with reproduction. But reproduction is not the only important factor in perpetuating the human race. Human adaptation and survival is facilitated by pair-bonding. A good deal of sexual behavior has the function primarily of cementing the pair-bond and secondarily of leading to reproduction.

Both the social psychologists and the sociobiologists acknowledge the fact that sex involves something more than instinct. Humans are rational creatures. They interpret. They assess. They attribute meaning. They evaluate. Furthermore, they take into account the thoughts of others on a topic. Sex may be rooted in our biological makeup, but our actual sexual behavior is the result of our thinking and our interaction in a social context.

As we investigate the various utopian communities we shall find that they invested a good deal of thought in their sexual arrangements. In the great bulk of the communities, the people believed that sexual behavior both could and should be controlled in accord with their system of thought. In other words, the utopians accepted a sociopsychological perspective, and attempted to create an environment in which each individual would conform to a particular sexual ideology. Some succeeded remarkably well in this endeavor. And in some cases, the very success carried within it the seeds of future decline.

Notes

1. Sir Thomas Browne, quoted in Will and Ariel Durant, The Age of Reason Begins (New York: Simon and Schuster, 1961), p. 195.

2. Margaret Mead, New Lives for Old (New York: William Morrow, 1956), p. 405.

3. John C. Messenger, "Sex and Repression in an Irish Folk Community," in D. S. Marshall and R. C. Suggs, eds., Human Sexual Behavior (New York: Basic Books, 1971), pp. 14-15.

4. Ibid., p. 16.

5. Karl G. Heider, "Dani Sexuality: A Low Energy System," Man 11 (June, 1976):192.

6. Janet Shibley Hyde, Understanding Human Sexuality (New York: McGraw-Hill, 1979), p. 256.

7. Paul H. Gebhard, "Human Sexual Behavior: A Summary Statement," in Marshall and Suggs, eds., Human Sexual Behavior, p. 211.

8. Alan P. Merriam, "Aspects of Sexual Behavior Among the Bala," in Marshall and Suggs, eds., Human Sexual Behavior, pp. 89-90.

9. Donald S. Marshall, "Sexual Behavior on Mangaia," in Marshall and Suggs, eds., Human Sexual Behavior, p. 123.

10. Ibid., p. 160.

11. Clelland S. Ford and Frank A. Beach, Patterns of Sexual Behavior (New York: Harper Torchbooks, 1951), p. 41.

12. Bronislaw Malinowski, The Sexual Life of Savages in North-Western Melanesia (London: George Routledge, 1932), p. 284.

13. Ibid., p. 285.

14. Weston La Barre, "Anthropological Perspectives on Sexuality," in D. L. Grummon and A. M. Barclay, eds., Sexuality: A Search for Perspective (New York: Van Nostrand Reinhold, 1971), p. 42.

15. Donald Marshall, "Sexual Behavior on Mangaia," p. 120.

16. Julia S. Brown, "A Comparative Study of Deviations from Sexual Mores," American Sociological Review 17 (April 1952):138.

17. Jules Henry, "The Social Function of Child Sexuality in Pilagá Indian Culture," in P. H. Hoch and J. Zubin, eds., Psychosexual Development in Health and Disease (New York: Grune & Stratton, 1949), p. 94.

18. Vern L. Bullough, Sexual Variance in Society and History (New York: John Wiley, 1976), p. 505.

19. Edmund S. Morgan, The Puritan Family (New York: Harper Torchbooks, 1966), pp. 62-63.

20. Quoted in Bullough, Sexual Variance, p. 512.

21. Ibid.

22. Benjamin Franklin, The Autobiography of Benjamin Franklin (New York: Washington Square Press, Inc., 1955), p. 86.

23. Quoted in Philip Greven, The Protestant Temperament (New York: Alfred A. Knopf, 1977), p. 248.

24. Ibid., p. 249.

25. Quoted in Ronald G. Walters, ed., Primers for Prudery (Englewood Cliffs, N.J.: Prentice-Hall, 1974), p. 27.

26. Ibid., p. 21.

27. Milton Rugoff, Prudery and Passion (New York: G. P. Putnam's Sons, 1971), p. 61.

28. Carl N. Degler, At Odds (New York: Oxford University Press, 1980), p. 253.

29. William Acton, The Functions and Disorders of the Reproductive Organs in Youth, in Adult Age, and in Advanced Life (London: J. & A. Churchill, 1871), p. 133.

30. William W. Sanger, The History of Prostitution (New York: Harper & Brothers, 1858), p. 489.

31. John Cowan, The Science of a New Life (New York: J. S. Ogilvie, 1869), p. 116.

32. G. J. Barker-Benfield, The Horrors of the Half-Known Life (New York: Harper and Row, 1976), pp. 179-81.

33. Bullough, Sexual Variance, p. 544.

34. Dio Lewis, Chastity; Or, Our Secret Sins (Philadelphia: Maclean, 1874), p. 25.

35. Walters, Primers for Prudery, p. 82.

36. Cowan, Science of a New Life, p. 106.

37. Nicholas Francis Cooke, Satan in Society (Cincinnati, Ohio: C. F. Vent, 1876).

38. Dr. Sylvester Graham, Chastity, in a Course of Lectures to Young Men (New York: Fowler and Wells, n. d.), p. 15.

39. Cowan, Science of a New Life, pp. 116-17.

40. James Reed, From Private Vice to Public Virtue (New York: Basic Books, 1978), pp. 3-18.

41. Cowan, Science of a New Life, p. 354.

42. Bullough, Sexual Variance, p. 547.

43. Barker-Benfield, Horrors of the Half-Known Life, p. 122.

44. Cowan, Science of a New Life, p. 117.

45. Time, January 24, 1964, p. 54. Wilhelm Reich, a trained psychoanalyst, developed sexual theories that were more radical than Freud's, including the notion that sexual repression is a tool of social control in capitalist society.

46. Ibid., p. 59.

47. Arthur Schlesinger, Jr., "An Informal History of Love U. S. A.," in Focus: Human Sexuality (Guilford, Conn.: Dushkin, 1977), p. 6.

48. James West, Plainville, U. S. A. (New York: Columbia University Press, 1945), pp. 177, 191.

49. From a letter to the editor in Christian Life, June 1965, p. 3.

50. Greven, The Protestant Temperament, p. 129.

51. See M. S. Weinberg and C. J. Williams, "Sexual Embourgeoisment? Social Class and Sexual Activity: 1938-1970," American Sociological Review 45 (February 1980):33-48.

52. Degler, At Odds, pp. 262-64.

53. See, for example, Jody Gaylin, "Those Sexy Victorians," in Focus: Human Sexuality (Guilford, Conn.: Dushkin, 1977), p. 56-47.

54. Sigmund Freud, Three Essays on the Theory of Sexuality, trans. and revised by James Strachey (New York: Basic Books, 1975), p. 57. To Freud, irregularities or perversions were anything other than intercourse by genital union.

55. Ibid., p. 27.

56. Sigmund Freud, A General Introduction to Psychoanalysis (New York: Pocket Books, 1953), p. 330.

57. Ibid., p. 322.

58. Sigmund Freud, Civilization and Its Discontents, trans.

and edited by James Strachey (New York: W. W. Norton, 1961), p. 29.

59. Ibid. , pp. 50-51.

60. Ibid. , p. 62.

61. See, for example, Robert H. Lauer and Warren H. Handel, Social Psychology: The Theory and Application of Symbolic Interactionism (Englewood Cliffs, N. J. : Prentice-Hall, 1982), chap. 7; and Lawrence S. Wrightsman and Kay Deaux, Social Psychology in the 80s, 3rd ed. (Monterey, Calif. : Brooks/Cole, 1981, pp. 192-93).

62. Jeffrey S. Victor, Human Sexuality: A Social Psychological Approach (Englewood Cliffs, N. J. : Prentice-Hall, 1980), p. 122.

63. Edward O. Wilson, On Human Nature (New York: Bantam Books, 1978), pp. 130, 146-47.

Part II

Sex in Utopia

If variety is the spice of life, the utopian communities offer us a delectable field of study, for they are no less diverse than humankind itself in the range of sexual practices that they have approved. Most of the communities endorsed only one kind of sexual arrangement. But some have taken an "anything goes" stance. A better understanding of this sexual diversity is obtained when we recognize the diverse nature of the utopian movement as a whole. In chapter 2, therefore, we will provide an overview of the utopian quest in America. The following chapters will examine the various sexual practices, the ideologies that justified the differing arrangements, additional mechanisms of control, and the experiences of the participants.

2. THE UTOPIAN QUEST

Analysts have given a number of different names to those groups engaged in what we call the utopian quest: utopian communities, communitarian societies, collective societies, communistic societies, socialisms, communes, and communal groups, among others. We make no attempt here to suggest a preferred term or to offer a definition that clearly includes all of the groups that have been studied. Rather, we will state the elements that comprise the groups we call utopian.

First, a utopian community is intentional. The members voluntarily choose to unite to achieve their purposes. Second, the community is founded upon an ideology that incorporates some vision of an ideal society. Third, the members are committed to the notion that the pursuit of the ideal must be a collective rather than an individual effort. Finally, the community makes some kind of shift away from a money economy. Changes may or may not be made in various other institutions, including marriage and the family, but the utopian community always alters its economic basis to avoid a strictly money-based economy. The change may involve the establishment of communism, some kind of co-operative or joint-stock enterprise, or a system of bartering and exchange like that established at the anarchistic community, Modern Times. But some change is always made, because the utopians all share the notion that many American ills flow directly from the nation's economic structure.

Given, then, the above characteristics of a utopian community, what can we say about the utopian quest in the United States? We will first discuss the various types of communities, then show the pattern of development over time, and conclude with a discussion of the social contexts in which the communities emerged.

TYPES OF UTOPIAN COMMUNITIES

There are different ways to create utopia. In trying to categorize these diverse ways, observers focus on the type of ideology, on the economic structure, and on the founders. For example, Julia Williams divided the communities into the religious, the cooperative or socialistic, the Owenites, the Fourierist, miscellaneous, and the single tax groups. [1] Since she wrote at an earlier date, her categories do not account for the communes of the 1960s. Other observers, however, have attempted to classify these more recent communes. For example, Zablocki identifies eight kinds of communes, based on their ideologies: two religious types (Eastern and Christian), and six secular types (psychological, rehabilitational, cooperative, alternative family, countercultural, and political). [2]

There are problems with any classification of these more recent communes for the categories tend to overlap. Religious groups may also be socialistic. Countercultural groups also may be political. Sometimes, a group may move from one type to another: the "New Age Brotherhood" changed from an Eastern to a Christian ideology. [3]

In spite of the difficulties, it is important to classify the communities in some way in order to get a sense of their diverse nature. We will, therefore, discuss them under five types: religious communistic, secular communistic/socialistic groups, joint-stock, anarchistic, and modern communes. Obviously, the first four types refer to those communities established prior to World War II. The modern communes can be, and have been, divided into various types that are not wholly appropriate for the earlier communities.

Religious Communistic Communities

Among the important religious communistic communities were Ephrata, the Pennsylvania cloister that existed from 1732 to the end of the nineteenth century; the Shakers, who arrived from England in 1774 and still have a few remaining members; the Rappites, who maintained communities from 1805 to 1903; Amana, which began in New York and then established a number of communities in Iowa, lasting from 1843 to 1933; Zoar, which existed in Ohio from 1817 to 1898; and Oneida, a New York community that lasted from

1848 to 1881. There were considerable differences in such matters as marriage, family, and sex roles in these communities, but all asserted a biblical basis for their practices. Of course, contrary interpretations could be put to the same biblical passage. For example, the teaching of Christ that there will be no marriage in heaven led the Shakers to insist upon celibacy and John Humphrey Noyes to institute what he called complex marriage at Oneida. In complex marriage, no individual can be the exclusive sexual partner of any other single individual. We will explore such matters in considerable detail in subsequent chapters.

As with all other matters, the communism of these groups was justified on biblical and theological bases. Framers of the ideologies found their most direct support for biblical communism in Acts 2:44: "And all that believed were together, and had all things common." But there were other, more indirect, biblical grounds for support as well as theological arguments. F. W. Evans, a noted Shaker writer, summed up the defense of communism as follows:

> Sin and self produce private property.
> Innocence and self-denial produce community of property.
> The first Christian Church set before men an example of love--a oneness of interest in all things. [4]

A more elaborate discussion is found in the first annual report of the Oneida community. The section on the theory of the rights of property begins with a condemnation of the economic system of the larger society:

> ...all the systems of property getting in vogue in the world, are forms of what is vulgarly called the "grab-game," i. e. the game in which the prizes are not distributed by any rules of wisdom and justice, but are seized by the strongest and craftiest; and that the laws of the world simply give rules, more or less civilized, for the conduct of this game. [5]

These unjust systems, the report argues, are based on the false assumption that humans have a right to lands and goods. In reality, "God the Creator has the first and firmest title to all property whatsoever." Only when people acknowledge God's ownership will they be able to escape from

the wretchedness of the "grab-game." The Oneida community was established on the basis of a joint ownership with
God of all things. In essence: "...all believers constitute
the family of God ... all valuables, whether persons or
things, are family property ... all the labors of the family
are directed, judges and rewarded in the distribution of enjoyments by the Father." [6]

Thus, while the details of the arguments vary, the
general principle is shared by the religious, communistic
groups: both biblical teaching and apostolic example indicate communism as the godly way of life for humans.

Secular Communistic Socialistic Communities

Prominent among the early secular, communistic/
socialistic groups were the Owenites and Icarians. The
Owenites followed the teachings and inspiration of Robert
Owen, a Scotch industrialist and philanthropist. Owen had
tried to provide optimal conditions for the workers in his
textile mills in Scotland. In 1825, he purchased New Harmony, Indiana from the Rappites (who were moving back to
Pennsylvania). There, and in a number of other communities, he hoped to establish his new social order.

The Owenites (and Icarians) were not secular in the
sense of disavowing religious practices in the utopian community. But the justification of the community and the solu-
tions to human problems were couched in secular rather than
religious terms. Owen, for instance, argued that the existing social system was ignorant and selfish, focusing on the
individual. As long as the individual system prevails, he
said in an address at New Harmony in 1825, "the great
mass of mankind must remain, as they comparatively are
at present, ignorant, poor, oppressed, and, consequently,
vicious, and miserable." [7] The system must be changed,
and the change must be on the basis of accurate knowledge
of human nature and of the laws of society. Owen, incidentally, did not believe that people could be quickly changed,
that selfish interests could be easily transformed into collective interests. New Harmony, therefore, was to be a
kind of "half-way house" on the journey from misery to
utopia, at least for the first three years. The goal was an
independent community, with common property, absolute
equality, and supreme happiness. Communism would achieve
the goal because it would eliminate the ruinous competition
between individuals.

The Icarian communities, which were located in various places in the nation throughout the latter half of the nineteenth century, grew out of the writing and efforts of Etienne Cabet, a French journalist. One of Cabet's works illustrates the nature of the secularism involved. [8] In chapter 2 of History and Constitution of the Icarian Community, Cabet asserts that the Icarians believe that the world was created by God, not by chance. God is the Father of the human race, and He loves all of His children equally. As a loving Father, God wills that all humans shall be happy. In spite of God's will, the history of humankind is replete with poverty, vice, crime, and wretchedness of all sorts. And what is the remedy for human misery? At this point, Cabet abandons his religious line of reasoning: "We believe that the cause [of evil] is in a bad social and political organization, resulting from the ignorance, inexperience and error of Humankind from its beginning." [9] The remedy follows logically--humans need a new social organization. But not every kind of new social organization can achieve human well-being. Rather, people need, Cabet insisted, to organize society on the basis of certain principles--brotherhood, equality, solidarity, and the suppression of poverty and individual property. In other words, the remedy to human ills is communism.

Later in the nineteenth, and early in the twentieth century, a number of groups arose that were somewhat more influenced by Marxist thought. They tended to call themselves socialist communities. For example, the Ruskin Commonwealth existed in Tennessee in the 1890s. Again, the appeal was to those who were distressed by the dislocations of capitalist America; in a newspaper published by Julius Wayland, founder of the community, the appeal was explicit:

> Would you like to know that your wife and babies would be placed beyond the possibility of want, whether you live or die? Would you like to know that your children grown up would be supplied with comfortable homes without paying rent or slaving years perhaps under a load of interest bearing mortgage? Would you like to know that employment would always be open to them where their wages would be the price of the goods they made brought on the market without deduction for rent, profit, dividends, high salaries, etc. ? ... this is just what will be the conditions when the co-operative commonwealth is instituted. [10]

The Ruskin Commonwealth openly advocated the Marxist principle of "from each according to his ability to each according to his needs." People were asked to pay $500 to join. Once a member, an individual worked at one of the various enterprises operated by the community. Workers received "hour checks" for their labor. The checks could be used to buy goods at the store or could be exchanged for U. S. currency (at the rate of two cents per "hour"). Goods at the store were sold at wholesale rates. Meals, lodging, laundry service, schools, and health care were free to all members.

Clearly, the secular communistic/socialistic communities were formed to address the same problems in human society as those that were the concern of the religious communists. Both the religious and the secular communists abhorred the human wreckage that they saw as inevitable in a capitalistic society. Both saw communism as a way to resolve the problems. But the religious communists insisted on undergirding communism with Christian beliefs and practices. The secular communists used a humanistic philosophy of the nature of people and of society as a rationale for their communities.

Joint-Stock Communities

Fourierism epitomizes the joint-stock approach to utopia. Charles Fourier was a French socialist writer who attempted to lay out a utopian scheme in which every detail was carefully specified. His complicated scheme attracted the attention of a number of Americans, who adapted his thought to the exigencies of American life and began more than 40 different communities in various parts of the country.

As with the communists, the Fourierists were concerned about the perceived evils of capitalism. As one of them wrote, our country has had a great many political and legislative reforms, but human happiness has not thereby increased. In fact, far from moving on toward a destiny that generates enthusiasm, "social evils have increased ... and the future offers us in the political world the prospect of bitter party strife, of dissensions and discord, and in the social world, of poverty and degradation for the mass." [11]

The Fourierists saw the solution to human misery not in communism, but in what they called "association." Association involved, ideally, a community of about 1800 individuals. The large number was required to fulfill Fourier's complex arrangement. For Fourier himself advocated a community built upon groups, which would consist of at least seven individuals so that each group could be subdivided. The groups would be formed for every possible function in the community, from growing flowers to cooking food to managing files. A number of groups formed a series. Each series had an area of responsibility, such as horticulture, livestock, and so forth. Finally, all of the series combined to form a Phalanx, which required around 1800 members if all of the functions of the ideal community were properly performed.

Size was one of the compromises that Americans made with Fourier's system, for none of the American communities were as large as 1800. Americans did retain the notion of a joint-stock enterprise. Each individual who joined a community contributed a certain amount, his or her investment, and each was promised a corresponding share of the profits in accord with that investment. American followers of Fourier stressed the fact that their communities offered "attractive industry," that is, an industrial setup that would resolve the problems that plagued the existing society. The joint-stock company would merge the interests of labor and capitalists. Capitalists could come into the community and make as much profit as before because of the efficiency of operation in the utopian group. Poor workers could come and get not only the prevailing wage, but also a portion of the surplus and the security of membership in the community. Everyone would benefit. At last, there would be abundance for all.

Anarchistic Communities

While expressing distress at the same kinds of problems that concerned the other utopians, the anarchists saw the solution in the abolition of authority structures rather than in the creation of new types of authority. Anarchism is much more likely to be chosen as a utopian model by modern communes than it was by earlier groups. Very few nineteenth century utopians opted for anarchism. A notable exception was Josiah Warren, who founded the communities of Utopia in Ohio and Modern Times in New York around the middle of the nineteenth century. Warren was a businessman who had been a member of Robert Owen's community at

New Harmony. The disintegration of New Harmony convinced Warren that future utopian communities would have to be based on the principle of individuality.

The essence of the principle of individuality was well expressed by Stephen Pearl Andrews, a friend of Josiah Warren and an advocate of Warren's ideas:

> ... every Individual is the rightful Sovereign over his own conduct in all things, whenever, and just so far as, the consequences of his conduct can be assumed by himself; or, rather, inasmuch as no one objects to assuming aggreeable consequences, whenever and as far as this is true of the disagreeable consequences. ... Hence the exact formula of the doctrine, with its inherent limitation, may be stated thus: "The Sovereignty of the Individual, to be exercised at his own cost." [12]

In accord with this principle of individuality, Warren tried to establish communities with no rules and no formal sanctions. People's needs would be fulfilled through negotiation and the exchange of skills. Free of all formal authority, people would be able to pursue their own interests and maximize their own well-being as they pleased in the context of a group of like-minded others.

Modern Communes

Modern communes are so variegated that they make categorization difficult. The scheme of Zablocki mentioned above is based on two fundamental dimensions, strategic philosophy and locus of attention. Strategic philosophy refers to the difference between a focus on changing people's consciousness and an emphasis on direct action in order to bring about social change. Locus of attention refers to the dominant concern, whether the spiritual world, the individual, the community, or the larger society. A much simpler scheme is offered by Gardner, who argues that there are two basic types that are most important. One type he describes as "anarchistic, libertarian, individualistic, voluntaristic, free-form, unstructured, or open," while the other type is "religious, disciplined, structured, authoritarian, hierarchical, transcendental." [13]

Perhaps the easiest thing to say here is that modern communes recapitulate all of the themes of the earlier communities and add a few of their own. In all cases, however, they share with the earlier communities a sense of the inequities and inadequacies of the existing society and a determination to create an alternative that will enable people to fulfill themselves.

Something of the enormous diversity in modern communes can be illustrated by briefly noting two groups in New Mexico: The Family and Lama. The Family began as an effort to overcome the limitations of individualism. Its purpose was "to create self-aware individuals" by means of "a specialized group or community epitomized by group marriage." [14] The emphasis on the collectivity was applied to all spheres. All economic activities had to be collective efforts in some sense; The Family rejected purely individual methods of securing income (such as a member of the group working somewhere with outsiders). Privacy of any kind was virtually unknown. For instance, one visitor reported that about sixty people had to sleep in three rooms. [15] The floors were completely covered with mattresses. There were also a number of double-decker beds, which belonged to women. A man who wanted to sleep with a woman on any particular night had to get her permission and to indicate whether he merely wanted to sleep or to have sexual relations. Often, three people would sleep in the same bed.

In contrast to The Family, Lama was formed to bring about a spiritual awakening in individuals. Members lived in individual A-frames and had separate sources of income. Each member sought the state known as self-realization. To achieve self-realization, the insights of many different religions were utilized. A researcher who visited Lama reported that he saw Tibetan prayer flags, prayers directed to both Allah and the Lord, and a photograph of a Persian mystic hanging in a wash room next to a Hindu symbol of devotion. [16] There were some restrictions on sexual activity at Lama and a fairly strict, daily regimen that began at 5:00 a. m.

Thus, as with earlier communities, modern communes invoke a variety of different means and paths to utopia. There has been consensus among all utopians that the existing order has gone awry, that considerable human misery is the result of existing social arrangements, and that a new, fulfilling social order can be created. Beyond those points of agreement, the utopians have gone in diverse directions to fulfill their dreams. We have sketched the major directions taken. We turn now to a consideration of how the utopian quest fits into the broad sweep of American history.

PATTERNS OF DEVELOPMENT

How many communities were there? How many people were involved in them? How long did they last? Where were they located? Is there any kind of pattern to their emergence? These are the questions we address in this section, beginning with the last.

The Historical Pattern

The earliest utopian communities in the nation pre-date the Revolution. All of them were religious. The first of which we have any information was Plockhoy's Common-wealth. It was established by Pieter Plockhoy and a group of Mennonites in 1663 near the Delaware River. Twenty years later, in 1683, the Labadists established communities in Maryland. The Labadists followed the teachings of the French Separatist pastor, Jean de Labadie. They survived for over 40 years.

A number of other religious, communistic communi-ties arose prior to or shortly after the American Revolution, including: Ephrata Cloister (established in 1732); Shaker villages (beginning in 1787 at Mount Lebanon, New York); Harmonie, or the Rappites (established 1805 in Pennsylvania); and the Zoarites (established in 1817 in Ohio). Religious, communistic communities have continued to spring up at various times into the present. But whereas the first wave of utopian communities all fell into this category, they com-prise only a minority of subsequent groups.

In 1825, the establishment of Robert Owen's group at New Harmony, Indiana marked the first wave of secular, communistic/socialistic communities. About a dozen Owen-ite groups appeared in 1825 and 1826, but none lasted more than four years. Two more Owenite groups began in the 1840s; each lasted about three years. After that, the Owen-ite movement was dead.

Joint-stock communities appeared on the American scene in the 1840s as the followers of Fourier built new

communities in over 40 different locations. Fourierist efforts dominated the period from 1840 to 1860. There were,
of course, a number of religious communities established
during the period, notably the Oneida Community (1848-1881)
and Hopedale (1841-1858). The Icarians also settled in a
number of places in the 1840s and 1850s. But the Fourierists were by far the most active of all. Albert Brisbane,
a social reformer, was the primary moving spirit of the
Fourierist advance. Brisbane had traveled in Europe,
where he came into contact with, and became enamored
of, Fourier's system of thought. Brisbane translated
Fourier and interpreted him for Americans. He wrote and
lectured extensively in support of Fourier's system. His
enthusiasm was contagious. Nevertheless, very few Fourier
communities began after the 1840s, and the movement was
virtually dead by 1850.

The utopian dream seemed to wane between 1860 and
1890, with only a scattering of new communities appearing
in the nation. But the number surged again during the 1890s
with a second wave of secular, communistic/socialistic
groups. In many cases, the new utopians were influenced
by Marxist thought and/or by the popular futurist novel of
Edward Bellamy, Looking Backward. The novel, published
in 1888, described a society of the future marked by cooperation, affluence, equality, and a humane pattern of industrial production. Bellamy's novel, incidentally, was not the
only utopian fiction to appear at the time. In fact, the
1890s saw a proliferation of novels as well as actual communities. From 1890 through 1900, writers published a
total of 72 utopian novels; only 39 had been published from
1800 to 1889. [17]

After the turn of the century, however, utopian interest declined again. There was a slight increase during
the Great Depression in the number of communities founded,
but the next large surge did not come until the 1960s when
communes sprang up throughout the nation. The modern
commune movement has surpassed all previous phases in
extensiveness and diversity. As Gardner put it, "everything
communal that happened in America in the three hundred
years before 1965 was dwarfed by what happened in the short
years that followed." [18] We will see the basis for such a
statement as we look at the numerical data.

The Statistics of Utopia

How many utopian communities have emerged in America? It is not possible to give an exact answer because not all groups have kept records. Arthur Bestor identified 130 groups that began between 1663 and 1860. [19] Julia Williams listed 262 communities that had been founded up through 1939. [20] Doig gives as good an estimate as possible when he notes that about 130 communities emerged through 1860 and another 200 appeared in the next hundred years. [21] The problem of numbers is greater, however, when we try to give estimates of the number of modern communes. Doig put the number at around 2000. Other estimates range as high as 50,000. In the mid-1970s, Jaffe and Kanter located almost 300 self-identified communes, collectives, or extended families just in the Boston area. [22] At any rate, in contract to the hundreds of communities established prior to the 1960s, the period since then is marked by thousands and perhaps even tens of thousands of communal groups. A literal population explosion of utopian groups occurred in the 1960s and 1970s.

From the above figures, it is clear why a categorization of modern communes is an extremely difficult task. As noted before, the modern groups represent every type, but we do not know the relative proportions of the various types. On the other hand, Williams classified the 262 communities that existed before 1939 according to her types. She found that 48.1 percent were religious; 16.4 percent were socialistic/cooperative; 14.5 percent were Fourierist; 8 percent were Owenite; and the remaining 13 percent were miscellaneous types. [23] The information we have about modern communes indicates that a far smaller proportion would fall into the category of religious. Gardner notes that, in his twofold typology, the religious groups were in a distinct minority in the 1960s but were probably as frequent as the anarchistic groups in the 1970s. If the average of a "distinct minority" and 50 percent is about one-third, then Gardner agrees exactly with Zablocki in the latter's estimate of the proportion of religious communes. The proportions of other types depend upon the classification scheme used, but in any case must be gross estimates. For our purposes, it will suffice to say that about one-third of modern communes are religious and two-thirds are various other types.

How many people are we talking about? How many

people have been members of the various communities?
Again, it is easier to give estimates for those communities
founded before the 1960s than for those that emerged sub-
sequently. In general, the earlier communities ranged in
size from about 15 people to as many as 800 to 900. In
terms of total membership for the duration of the communities, the Shakers were the largest group. In their varied
communities they had nearly 15,800 members from 1787 to
the present. [24] Noyes estimated the number of Owenites
and Fourierists at 8,641. [25] Holloway put the total number of members in all communities in the nineteenth century at more than 100,000. [26] A reasonable figure to us,
for all communities prior to the 1960s, would be somewhere
between 100,000 and 125,000 individuals.

As far as modern communes are concerned, estimates of the total number of members vary as wildly as
estimates of the number of communes. In his study of 120
communes, Zablocki found that the size ranged from 4 to
320 people, with an average size of 39 for rural groups and
11 for urban groups. [27] If those averages are typical,
there must be well over 100,000 Americans who are or
have been members of modern communes. In fact, Jerome
puts the total at 750,000. [28] Others offer smaller estimates, although the differences are due in part to differing
definitions of the kinds of groups that should be included.
Whatever estimate one chooses, it seems clear that the
number of people who have entered a utopian community
since 1960 is greater than the total who entered during the
previous three centuries.

The total number of utopians is small compared to
the total American population. But the utopians were large
in spirit and determination. Most made considerable financial and psychological investments in the communities they
joined. Those who entered communistic groups turned over
all of their property and possessions to the group. Those
who joined other groups often had to pay a fairly sizable
entrance fee. All groups have had various commitment
mechanisms to insure the retention and stability of their
memberships. [29] People, for instance, might be asked
to make certain sacrifices, to abstain from sex or alcohol
or meat or tobacco. Such mechanisms deepened the psychological investment of the members.

In some cases, the very act of getting to and setting
up a community represented a considerable investment. For

example, a group of men set out from Reunion, Missouri
in January, 1871 to establish a utopian community in Kansas. The Progressive Community, as it was called, was
built on a foundation of considerable agony and frustration
and deprivation. The warm weather in which the trip began
turned to a snowstorm on the second day out. One of the
men got frostbite on three of his toes. One day they were
able to travel only three and one-half miles with two of the
men using shovels to open the road in front of the rest of
the group. William Frey, the leader of the group, put the
following in his diary for January 20: "We went again but
evidently God was against us and wishes to punish us like
Israel on their way to the promised land." [30] After numerous problems, they arrived at their land and began to
build their community. Life was difficult in the early days.
Frey recorded the meals they had during February. They
ate breakfast and dinner. A typical breakfast consisted of
corn bread, graham bread or dumplings, corn gruel, and
an occasional apple or egg. Dinner featured graham or
corn bread or gruel, bean soup, and apples. Occasionally
a dinner might consist of nothing more than graham dumplings and corn bread.

The situation at Progressive improved somewhat as
time went on. Frey insisted that the experience of shared
difficulties, combined with mutual love and respect, acted
as an unbreakable bond for the community. One might indeed expect that, given the sacrifices and investments made
by the founders, the community would have a good chance
for long-term survival once the initial difficulties were overcome. But the Progressive Community lasted only six
years. Internal ideological dissension led to the collapse.
A clash of ideals killed the community for which men and
women had willingly sacrificed their fortunes and imperiled
their health.

And what of the other communities? How did they
fare after people built them on a foundation of high expectations and heavy investments? The answer has two related
aspects--the rate of turnover, and longevity. With respect
to turnover, the rates vary considerably from one kind of
community to another. For communities prior to the modern communes, the religious groups appear to have less
turnover than others. Oneida, which reached a population
of about 300, had on the average three to five people leave
each year. [31] In groups like the Hutterites and Amanaites,
fewer than 5 percent left the community permanently. Among

the Shakers, a very high proportion of young children who had been brought into the communities left before they were twenty years old. But few adults left. Kern calculated the attrition rate through apostasy at an average of 0. 5 percent per year. [32]

Available information on nonreligious communities indicates a much higher turnover rate. Noyes reported a rate of between twelve and twenty percent at the Wisconsin Phalanx, a Fourierist group. [33] A member of Llano claimed that three of every four who came into the group eventually left. [34] At the Equality Colony, in the state of Washington, "there was always a steady stream in and out of the colony, the average family remaining about three months. " [35]

Turnover rates are also high for modern communes. Zablocki reported that about half of the members in the 120 communes he studied leave each year. At Ananda Cooperative Village, one of the most prosperous of the thirteen rural communes studied by Gardner, only half of the 1973 members had been in the community in 1970. [36] Finally, Twin Oaks is one of the most successful of modern communes. It was founded in 1967 in Virginia. B. F. Skinner's utopian novel, Walden Two, was the inspiration and guiding ideology for the community. But there has always been a high turnover in the group; an anthropologist who studied Twin Oaks reported that by January, 1978, 31 of the 72 individuals who were there in June, 1976 had left. [37]

There appears to be some relationship between turnover rate and survival of the community, although we cannot make a judgement about the relationship with respect to modern communes. Twin Oaks has survived for well over a decade in spite of its high turnover rate. Many modern communes, however, have dissolved within a few years. Unfortunately, we simply do not have information on the survival rates of the multitude of modern communes. The evidence is more clear-cut for earlier communities. And again, the major difference is that between religious and nonreligious groups. A number of the religious groups have survived for more than a century. None of the nonreligious groups lasted even half a century. Williams found religion to be the differentiating factor in the longevity of the 262 communities included in her study. [38] For example, she found that nearly a third of the nonreligious communities, but only about 8. 5 percent of the religious, failed to survive one year. And 97 percent of the nonreligious, but only 40 percent of the religious communities, failed to survive 25 years. The religious communities have both longer survival rates and lower turnover rates.

THE SOCIAL CONTEXT

Why did they embark upon their quest? Why, in this land of freedom and opportunity, have hundreds of thousands of people turned their backs on the larger society and sought refuge in a utopian community? Obviously, they found some deficiencies in American society. They perceived the social context not as one of unlimited opportunity to pursue one's well-being, but as one that imposed intolerable constraints or unjustifiable inequities. The point is that we must understand the social context of utopian communities in order to fully grasp the meaning of the quest.

The earliest groups were reacting to European rather than American society. Many of the religious communists came to this country to escape persecution in Europe, a persecution rooted in their variant beliefs and practices. Although immigrant communists continued to bolster membership during the first half of the nineteenth century, many of the utopians who entered communities during these years were reacting to the structure of American society. What kind of society was it?

Historians generally agree that American society changed significantly after the War of 1812. The changes were structural, and they occurred rapidly. Economic and political equalitarianism, spatial and social mobility, industrialization and urbanization, and secularization and immigration all combined to bring about a fundamentally different social order. Factories replaced domestic and craft shop manufacturers. Many skilled workers found themselves less in demand than the unskilled (whose ranks were swelled by immigrants). The cities grew rapidly in the 1840s and 1850s. The total value of manufactured goods increased fourfold from 1840 to 1860. The American people experienced the full impact of a "radical departure from the agrarian past." [39]

Many Americans perceived the decades between the War of 1812 and the Civil War as an era of extreme flux. Indeed, to some, society seemed to be "in a state of chaos." [40] James Fenimore Cooper epitomized the feelings when he had one of his characters say: "The whole country is in such a constant state of mutation, that I can only liken it to the game of children, in which, as one quits his corner another runs into it, and he that finds no corner to get into, is the laughing stock of the others." [41]

The breathless pace of change generated considerable distress. William R. Taylor characterized the 1830s as an "age of anxiety," [42] and it does not overstate the case to label the entire period in those terms. Anxieties manifested themselves in several ways: pervasive fears that sometimes bordered on paranoia; strenuous efforts to order and make sense out of life; a deeply felt need for a sense of community; irrational reactions to real and imagined threats; and personal pathologies. It is not surprising, as Taylor points out, that there was "something like an epidemic of catastrophic fiction which swept the country in the eighteen-thirties," nor that from both clergymen and public speakers came a message of the need for inner strength in the face of continuing crisis. [43] Public figures continually warned their fellow Americans that the nation hung precariously at the edge of an abyss of doom.

In some cases, fear took the form of a conspiracy mentality, an irrational fear bordering on paranoia of such groups as Roman Catholics, Mormons, and Masons. In the South, the conspiracy mentality focused on the slaves. Southerners were constantly on guard for a slave conspiracy and uprising. Freehling pictures the slave-holding aristocracy of South Carolina, because of their obsessive fear of a slave insurrection, as reacting hysterically to the relatively harmless abolitionist crusade of the 1820s. [44]

Thus, Americans saw themselves embedded in a social milieu abounding with enemies. The land of opportunity was also a land of subtle dangers, a land envied by and sought by those who would seize it and remake it into their own image. Conspiracies were everywhere. Vigilance and counterattack were the orders of the day.

But there was another prominent strain of thought: optimism, hope, and faith in the progress of the individual and the nation. Americans felt that the future would inevitably be better than the past. In spite of the serious problems and enemies, progress was as certain as the sunrise. "Progress" here means material progress. Americans pursued prosperity with the passion of the young lover. But prosperity eluded the masses. And financial security of even the minimal kind was unknown to most. There were, after all, no Social Security programs, no welfare, no package of fringe benefits for workers, no unions to protect jobs, and no federal programs to support farmers.

Thus, many of those who joined utopian communities in the first half of the nineteenth century came from a rapidly changing society where optimism clashed with fear, and faith in progress struggled with the precarious realities of everyday life. The utopians were not the only ones seeking to resolve these contradictions through social action. Numerous social reform movements also marked the period.

However, even before the Civil War both reform movements and utopian efforts had subsided. Neither had proven very effective in solving the problems or soothing the anxieties of the rapidly changing society. As the war dragged on, weariness with the "do-goodism" which many believed had inspired it intensified. And by war's end, Americans were ready to return to economic pursuits with renewed vigor and with little regard for humanitarian concerns. Indeed, in the decades following the Civil War material values seemed to triumph as industrialization proceeded at a rapid pace accompanied by waste, exploitation, and corruption.

To be sure, there were those who believed that their pursuits were just and moral and who saw in industry and technology the foundations for an equitable and affluent society. As late as 1890, one American spoke of science in lyrical terms as "a great comforter, civilizer, and enlightener" to the peoples of the world. [45]

By the late nineteenth century a number of Americans had begun to have second thoughts about the direction of the nation. Urbanization, industrialization, and a rising flood of immigrants were creating a different America with a host of new problems. Frequent economic crises accompanied by severe dislocation intensified human suffering and exacerbated the problems. In the 1890s, not surprisingly, people reacted to the situation through a new wave of social reform movements and utopian communities.

The above sketch suggests that those times of greatest activity in the building of nineteenth-century utopian communities were also times in which many people sensed that they were the victims of social and economic dislocation. The beliefs of the utopians support the point. As Bliss and Olin point out, all nineteenth-century utopians shared a concern about the consequences of the fundamental economic changes that were occurring in the country. As the market economy displaced the small village economy, numerous Americans experienced a dissociation from a local community where each person had a place. The utopians reacted to this change, and sought to improve the quality of life of people and to restore each individual to an important place in a network of like-minded people. [46]

The reasons that people gave for wanting to join or to remain in the communities also reflects their concern with social and economic dislocation. In his analysis of the applications for membership to the Zoar Society, Nixon points out that some were German immigrants who were disillusioned by problems in this land of opportunity; some were farmers or mechanics primarily concerned about security which they could not find in the larger society; and some expressed religious concerns as their primary motivation. [47] A visitor to the Trumbull Phalanx, a Fourierist group in Ohio, reported:

> They spoke of the near relations they sustained to each other, and of the many blessings they look to receive in the future; meanwhile the present unity gave them an idea of heaven. One spirit of joy and gladness seemed to animate them, viz, that they had escaped from the wants, cares, and temptations of civilization, and instead were placed where public good is the same as individual good. [48]

Finally, a popular hymn among the Shakers speaks of the appeal of the home "in Zion" where each Shaker has food, clothing, and "shelter from the storm" while people on the outside are searching desperately and not always successfully for the same benefits. [49]

And what of the modern commune, representing the latest surge in utopian community-building? The 1960s were, like the earlier periods mentioned, a time of social movements. Furthermore, the modern communal groups are, like their forebears, reacting against what they perceive as the shortcomings of an industrial nation. Gusfield points out that the communes share a romantic and anti-industrial perspective. [50] This perspective includes an emphasis on naturalness, on the communal, and on transcendentalism. Naturalness is the belief that such things as food, clothing, and the human mind are better in their natural state than in a processed form. The communal emphasis exalts the group over the individual and relationships over privacy. Transcendentalism refers to the tendency of the groups to value the mystical over the scientific. In his survey of 50 respondents in twelve different communes, Westhues found that 90 percent supported the following values: "close interpersonal relationships, total honesty with other people, doing things with other people, a sense of community, greater sensitivity to other people, and opportunity to be creative." [51]

There is one aspect of the social context that appears to differ significantly between the modern communes and earlier communities, namely, the emphasis on economic security in the latter. In the 1960s, as compared to earlier eras, the American people were more affluent, shared more equally in that affluence, and had greater access to various kinds of programs that offered economic security. We would not expect people in the 1960s to respond as much to the appeal of economic security that was so prominent in earlier communities. Thus, Zablocki found in his survey that 25 percent of all urban communards and only 10 percent of all rural communards gave "economic advantages" as a primary reason for joining a commune. [52] And for many of those the "advantages" were tax breaks or lower housing costs rather than security against a precarious economic situation.

In sum, the periods of greatest activity in the establishment of utopian communities have been periods when social movements flourished. They have been periods of rapid change when people have experienced a good deal of social and economic dislocation. Americans have adjusted to such times in various ways. For hundreds of thousands, the adjustment has taken the form of seeking refuge in a utopian community.

Notes

1. Julia Elizabeth Williams, An Analytical Tabulation of the North American Utopian Communities by Type, Longev-

ity, and Location. Unpublished M. A. Thesis, University of South Dakota, 1939.

2. Benjamin Zablocki, Alienation and Charisma: A Study of Contemporary American Communes (New York: Free Press, 1980), pp. 204-207.

3. Ilse Martin, "Inequality, Chastity, and Sign Endogamy in the New Age Brotherhood," in Jon Wagner, ed., Sex Roles in Contemporary American Communes (Bloomington, Ind.: Indiana University Press, 1982), p. 86.

4. F. W. Evans, Tests of Divine Inspiration (New Lebanon, Ohio: United Society Called Shakers, 1853), p. 84.

5. First Annual Report of the Oneida Association (Oneida: Leonard & Company, 1849), p. 14.

6. Ibid., p. 15.

7. New Harmony Gazette, October 1, 1825.

8. Etienne Cabet, History and Constitution of the Icarian Community, trans. Thomas Teakle, Iowa Journal of History and Politics 15 (1917):214-86.

9. Ibid., p. 234.

10. The Coming Nation, January 27, 1894.

11. "On Association and Attractive Industry: By a Fourierist," United States Magazine and Democratic Review 10 (January 1842):32.

12. Stephen Pearl Andrews, The Science of Society, Vol. 1 (New York: Fowlers and Wells, 1852), p. 63.

13. Hugh Gardner, The Children of Prosperity (New York: St. Martin's Press, 1978), p. 243.

14. John Hostetler, Communitarian Societies (New York: Holt, Rinehart & Winston, 1974), p. 9.

15. Elia Katz, Armed Love (New York: Holt, Rinehart and Winston, 1971), p. 118.

16. Michael D. Whitesage, We and Thou: The Evolution of American Communal Monasticism, Unpublished Ph. D. dissertation, University of New Mexico, 1975, p. 92.

17. James Harvey Sweetland, American Utopian Fiction, 1798-1926, Unpublished Ph. D. dissertation, University of Notre Dame, 1976, p. 11.

18. Gardner, The Children of Prosperity, p. 3.

19. Arthur Eugene Bestor, Jr., Backwoods Utopias (Philadelphia: University of Pennsylvania Press, 1950), pp. 235-42. See Rosabeth Moss Kanter, Commitment and Community (Cambridge, Mass.: Harvard University Press, 1972), pp. 244-45 for a discussion of the problems of arriving at accurate numbers.

20. Williams, An Analytical Tabulation.

21. Ivan Doig, Utopian America: Dreams and Realities (Rochelle Park, N. J.: Hayden Book Company, 1976), p. 9.

22. Dennis T. Jaffe and Rosabeth Moss Kanter, "Couple Strains in Communal Households: A Four-Factor Model of the Separation Process," Journal of Social Issues 32 (No. 1, 1976):171.

23. Williams, An Analytical Tabulation, p. 17.

24. As of this writing, a few Shaker women are still living in New England. The estimate on the total number of Shakers comes from Edward Deming Andrews, The People Called Shakers (New York: Dover, 1953), pp. 290-91.

25. John Humphrey Noyes, Strange Cults & Utopias of 19th-Century America (New York: Dover, 1966; 1st publ. 1870), p. 18.

26. Mark Holloway, Heavens on Earth (New York: Dover, 1966), p. 18.

27. Zablocki, Alienation and Charisma, p. 83.

28. Judson Jerome, Families of Eden: Communes and the New Anarchism (New York: Seabury, 1974).

29. Kanter, Commitment and Community.

30. William Frey Papers, Box 2, Jan. 20, 1871. Rare Books and Manuscript Division, The New York Public Library, Astor, Lenox and Tilden Foundations.

31. Maren Lockwood Carden, Oneida: Utopian Community to Modern Corporation (New York: Harper Torchbooks, 1969), p. 77.

32. Louis J. Kern, An Ordered Love (Chapel Hill, N. C.: University of North Carolina Press, 1981), p. 101.

33. Noyes, Strange Cults, pp. 434, 439.

34. George Pickett, "The Whole-Souled Ones," ms. in the Robert Carlton Brown Collection, Illinois Historical Survey Library, University of Illinois.

35. Worth W. Caldwell, "The Equality Colony," Sunset 52 (February 1924):27.

36. Gardner, The Children of Prosperity, p. 167.

37. Lani Wheeler Higgins, Not Yet Utopia: A Study of Twin Oaks Community, Unpublished Ph. D. dissertation, University of Virginia, 1979, p. 144.

38. Williams, An Analytical Tabulation, p. 16.

39. Douglas T. Miller, Jacksonian America (New York: Oxford University Press, 1967), p. 121.

40. Ibid., p. 22.

41. Quoted in Marvin Meyers, The Jacksonian Persuasion (Stanford, Cal.: Stanford University Press, 1957), p. 75.

42. William R. Taylor, Cavalier and Yankee (New York: Harper Torchbooks, 1967), p. 96.

43. Ibid., pp. 99-100.

44. William H. Freehling, Prelude to Civil War (New York: Harper & Row, 1965), p. 17.

45. R. H. Thurston, "The Border-Land of Science," The North American Review 150 (1890):67.

46. Nathaniel L. Bliss and Spencer C. Olin, Jr., "In Praise of Utopian Socialism in America," Alternative Futures 3 (Winter, 1980):54-5.

47. Edgar B. Nixon, "The Zoar Society: Applicants for Membership," Ohio Archaeological and Historical Quarterly 45 (No. 3, 1936):342.

48. Quoted in Noyes, Strange Cults, p. 331.

49. Quoted in Daryl Chase, The Early Shakers: An Experiment in Religious Communism, Unpublished Ph. D. dissertation, University of Chicago, 1936, p. 146.

50. Joseph R. Gusfield, Utopian Myths and Movements in Modern Societies (Morristown, N. J.: General Learning Press, 1973), p. 27.

51. Kenneth Westhues, "Hippiedom 1970: Some Tentative Hypotheses," The Sociological Quarterly 13 (Winter, 1972):84.

52. Zablocki, Alienation and Charisma, p. 105.

3. THE UTOPIAN PRACTICE OF SEX

Lewis Coser identifies the American utopian communities as one example of what he calls the "greedy institution." [1] Greedy institutions consume their members. They demand total allegiance and brook no rivals for their members' time and energy. In the case of the utopian communities, Coser argues, sexual attachments were viewed as "an unwelcome diversion of energies and hence a subversion of professed goals." [2] In particular, the communities could not tolerate exclusive sexual attachments, because the sexual bond between a man and a woman would threaten their allegiance to the total community. Both celibacy and free love eliminated exclusive relationships, so that these contrary types of arrangements performed the same sociological function.

Coser's argument has been echoed by a number of other analysts. But when we look at the total range of sexual practices in the communities, the argument becomes a limp one. Celibacy was a common arrangement, and free love was practiced in a few of the communities, but many communities (including some that lasted a number of generations) preferred or at least approved of monogamous unions. In this chapter, we will examine the various types of arrangements. They ranged from celibacy to group marriage to free love. The communities also differed in whether the ideal arrangement was voluntary or mandatory.

THE CELIBATES

The celibates have all been religious groups. A form of either Christianity or Eastern religion has provided the basis for the celibacy. But we can distinguish among three different experiences of utopian communities with celibacy: some have preferred though not demanded it; some have practiced it as the norm for the group; and some have tried it only to abandon it.

Celibacy Preferred

At Jerusalem, Amana, Bethel-Aurora, St. Nazianz, and the New Age commune, celibacy was clearly the ideal way. But it was not a condition of membership. Jerusalem was founded in 1788 by Jemima Wilkinson. She taught her followers that celibacy is a higher spiritual state, but she did not forbid marriage. Most of her followers opted for the lower state of marriage. St. Nazianz was a Roman Catholic community in Wisconsin and celibacy was a voluntary step taken by those who wished to pursue spiritual perfection in the traditional Catholic way. At Amana, celibacy was exalted but few people except some of the elders remained celibate. Nevertheless, the Amanaites never stopped proclaiming celibacy as the better way. One of the group's teachers warned the young men to "fly from intercourse with women, as a very highly dangerous magnet and magical fire." [3] When the Amanaites first came to Iowa, they were debating the question of marriage. Christian Metz, their leader, decided that marriage should be approved by the community as long as it was closely controlled and supervised. However, a number of the other leading members wanted to denounce marriage as unchristian. Metz prevailed, but pious members of the group insisted even in the early years of the twentieth century that a marriage should be made only by God's consent as signified through a charismatic leader. [4]

Thus, at Amana the official teaching was that God preferred people to follow the celibate way. The actual practice was for all but a few to be married and have children. Most of those who accepted the celibate life were elders (religious leaders). At Bethel-Aurora and the "New Age" commune in New Mexico, on the other hand, the leaders attempted to dissuade their followers from sex and marriage even while they exempted themselves. At the New Age group, sex was barely tolerated though the leader felt free to express his own affection to a number of the female members. [5] Dr. William Keil, founder and leader of Bethel Aurora, told his followers to remain celibate even though he was married and fathered nine children. Keil allowed some couples to marry but forbade others. And no one was allowed to marry an outsider. Why Keil urged celibacy, and why he was selective about who was allowed to marry are matters of speculation. One student of the Aurora, Oregon branch of the community pointed out that single people meant more workers at less cost than providing for a home and the children of a married couple, plus Keil received the property of those who died without heirs. [6] At any rate, Keil frequently did his best to dissuade people from desiring marriage:

> In his most graphic, persuasive, and powerful language he would describe to the women a beautiful wedding, the lovely bride, the proud groom, the procession to the church, the ceremony, the march home and the festivities--then he would depict in sharp contrast a year later when the little bride lay dead in childbirth, the crepe on the door, the despair and grief. He would then argue that it would be much better not to marry than to risk such sorrow. [7]

Celibacy the Norm

In a number of other communities, celibacy was either practiced or insisted upon by most or all of the members. In these communities, celibacy was spoken of as not merely an ideal but a necessity as well. Many of these groups taught that it was extremely difficult, if not impossible, to attain the desired spiritual state without adopting celibacy. For instance, Benjamin Purnell, founder and long-time leader of the House of David, taught his followers that they could all attain immortality. But they needed more than good works for such an achievement. Their blood must be purified of every bit of evil that was within them as a result of Adam's sin. And such a purification could be accomplished by foregoing all sexual activity. [8]

The Shakers took the most extreme stance. They were ambiguous in their writings regarding the status of non-Shakers. Sometimes they seem to suggest that non-Shakers can be Christians (though certainly inferior Christians) while at other times they assert that the only Christians are those who have entered with them into the celibate life. In any case, they insisted that every Shaker must be celibate--no exceptions whatever would be allowed. Furthermore, they insisted that sexual relations among non-Shakers

for any reason other than propagation was evil. A female
writer in the middle of the nineteenth century gave the following advice to non-Shaker females who married:

> Thou who has become the wife, and bosom friend
> of thy choice, remember the law of the Lord, for
> the direction of natural people, to do and to keep
> it. Honor thy husband that he may honor thee;
> yield and subject unto him, but go no further in
> sexual connexion than accords with the laws of God,
> given in the beginning, and the regulations of his
> servant Moses respecting times and seasons, for
> the protection of men in the flesh, while following
> the path of nature, to prevent uncleanness and
> brutality in their desires and gratifications. [9]

Another Shaker writer, in the last decade of the nineteenth
century, said that all people--whether Shakers or not--are
"morally and religiously obligated" not to have sexual relations except when the conditions are right for conceiving a
child. Otherwise, the couple would be engaged in "a debasing prostitution, and of the nature of whoredom. " [10] Sex
is meant by God for one purpose only--reproduction. Those
who engage in it for any other reason make it "a sore, an
ugly ulcer, on creation's organism. " [11]

    In spite of such grim portraits of sex, none of the
groups pretended that celibacy was easy. Constant vigilance
and continual encouragement were necessary to maintain the
celibate life (see chapters 4 and 6). Thomas Lake Harris,
leader of the Brotherhood of the New Life, said that the
sexual impulse was particularly strong in the milder climates,
so that "a morality is possible in Iceland that will not endure
the climate of Mexico. " [12] Moreover, he taught, as humankind improves the conditions of living and advances in
civilization, the sexual impulse becomes more and more
stimulated. It is, therefore, no easy thing to adopt the
celibate way. Harris believed that people had to grow
spiritually before they could abide by celibacy. We even
find a confession of temptation from Shaker lips. In response to a question as to whether he had ever "felt at least
a streak of love" for a woman and a desire for marriage, a
Shaker preacher replied "O yea, I have been tempted in all
points as Christ was, but in the particular cases you mentioned, I found upon critical and minute self-examination, as
many streaks of lust as there were of love. " [13] Sensing
that his feelings included lust, he continued, he was able to
exercise his faith and resist the devil's temptation.

Undoubtedly, celibacy was easier for some people than for others. It is reasonable to assume that some women in the nineteenth century found celibacy at least as attractive as continual child-bearing. In the society at large, family size decreased during the nineteenth century in spite of the fact that birth control methods were not generally approved or available. In 1800, American women bore on the average 7.04 children. By 1900, the figure dropped to 3.56. [14] Some feminists were explicit about women's right to decide when they would become mothers and they advocated abstinence as a way of limiting childbirth. [15] Women generally were concerned about the problem of continual pregnancies. Undoubtedly, some of the women who came into the utopian communities shared that concern. In fact, two female founders of communities had good reason for concern. Ann Lee, founder of the Shakers, had the traumatic experience of bearing four children, all of whom died in infancy. Martha McWhirter, founder of the Sanctificationists, had borne twelve children (half of whom lived to maturity) when she had an experience of "sanctification" while walking home one evening from a church service. She was convinced from that point on that she must live a celibate life.

Even in the twentieth century there have been women who have found celibacy attractive as an alternative to continual pregnancies. The poor black women who came into Father Divine's group had to give up both their money and their sex. But as Lawson has pointed out, that represented little sacrifice "in those beaten lives." For they had very little, if any, money. And for a good many, "sex meant too many children to feed, or painful abortions, or disease, or marriages broken by intolerable stress." [16] When Father told them that sex was evil, therefore, they readily agreed.

Religious fervor and a belief that celibacy was God's will for humans also made celibacy easier to maintain (see chapter 4). Consequently, while celibacy was imposed on people in most groups, in some there was a kind of grassroots movement that demanded it. Notably, the adoption of celibacy among the Rappites seems to have come from the demands of the people themselves following a religious revival in 1807. [17] The Rappites had come from Germany, but there is no evidence that there was any inclination towards celibacy while they were there. Moreover, Rapp did not initiate the custom. Apparently, the young people of the community, caught up in the glow of revival, led the way in establishing celibacy as the norm. Rapp accepted the idea and supported it with his sermons. The bulk of the Rappites adopted the new rule with little complaint and even with some enthusiasm.

And what of those who were already married? In Rapp's community, they continued to live together, but as brother and sister. So committed were they to the celibate way, wrote William Hinds in 1878, that it wasn't necessary to separate the sexes nor to separate parents from their children, "and to this day the men and women live together in the same house, relying upon their religious restraints alone to keep them from falling into 'temptation and a snare.'" [18] All of the celibates faced the problem of what to do with married couples who came into the communities. Generally, where celibacy was the norm the married couple would be expected to abide by it even if they continued to live together in the same house.

Some leaders have allowed themselves privileges that they denied their followers, but some others have set the example in the matter of celibacy during marriage. Ann Lee refused to have sexual relations with her husband once she became a leader of the Shakers. Martha McWhirter continued to live with her husband after her experience of sanctification. But she had no sexual relations with him for the remainder of his life. Thomas Lake Harris had two celibate marriages, one of which lasted about thirty years.

Furthermore, outsiders criticized the practice of severing sexual relations between a husband and wife, but the Shakers spoke of it as though it were a high privilege. One Shaker writer pointed out that a man and woman who were married had mutually agreed to enter such a relationship:

> Now, have they not the same right to agree to live no longer as husband and wife, but as brother and sister, that they may rise to a higher plane, and by the cross and self-denial, devote themselves to the cause of God and humanity?... By the first agreement, they became one flesh, by the second, one spirit by being jointed to the Lord. [19]

In some groups, including the Shakers and the modern commune of Trabuco, married couples who visit have been required to abstain from sexual relations while in the community. The Shakers facilitated the abstinence by putting the man and woman into separate quarters.

In spite of their insistence that celibacy is necessary, a few of these groups allowed at least some marriages. At Ephrata, the celibates lived together in the cloister. Married brothers and sisters lived in homes nearby and attended church with the celibates. But a clear distinction was made between the married members and the celibates. As a contemporary visitor pointed out, those who marry "are no longer considered in full communion, or suffered to live under the same roof." [20] The married members continued to wear the habit adopted by the celibates and in most respects continued to be thought of as members. But they clearly dropped in status. Similarly, the Rappites, for all their fervor, never insisted that celibacy was mandatory for everyone. Father Rapp united a number of couples in wedlock even while he continued to speak of marriage as an expression of the lusts of men. But, he wrote in a letter to his son, "it is difficult to reform sensuous man into a moral being." [21] Consequently, he married a few people but hoped that all would grow into a spiritual state where they could live the celibate life. Rapp's son, Frederick, expressed the ideal in a letter to an editor:

> The Harmonie Society consists only of people who live the religion of Jesus practically and who pursue sanctification. Among these there are some of both sexes who have so advanced in sanctification and who by means of the power of the gospel of Jesus Christ and His vicarious atonement have been so ennobled in their virtue, that they of their own free will have given up carnal intercourse and devote themselves fully to prepare for Christ and His Kingdom. [22]

Celibacy Tried and Failed

In at least three communities, the people attempted to institute celibacy but the experiment failed. At Zoar, Joseph Baumeler taught that celibacy is preferable because it enables the individual to focus on the eternal rather on the things that are transient. The principles which the Zoarites had brought with them from Germany included the statement that sexual relations except for the purpose of propagation is "sinful and contrary to the order and command of God. Complete virginity or entire cessation of sexual commerce is more commendable than marriage." [23] Initially, they prohibited marriage, but in the late 1820s they began to allow it, with Baumeler himself taking a wife. According to a member of the community, one of the main arguments for the change was that the community could raise its own members, who would become "natural Communists." [24] But the Zoarites seemed to be somewhat uncomfortable with either arrangement. Another member pointed out that marriage is unfavorable to communal life, that celibacy is preferable. But marriage is not, he continued, "in our experience, fatally adverse. It only makes more trouble; and in either case, whether a community permit or forbid marriage, it may lose members." [25]

Bishop Hill was a Swedish colony established in Illinois in 1846. The founders were religious dissenters who came to America to settle in a "New Jerusalem" from which true faith would be broadcast to all the world. They called themselves Janssonists because their leader and preacher was Erik Jansson. For a time, Jansson forbade the people to marry possibly because of the lack of adequate housing and the vicissitudes of beginning a new community on the frontier. Once housing was available, Jansson ordered the young people to marry and there was a literal flood of weddings. But in 1854, Nils Hedin, one of the twelve apostles appointed by Jansson to spread the faith in America, visited a Shaker group. The Shakers convinced him that celibacy was the best way for a Christian group. When he returned to Bishop Hill, he convinced Jonas Olson (Jansson had died) that the group should adopt celibacy. Olson and Hedin, along with the trustees, issued an edict forbidding marriage. The preachers of the community provided ample religious justification. They said that it was contrary to God's will for a husband and wife to live together, and that natural generation was the will of the devil. They also pointed out that when the young women married they could no longer perform their outdoor work in the fields and stables. [26] Married people could continue to live together as long as they remained celibate; young people, however, were not allowed to get married. A number of people left the community immediately when the ban on sex was put into effect. Those who remained were discontented. A number were expelled, while others formed a "secret league" to oppose the doctrine and, eventually, to depose the leaders. [27] The community only lasted a few more years. The attempt to enforce celibacy was one of the major reasons for its demise.

Finally, Fruitlands was founded in 1843 by a group of New England transcendentalists, including Charles Lane and A. Bronson Alcott. They organized their community at Harvard, but it lasted only about seven months. Lane strongly argued for celibacy, and came close to convincing Alcott. But Alcott could not accede to such a rule, and he and his wife left the community. Lane convinced the others that the lack of celibacy was ruining the experiment. After much persuasion, discussion, and prayer, Fruitlands became a celibate community. But the adoption of celibacy did not save the group. It was only a brief moment in the history of communal societies. Lane and his son joined the Shakers. The others went their different ways, some relieved and some despondent over the failure.

The Success of the Celibate Rule

Many people find it difficult to believe that a group can enforce celibacy on all its members. Indeed, the experience of the Janssonists underscores the difficulty of the task. On the other hand, the ease with which the Rappites followed the celibate way suggests that a celibate rule can be quite successful. In general, then, what does the evidence say about the extent to which the people adhered to the rule of celibacy? There is not a great deal of evidence, but what we have indicates a fair amount of success with some failures and rule-breaking.

For one thing, charges of sexual immorality were leveled against most, if not all, of the groups. Before they managed to build a reputation for integrity, the Shakers were accused by some of engaging in sexual orgies. At Ephrata, a number of the brethren, including their long-time leader Conrad Beissel, were charged with sexual indiscretions. It must be admitted that some of Beissel's behavior provided a good basis for rumors. For instance, he held love-feasts with the sisters; none of the other brethren were present. [28] As another example, Thomas Lake Harris left Brockton, New York in the face of charges of sexual immorality. He settled in Fountain Grove, California, but was forced to flee to England after a female reporter disguised herself as an interested seeker and wrote a series of scandalous articles about him. She accused Harris of gross immorality. But

her accusations were based mainly on his own accounts of
his relationships with women (see chapter 4 for a description of Harris' abundant use of sexual imagery). Moreover,
she claimed that Harris acted improperly towards her (he
was 68 years old at the time). [29]

One of the more sensational episodes of alleged sexual
immorality was that of Benjamin Purnell in the House of
David. The case against Purnell was actually a multifold
one, brought by the state of Michigan in 1927. Among other
things, Purnell was charged with maintaining a fraudulent
religious operation, teaching members to commit perjury in
order to protect the leaders, and committing gross immoral-
ities with women and girls in the community. Purnell stead-
fastly denied all charges. But a number of females testified
that he indeed had sexual relations with them under the guise
of engaging in a Purification Rite. One woman wrote about
her own experience with the rite when she was a girl. She
was walking down a hall one day when she heard Benjamin
call her into his room. He reminded her that she must be
obedient to him in all things, and told her to sit on the bed.
Then he explained to her that the rite of purification was an
important part of spiritual growth, and that women are "a
cleansing fountain." Since he had already been cleansed by
God's grace, the rite would cleanse her even as it made
him immortal. According to her, he said that as he emitted
"the emanation which is of the blood," he would become an
immortal one. "Man has not the power to lift himself. According to His word, this can only be done through woman." [30] When they were finished, he admonished her not
to tell anyone, for what they had done was a secret of the
Lord.

Benjamin denied at the trial that he had ever engaged
in such rites of purification. But after 51 days, 225 witnesses, more than 500 exhibits, and 15,000 pages of testimony, the court ruled that Benjamin and Mary Purnell had
to leave the community. The judge placed the community in
receivership. A month later, Benjamin died.

Undoubtedly many of the charges of sexual immorality
by outsiders were false. But some were undoubtedly true.
Certainly, no one would argue that every member of all the
celibate communities abided by the rule without fail. But if
we judge by the number of children born, the rate of failure
was not very high. Few children, according to the testimonies of a number of observers, were born in the Rappite

community. At Ephrata, some members decided to leave
the cloister and get married. One visitor to Ephrata said
that he saw a brother and a sister who were married: "That
is to say, he had got her with child in the Cloister." [31]
Two different physicians who treated the Shakers testified
before the New Hampshire legislature. One said that he
had never been called to deal with a case of pregnancy
among the Shakers, while the other said that during ten
years of irregular consultations, he only had one instance
of delivering a baby. [32] Interestingly, the doctor said
that he told them to keep the birth a secret, but they "were
for letting it be known." The Shakers despised an illicit
sexual encounter and the resulting pregnancy, but they gave
no indication of wanting to hide the fact. Finally, in depositions taken in a court case against Zoar, a couple of witnesses testified that there were some instances of sexual
relations while the community was supposedly celibate, and
that at least one illegitimate child was rumored to be Baumeler's.

Even people who were disenchanted with the communities indicated that the violations of the celibate rule were
occasional rather than typical. Thus, the bulk of the evidence suggests that the celibates were rather successful in
maintaining sexual abstinence. They may have had other
outlets--the kind of outlets that would scarcely be hinted at
in the nineteenth century. For instance, a young man who
had been in the Shakers for about 13 years and held many
offices said that the lack of sexual relations was a continual
source of discontent. To see the extent to which the Shakers
were consumed by sexual passion, he pointed out, one need
only consider the "effects of dreams" in a majority of the
men. [34] In spite of their wet dreams, the young man
said, the Shakers were generally a very holy group of people. Their dreams and their confessions simply showed that
they had not been able to quell their sexual passions totally.

Some of the celibates may have found relief in masturbation. It was mentioned in 1927 as practiced by some
members of the House of David (although the charge was
brought by an ex-member, which always means that we must
be cautious in accepting it as fact). [35] And members of a
modern celibate commune have also confessed to masturbation
as well as wet dreams and thoughts about sex. [36]

On balance, the evidence we have indicates that at
least some members broke the celibacy rule, some used

alternative outlets such as masturbation or wet dreams, but most seem to have kept the rule while they remained in the community. Most no doubt also struggled with their own persistent impulses. The celibate road was strewn with the jagged rocks of temptation, but a good many Americans traversed it successfully.

THE TRADITIONALISTS

The notion of a "traditional" arrangement in a utopian community appears somewhat of a contradiction in terms. Nevertheless, a number of communities took a strictly traditional approach to the question of sex. That is, they argued that sex must be confined to monogamous marriage. The traditionalists are found in both the nineteenth and twentieth centuries. In spite of the presumed sexual freedom of the present, today's utopians are not necessarily sexual adventurers. The Browns' study of a modern commune even reported that the members found it difficult to openly discuss the question of sexuality; they opted for exclusive sexual relationships. [37] And Zablocki reported that monogamous relationships were the modal type in the 120 communes he studied; 47 percent had either licensed or unofficial monogamous marriages as their sexual arrangement. [38] The monogamists also included Brook Farm, Hopedale, the Icarian communities, Shalam, Kaweah, and The Farm.

The Meaning of Sex

Some of the traditionalists had a negative and some had a positive attitude towards sex itself. Their common commitment to marriage does not mean that they viewed sex or marriage in the same way. For example, in the modern commune "Christ Communal Organization" women are viewed as sensuous beings who may tempt men in an evil way. The female body can cause a man to "have fleshly desire," so women must avoid creating "sexually charged situations and must take care not to 'stumble' (sexually arouse) the brothers." [39] In CCO, a romantic relationship should develop only when the two people feel that God is directing them to their relationship and only as long as their primary shared interest is their love of God rather than each other. With sex being devalued, courtship must take subtle forms, such as tone of voice or manner of looking at the other. A somewhat less negative view is held by the Hutterites, who are one of the more successful groups in American history. The Hutterites are an Anabaptist group who began settling in this country in 1874. They continue to flourish and to practice their traditional ways in spite of the developments in the larger society. The Hutterites believe that sex is only for procreation, but that it is for procreation. That is, sex should be used in order to produce children (as opposed to some other groups who emphasized abstinence unless a child was wanted). As a result, they may be one of the fastest growing groups in the world. [40] Their birthrate is more than double that of the American population as a whole.

Other groups have taken a more positive view towards sex itself. At Kaweah, a socialist colony organized in California in 1885, Burnette Haskell called the "enforced celibacy" of young people one of the "greatest evils" of the existing economic system. Young people had to remain celibate because they could not afford to marry. Kaweah, he declared, would remedy the situation by creating a new economic order. [41]

Similarly, at The Farm, a modern commune in Tennessee, sex is viewed positively and discussed openly. The members of The Farm came out of the hippie movement in the Haight-Ashbury district of San Francisco. Nevertheless, the group's leader, Stephen Gaskin, teaches them that any kind of promiscuity is wrong. Premarital sex and adultery are both taboo at The Farm. Sex itself, however, is considered good. In fact, members are taught to recognize the importance of the female orgasm. [42] And Stephen advocates "tantric loving." Tantric loving avoids the typical male-centered approach in America by recognizing the needs and capacities of both the male and the female. In sex, Stephen has written,

> we're not so much interested in the friction or the position or something like that as in moving the energy back and forth between us. Feels lovely when it moves too. And it gets you well, gets you sane, gets you healthy. Good for your body. Good for your mind. [43]

Tantric loving includes massaging and caressing the body of the other as a form of foreplay. The emphasis is on a gradual building up of desire and mutual gratification.

Sex Is Confined to Marriage

Whatever else sex means to the traditionalists, it always means an activity that is confined to marriage. As at The Farm, any kind of sexual activity outside of marriage is forbidden. The only alternative to marriage was celibacy, as some of the groups explicitly pointed out. For example, Shalam was founded in 1884 in New Mexico by John Newbrough. The community was set up to care for foundlings and orphans. "Oahspe," a "new Bible" written by Newbrough, provided the inspiration and guidance for the group. The book's guidance on sex is terse and clear: "For, after thou hast purified thyself as to flesh and spirit, two conditions are open to thee, celibacy and marriage." [44]

The Icarians also believed that people should only have sex in marriage, but they went a step further and argued that everyone should be married. Etienne Cabet incorporated a strict sexual morality into his utopian novel, Voyage to Icaria. In his ideal community there would be no adultery, no prostitution, no sexual crimes of any kind. Neither would there be any unmarried adults, for Cabet believed that people could only find true happiness in the married state. Hence, the Icarian Constitution not only stated that marriage and the family were to be a part of the community, but also asserted that "voluntary celibacy, when not induced by any physiological reason, is regarded as a transgression of natural laws." [45] Divorce was permitted, but the parties to the divorce were expected to remarry as soon as possible.

Among the traditionalists, then, sex apart from marriage was taboo. Some called it a sin, while others called it a violation of the community's well-being. Whenever any kind of extramarital sex was detected, it was treated as a serious offense. Even sexual experimentation has been viewed as an affront to the community. For example, in the Bruderhof, a group of religious communities that came to America in the 1950s, children are not expected to have any knowledge of sexual matters until they are adolescents. Any kind of sexual experimentation, including "masturbation and adolescent flirtation, are not merely frowned upon, but if detected are treated as abhorrent." [46]

An interesting example of the horror of the traditionalists at any extramarital sex occurred at Hopedale, Adin Ballou's religious community in Massachusetts (1842-1867).

The people uncovered a case of "free love" in the community in 1853. A man had sexual relations with a woman in his household. He presumably repented, but continued the affair. When confronted the second time with his trespass, he defended it in terms of individual liberty. He and the woman both admitted to being free lovers in their philosophy. Consequently, they were forced to leave, and the community felt constrained to set forth its position on the matter. A set of ten resolutions was passed in July, 1853 setting forth the group's beliefs about Christian Chastity. Among other things, they asserted:

> ... we contemplate as utterly abhorrent the various "Free Love" theories and practices insidiously propagated among susceptible minds under pretext of higher religious perfection, moral exaltation, social refinement, individual sovereignty, physiological research and philosophical progress; and we feel bound to bear our uncompromising testimony against all persons, communities, books and publications which inculcate such specious and subtle licentiousness. [47]

The next month the community adopted a revised constitution in which it resolved that a "sacred and vigilant maintenance of pure chastity" is absolutely necessary for the welfare of the community, and that "no decent community ever can be permanently established which does not insist on sexual purity as one of its fundamental vitalities." [48]

Nor did that end the matter. Ballou continued to debate the issue with a Mr. Kent in the community's paper, The Practical Christian, and to publish articles in defense of traditional marriage. One article, published in the paper in 1854 and in 1855 as a pamphlet, was the testimony of a "true hearted woman." The anonymous woman pointed out that when Love grips a man or woman, there is always "a desire to possess exclusively the affections of the beloved," a desire that is directly proportional to the "intensity and purity of the love." [49] In other words, free love so-called is actually not a form of love at all. Love by its very nature is exclusive, not free floating.

Even where there was no overt scandal, as at Hopedale, the traditionalists worried about the possibility of such a scandal. At Brook Farm, founded in 1841 by Transcendentalists and later turned into a Fourier group, the leaders had to deal with rumors that the young people had been affected by Fourier's nontraditional ideas about sex. Parents were worried that their children would be morally corrupted and adopt the philosophy of free love. [50] One who had been there as a child later wrote that she could understand why the adult leaders were so concerned about the "almost unrestrained companionship of so many young people of both sexes," but actually the relationships between them were "really noble and pure." [51] It was hard enough to try to maintain a utopian community without dealing with the accusations by outsiders of sexual immorality. For the traditionalists, such accusations would be doubly hard to bear because they abhorred extramarital sex as much as anyone else in American society. The traditionalists did not agree with other Americans about the best form of the economy and the polity, but they had no doubts that the traditional form of marriage and the family was as utopian as one could hope to find.

The Meaning of Marriage

Although the traditionalists all believed that sex should be confined to marriage, they did not believe that regulation of sex was the only purpose of marriage. As noted above, Cabet made marriage mandatory because he believed it necessary for human happiness. Their constitution itself stated that marriage and the family are the primary condition for people's happiness. At Hopedale, they also stressed the benefits of marriage for human happiness. One man gave his testimony in glowing terms (though admitting that not many marriages reached the ideal that he described):

> There will be no jealousy, discord, or divorce,
> WHEN THERE IS A SOUL-UNION. When loving
> souls are thus united, life's pathway is made
> smooth and pleasant, for the genial love-light of
> the higher spheres shine upon it; the rudest cottage
> is made a heaven, when love and affection have
> sanctified it. [52]

In contrast to the Hutterites, who believe that sex and marriage are designed to be used to produce children, the people at Hopedale explicitly denied that a marriage should necessarily produce offspring. The divine end of marriage is not the perpetuation of the race, for "man is somewhat more than a vegetable seed-vessel, or an animal germ-cell, cre-

ated for the humiliating end of mere use and decay. " [53]
Marriage, rather, should lead to the fulfillment of both the
man and the woman.

The Icarians believed that marriage and family life
were essential to social order as well as to human happiness. When all were married, there would be little disor-
der, scandal, crime, or "debauchery and prostitution. " [54]
Another group, the short-lived Champ d'Asile that was settled in Texas in 1818, also made marriage obligatory on the
basis that it was essential to social order. A member who
refused to marry after a "reasonable time" was excluded
from participating in public affairs. When a young male
announced that he was going to marry, the rest of the colony
built him a home, gave him land which they cultivated and
planted, and furnished him with sufficient supplies for a
year. [55]

A somewhat different approach is found in the Christ
Communal Organization. Marriage is encouraged in spite of
their negative view of sex, but the meaning of marriage takes
on a utilitarian tone. Members are undoubtedly motivated by
sexual and companionship needs, but marriage in the CCO
does not follow the American companionship model. Rather,
there is an emphasis on the difference between the two sex
roles and the fact that the couple should complement each
other in order to facilitate the tasks for which they are responsible. In other words, there is a "task-oriented family
structure reminiscent of frontier times. " [56]

With some exceptions like Christ Communal Organization, the traditionalists gave a traditional meaning as well as
a traditional form to marriage. They stressed the role of
marriage in securing the individual's well-being through affection and companionship. They pointed to the social benefits of stable relationships. One position which appears to
be rather unique in all this is that of the Friendship Community, a small communist group in Missouri that lasted
from 1872 to 1877. The group's newspaper declared its belief that communism is opposed to "free-love or promiscuous
and irresponsible intercourse. " Communism leads to a true
relationship between the sexes, and that relationship will be
marriage "of some kind or its equivalent. " Since the law
requires marriage, however, the form of relationship between the sexes in the community would be marriage. It is
only because the law requires it that marriage is needed in
the community,

but while we hold that that is the only reason, we also hold that that is an ample and sufficient reason; for as our Community is incorporated in accordance with the laws of the State and thereby made a legal body for the transaction of business, we could not reasonably expect the protection of the law in this respect unless we were law-abiding citizens in all other respects. And so we do not desire nor propose to set the law at defiance in regard to marriage. [57]

Traditional marriage at Friendship was obviously a matter of expediency more than of ideology.

THE SEXUAL DEVIANTS

While celibacy has been the most common arrangement in the past and monogamy or coupling the most common in recent times, the utopians have had a great many deviant arrangements as well. The popular image of the commune as a place of sexual license is not entirely without foundation. Sprague begins his account of communes with the following vignette from a rural group. [58] A number of young men and women are sitting around on the farmhouse porch. One male is sitting in a cane-bottom chair, playing his guitar and singing. A blonde woman kneels between his legs, performing fellatio. The rest of the people pay no attention to the two. As the male approaches orgasm, he stops playing and singing. Afterwards, he relaxes back into his chair and begins to enjoy his music again. The woman gets up, looks around and asks, "Anyone else?" Getting only negative responses, she goes into the house.

That rural commune is not typical of sexual arrangements, even among those who practice sexual deviance. The point is that virtually every type of sexual practice can be found among the utopians, including those that many Americans would label as immoral, disgusting, or animalistic. However, we can group the deviants into three types: those that practice group marriage; those that opt for free love of a laissez-faire arrangement; and the complex marriage system at Oneida.

Group Marriage

In a group marriage, each member is married to

every other member of the opposite sex. In one commune, an ordained minister performed a wedding service in which each member was married to all others. [59] This is not to say that there are no restrictions on sexual activity, however. At Kerista Village, a San Francisco commune, they talk about their arrangement as "polyfidelity," or simultaneous faithfulness to many others. But the many others do not include outsiders. Rather, polyfidelity means that the commune itself is a family, that each member has sexual relations equally with each other member of the opposite sex, that no one has sex with outsiders, and that all adults will act as parents to all children born in the community. [60]

One of the problems of a group marriage is the mechanics of the arrangement. How do they determine who has sex with whom? At Kerista Village, the community is broken down into "best friend identity clusters" (BFICs). A BFIC has a maximum of 24 members, twelve of each sex. Sexual relations occur within the BFIC on a "non-preferential" basis. That is, each member is expected to love every other member of his or her BFIC equally. Newcomers to the community live through a period of "transitional celibacy" until they decide upon, and are accepted into, a BFIC which has less than 24 members. A newcomer can also begin a new BFIC and wait for other newcomers with whom he or she feels an affinity.

According to the Kerista literature, this arrangement works very well. In other groups, it has not worked so well. Harrad West began in 1968 in the San Francisco area. The name was inspired by Robert Rimmer's novel, The Harrad Experiment, which describes a sexual experiment where college students learn the joys of having sex with a variety of partners. Although all adult members at Harrad West were married to all other adult members, there were also "pair-bond" relationships because most people had entered the group as couples. The goal at Harrad West was to create a group of people who had intimate, personal relations with each other, as opposed to the kind of relationships involved in sexual "swinging." Harrad West was never large. Yet even with six adults, there were problems about sexual relationships. At one point, the pattern was two or three nights a week with the pair-bond partner, and one night with each other member of the opposite sex. [62]

Toward the end of the experiment, Robert Houriet visited the group and found considerable tension and conflict. Houriet's description sounds like a summary of a soap opera:

Gloria was intimate only with Herb in a casual, almost brother-sister relationship. Both Alice and Daphne were becoming more independent of the roles they had played in the past with Herb and Bud, respectively. Herb actually welcomed Alice's new independence. However Daphne's self-assertion deeply disturbed Bud and forced him to find a separate identity. Bud keenly felt the lack of a brotherly tie with Moishe and Herb. Most of the lines of stress in the group marriage seemed to have converged on Bud. [63]

One day, Alice showed Houriet "The Chart." The chart was a kind of calendar. Fourteen days were listed vertically and the members of the group were noted horizontally. The chart showed the sleeping arrangements for the two-week span. They developed the chart, Alice explained, because too much time had been spent each day trying to decide who would sleep with whom. With the chart, there was an equitable distribution and no one was supposed to get jealous. But the chart did not solve their problems. As Houriet pointed out, the six adults seldom got together as a group "partly because no one can stand the house's highly charged atmosphere for long. When they do get together, it's like a scene from Who's Afraid of Virginia Woolf plus two." [64]

Various other groups have also had their problems trying to maintain a group marriage. In the four communes studied by Hawkins, there was an ideological commitment to group marriage, but in practice they all developed a pattern of serial monogamy. [65] Perhaps the most successful attempt to create a group marriage system was that at Oneida, which we shall discuss below.

Free Love/Laissez-Faire Groups

Groups that have practiced free love have believed in the individual's right to choose his or her sexual partner regardless of marital status. Sometimes, however, groups that opted for free love rejected the right of people to get married and have an exclusive relationship. At other times, free love really meant a laissez-faire arrangement, with each individual having the right to choose whatever sexual pattern he or she desired. We shall include both variants in this section, since both more or less affirm the right of individual choice in sexual matters.

As in the case of group marriage, advocacy of free love did not always mean actual practice. An interesting example is provided by the Fourier groups. Fourier himself advocated sexual fulfillment by guaranteeing every individual a "sexual minimum." He argued that while people can do without sexual intercourse, "it is certain that the need for tactile or sensual pleasures causes as many social disorders as does the need for subsistence." [66] Every individual, therefore, should have a minimum of sexual pleasure. Furthermore, sexual fulfillment can be aborted through the bondage of a traditional Christian marriage. Without "mutual attachment of heart," marriage is a hindrance rather than a means to the experience of love. [67] This frequently happens since the aim of Christian marriage is procreation. Hence, marriage actually debases love, approves "even the most brutal sort of sexual unions," and encourages "the worst kinds of tyranny." [68] People should act on the basis of sentiment, their love for each other, rather than on the basis of a legal union established to bring children into the world.

American followers of Fourier tried to avoid any public discussion of his ideas about sex and marriage. Albert Brisbane, one of the leading American Fourierists and a translator of much of Fourier's work, avoided translating the works that made sexual recommendations. [69] Nevertheless, by the middle of the nineteenth century, the name of Fourier was associated in the public mind with free love, and charges of free love plagued the various phalanxes. Indeed, some members did advocate free love as a principle, but there is no evidence that it was practiced. At the Wisconsin Phalanx, there was a strict moral code. One member pointed out that in the area of the family the group had modified Fourier's theory "to adapt it to American feelings and habits--in family independence, care of children, and mode of living." [70] There is no evidence of anything but conventional marital arrangements in Wisconsin or in any of the other Fourier groups. As Brisbane had written in 1846, they would "leave marriage as it is, and maintain it in its present condition" since it is not a question for "the present age." [71] Marriage, after all, said Brisbane, is not the cause of all of the evils of the present age. Still, he noted, when the other evils had been taken care of, in some future generation, women themselves will decide about the question of marriage.

Obviously, the Fourierists believed in the teachings of their master. But they also believed that they could not advocate those teachings in the United States. They first had to establish themselves, gain respectability, implement various social, economic, and political reforms, and then the question of sex and marriage would be raised and dealt with appropriately. What would actually be appropriate in the realm of sex and marriage was never made explicit, but Fourier's writings suggest free love as a way for people to find fulfillment.

Similarly, at New Harmony the actual arrangements were never quite consistent with Owen's views. Owen had harsh words for marriage. As he expressed it in a lecture delivered after his experiment at New Harmony had failed:

> And I now tell you ... that the marriages of the world, under the system of moral evil in which they have been devised and are now contracted, are the sole cause of all the prostitution, of all its incalculable grievous evils, and of more than one half of all the vilest and most degrading crimes known to society. And that until you put away from among you and your children for ever, this accursed thing, you will never be in a condition to become chaste or virtuous in your thoughts and feelings, or to know what real happiness is. [72]

Owen never advocated free love openly as an alternative, but, again, free love seems to be a reasonable alternative if indeed we are to eliminate that "accursed thing," marriage, from our midst. At New Harmony, however, people established sexual relations by getting married with the services of a clergyman. The only way in which they deviated was for a couple to explicitly state at the beginning of the ceremony that they took each other as husband and wife and that "I submit to any other ceremony upon this occasion only in conformity with the laws of the state." [73] They then had a regular marriage ceremony.

Other groups have not only advocated, but also practiced free love, including some nineteenth-century groups. Modern Times was founded in 1851 by Josiah Warren, the American anarchist. Modern Times was the third community established by Warren, who wanted to build a community with a system of cooperative, nonprofit labor along with exchange of commodities. At Modern Times, sexual and marital arrangements were left up to individual discretion. People could be married or could simply take up residence together.

The relationship could be dissolved at will without any formality. Because of the free, individual choice involved, and the right of individuals to engage in their own arrangements without any outside interference, a number of customs emerged. [74] It was not, for instance, polite to ask about the identity of the father of a newborn child, or about the identity of the husband or wife of any member. Members who considered themselves married wore a red thread on their finger. If the red thread was taken off, it meant that the marriage had been dissolved.

At Modern Times, then, sexual relationships tended to be one of two kinds--married couples and couples living together. In modern communes, there is a greater variety of sexual practices in the free love groups. In particular, there tends to be more promiscuity and more sexual experimentation. One female told of having sexual relations with eight to ten different males in a single day. [75] At Blue Mountain Ranch "some of us played man-and-wife, with the rest of us playing musical beds." [76] Individuals in the group experimented with various kinds of sexuality. One, named Myeba, had a baby by one man, lived awhile with another man, then lived with some women. She left the community for a short time, returned and moved in with another man; they lived as a celibate couple. Finally, she began experimenting with lesbian relationships and found them more satisfying. "My feelings about sexual relating with men are that it's a boring and frequently unpleasurable situation with no possibility for creative, sensual exploration. I feel I have begun to find a sexuality that is mine with women." [77]

Many communes, like Blue Mountain Ranch, have permitted any kind of sexual expression. As Kathleen Kinkade, the founder of Twin Oaks, pointed out, what liberals have talked about for a long time has been put into practice by her group, namely, a society in which each one can freely express his or her attraction to anyone else in the community. This did not mean that everyone began engaging in sexual orgies. But it did mean that whatever happened was approved by the others or at least the others kept quiet about it. [78] In addition to promiscuity and homosexuality, various groups have tolerated such things as public nudity, public sex, group sex, sex play between children, and adult-child sexual relations. [79]

But there are also some restrictions. Some groups

have made homosexuality taboo. At Twin Oaks, only jealousy
and possessiveness are said to be forbidden. But, according
to an anthropologist who studied the community, there are
subtle pressures on monogamists, so that monogamous couples invariably either split up or leave the community. [80]
Few groups, it seems, have been willing to tolerate literally
anything at all.

One other question about the sexual practice of the
free-love groups is the amount of sexual activity that occurs.
Given the permissive atmosphere, is sex a dominant concern
and activity? The evidence suggests that it is not. As a
member of a defunct community lamented, the abolition of
all sexual taboos did not lead to a situation of sexual adventure. "On the contrary, it seems to me that the abolition
of these taboos made such sexual adventurism significantly
less necessary and alluring." [81] And in the 120 communes
studied by Zablocki, the actual amount of sexual activity and
sexual experimentation appeared to be rather low. [82] Zablocki found that homosexual and multisexual activities tended
to decline somewhat after people joined a commune. Moreover, a survey of members showed that at the time of the
survey 42 percent of urban communards were not sexually
involved with another member of their commune. And among
those who were involved, 71 percent had a monogamous relationship.

Complex Marriage

The system of complex marriage at Oneida has been
called a form of group marriage by some and a form of free
love by others. The Oneidans called their system free love
at one point, then later denied it. In 1852, the Circular, a
community publication, affirmed the "cultivation of free
love." By 1865, the same publication carried an article that
took pains to distinguish the typical view of free love from
what was practiced at Oneida. [83] At any rate, the system
at Oneida was unique and we need to look at it separately.

John Humphrey Noyes, the charismatic minister and
founder and leader of Oneida, was struggling with the meaning of sex and marriage before he established the community.
In 1837, he discovered that the woman he deeply loved had
decided to marry someone else. Noyes expressed his agony
in a letter to a friend, in which he said, among other things,
that when God's will is done on earth as it is in heaven,

there will be no marriages. "The marriage supper of the Lamb is a feast at which every dish is free to every guest. ... I call a certain woman my wife--she is yours, she is Christ's and in him she is the bride of all saints." [84]

Eventually, Noyes worked out his system of "complex marriage" that reflected his early ideas. Complex marriage is group marriage; each member is married to every other member. But Noyes added a number of elements to the system that made it unique. Perhaps the most unique aspect was "male continence." The point of male continence was to prevent conception. Noyes had fathered five children in six years of marriage, all but one of which had been stillborn. The experience was so painful to both him and his wife that he resolved not to have sexual relations with her until something could be done to remove the burden of continual childbearing from her. That something turned out to be male continence, or what has become known as coitus reservatus. That is, the male does not ejaculate during intercourse. According to Noyes, this is easy once it is learned. He said that there are three parts to intercourse. In the first, the male has his organ in the female. In the second, there is a series of reciprocal motions. And in the third, there is ejaculation. All is voluntary, Noyes pointed out, up to the very moment of emission. All, therefore, can be controlled up to that point.

Noyes used the analogy of a man in a boat, floating down a stream in which there is still water, then rapids, then a waterfall:

> The skillful boatman may choose whether he will remain in the still water, or venture more or less down the rapids, or run his boat over the fall. But there is a point on the verge of the fall where he has no control over his course; and just above that there is a point where he will have to struggle with the current in a way which will give his nerves a severe trial, even though he may escape the fall. If he is willing to learn, experience will teach him the wisdom of confining his excursions to the region of easy rowing, unless he has an object in view that is worth the cost of going over the falls. [85]

The "object in view" of course is ejaculation and subsequent pregnancy for the woman.

Anticipating objections, Noyes argued that male continence is natural, healthy, conducive to love, and effective in controlling conception. It is natural because God surely did not design men to "sow seed by the way-side where they do not expect it to grow." [86] It is healthy because it saves women from continual childbearing and saves men from the drain of life (see chapter 4 on the spermatic economy). It is conducive to love because it enhances sexual pleasure (Noyes insisted that the most gratifying part of sexual intercourse was the union of the two people rather than the orgasm). Finally, it is effective by definition. It was also effective in practice, for in a twenty-one year period during which the method was used by all males in the community there were no more than thirty-one accidental conceptions. [87]

Noyes also argued that male continence is easy, as he found out by his own efforts to learn it. At Oneida, young males learned the method by having intercourse only with women who were past their childbearing years. After they mastered the method, they could have sex with younger women also.

According to an informant of a physician who examined a number of the women, females could be introduced to sexual relations (usually by Noyes himself or an older male) as early as nine or ten years of age, while males might begin having sex as early as thirteen or fourteen. [88] The same informant said that a girl as young as sixteen or seventeen could be called on to have intercourse as much as seven times a week or more.

How did they decide who would have sex with whom? Noyes was determined to prevent exclusive relations from developing. In the early 1860s, therefore, requests for sex were made through a third party, generally an older woman. This system not only made it easier for someone to decline the invitation, but also enabled the community to keep a record of sexual activity and prevent any one couple from developing an exclusive relationship. Either males or females could take the initiative in requesting a sexual encounter with someone. [89]

Additional information on the sexual practices comes from some studies made in the latter part of the nineteenth and early part of the twentieth centuries. According to Dr. Hilda Noyes, the position used (which presumably helped the male to restrain from ejaculating) was "wife on side--upper thigh bent--husband enters from rear, they play manually with each others genitals." [90] At first, she said, the sexual activity might go on all night. Later, there was a midnight curfew. She also said that the method was particularly satisfying to women, who did experience orgasm, and that both cunnilinctus and fellatio were "probably used."

Anita McGee, an anthropologist, interviewed a number of people in the 1890s who had been members of the community. According to her respondents, some men found it nearly impossible to avoid ejaculation, but the women avoided those men. The men, according to one respondent, found relief in nocturnal emissions. Some of the women were in greater demand than others. Those in lesser demand took the "overflow." Sexual relations for the average individual occurred every two, three, or four days. Women's sexual desire increased with experience, but it was generally less than the men's. [91]

The Oneida system of complex marriage lasted a generation, from 1848 to 1879. Interestingly, when the community finally began to break up, Noyes recommended that the people adopt celibacy (he was an old man at the time and had already fled to Canada). In his communication to the community, Noyes wrote that they should give up complex marriage because of public sentiment, not because they had changed their ideas about its validity. Secondly, he suggested that in its place the group adopt neither the standards of the Shakers nor of the world, but stand "on Paul's platform, which allows marriage but prefers celibacy." [92] The people decided to abolish the utopian community, and reorganize into a joint-stock company. Most of the members opted for marriage rather than celibacy and the Oneida Community officially became Oneida Community, Limited, a joint-stock company on January 1, 1881.

Notes

1. Lewis A. Coser, Greedy Institutions: Patterns of Undivided Commitment (New York: Free Press, 1974).

2. Ibid., p. 137.

3. Rev. M. Kaufmann, "Utopian Experiments and Social Pioneering," Leisure Hour 28 (1879):542.

4. Bertha M. H. Shambaugh, Amana: The Community of True Inspiration (Iowa City: The State Historical Society of Iowa, 1908).

5. Laurence Veysey, The Communal Experience (Chicago: The University of Chicago Press, 1973), p. 381.

6. Ione Juanita Beale Harkness, Certain Community Settlements of Oregon. Unpublished Master's Thesis, University of Southern California, 1925, p. 19.

7. Ibid.

8. Robert S. Fogarty, The Righteous Remnant: The House of David (Kent, Ohio: Kent State University Press, 1981), p. 53.

9. Paulina Bates, The Divine Book of Holy and Eternal Wisdom (Canterbury, N. H.: United Society, 1849), p. 516.

10. A. G. Hollister, Mission of Alethian Believers, Called Shakers (Mount Lebanon, N. Y.: n. p., 1892-1899), p. 5.

11. "Longevity of Virgin Celibates," Shaker Manifesto 12 (October 1882):217.

12. Thomas Lake Harris, A Voice from Heaven (privately printed, 1879), p. 7.

13. H. L. Eads, Shaker Sermons, 4th ed. (South Union, Kentucky: n. p., 1887), p. 313.

14. James Reed, From Private Vice to Public Virtue (New York: Basic Books, 1978), p. 4.

15. Carl Degler, At Odds (New York: Oxford University Press, 1980), pp. 271-73.

16. Donna Lawson, Brothers and Sisters All Over This Land: America's First Communes (New York: Praeger, 1972), p. 126.

17. John S. Duss, The Harmonists (Philadelphia: Porcupine Press, 1972), pp. 26-27.

18. William Alfred Hinds, American Communities (Oneida, N. Y.: Office of the American Socialist, 1878), p. 13.

19. Ruth Webster, "The Family Relation," The Shaker and Shakeress 3 (May 1873):39.

20. Felix Reichmann and Eugene E. Dollieds, "Ephrata as Seen by Contemporaries," The Pennsylvania German Folklore Society 17 (1952):100.

21. Karl J. R. Arndt, A Documentary History of the Indiana Decade of the Harmony Society, 1814-1824, Vol. 1, 1814-1819 (Indianapolis: Indiana Historical Society, 1975), p. 399.

22. Ibid., p. 775.

23. Charles Nordhoff, The Communistic Societies of the United States (New York: Schocken Books, 1965; 1st publ. 1865), p. 104.

24. Hinds, American Communities, p. 32.

25. Nordhoff, Communistic Societies, p. 108.

26. Sivert Erdahl, "Erik Jansson and the Bishop Hill Colony," Journal of the Illinois State Historical Society (October 1925):561.

27. Ernst W. Olson, ed., History of the Swedes of Illinois (Chicago: The Engberg-Holmberg Publishing Co., 1908), p. 251.

28. Lamech and Agrippa, Chronicon Ephratense (New York: Burt Franklin, 1786), p. 91.

29. Herbert W. Schneider and George Lawton, A Prophet and a Pilgrim (New York: Columbia University Press, 1942), pp. 534-53.

30. Mrs. Isabella Pritchard and Mrs. Harry Achterberg, The Truth About the House of David as Related by Former Members (Benton Harbor, Mich.: House of Antarrah, 1927), p. 35.

31. Reichmann and Dollieds, Ephrata, p. 123.

32. Shaker Examination Before the New Hampshire Legis-
     lature, November Session, 1848 (Concord, N. H. :
     Ervin B. Tripp, 1849), pp. 46, 48.

33. Depositions of Mathew Heilman and Martin Reily,
     Brief 209, U. S. Supreme Court Record. Ms. in the
     Nixon Family Papers, Ohio Historical Society.

34. Letter of Charles Byrd, July 25, 1827. In the Byrd
     mss., Lilly Library, Indiana University.

35. Pritchard and Achterberg, The Truth About the House
     of David, p. 14.

36. Ilse Martin, "Inequality, Chastity, and Sign Endogamy
     in the New Age Brotherhood." P. 100 in Jon Wagner,
     ed., Sex Roles in Contemporary American Communes
     (Bloomington, Ind. : Indiana University Press, 1982).

37. L. Dave Brown and Jane C. Brown, "The Struggle
     for an Alternative: A Case Study of a Commune,"
     Human Organization 32 (Fall 1973):262.

38. Benjamin Zablocki, Alienation and Charisma (New
     York: Free Press, 1980), p. 339.

39. James T. Richardson, Mary White Stewart, and Robert
     B. Simmonds, Organized Miracles (New Brunswick,
     N. J. : Transaction Books, 1979), pp. 140-141.

40. William F. Pratt, "The Anabaptist Explosion," Natural
     History 78 (February 1969):8.

41. Burnette G. Haskell, "A Pen Picture of the Kaweah
     Co-Operative Colony Company," The Commonwealth 3
     (November 1889):114.

42. Bryan Pfaffenberger, "A World of Husbands and
     Mothers." P. 203 in Wagner, ed., Sex Roles.

43. Stephen Gaskin, Hey, Beatnik! (Summertown, Tenn. :
     The Book Publishing Co., 1974), no page numbers.

44. OAHSPE: A New Bible in the Words of Jehovih and
     His Angel Embassadors (Boston: Oahspe Publishing
     Assoc., 1891), p. 767.

45. Brief History of Icaria (Corning, Iowa: Icaria, 1880), p. 21.

46. John McKelvie Whitworth, God's Blueprints (London: Routledge & Kegan Paul, 1975), p. 206.

47. Adin Ballou, History of the Hopedale Community (Lowell, Mass.: Thompson & Hill, 1897), p. 249.

48. Constitution, By-Laws, Rules and Regulations of the Hopedale Community: As Revised and Approved, August 31, 1853 (Hopedale, Mass.: n. p., 1853), pp. 34-35.

49. True Love vs. Free Love (Hopedale, Mass.: Hopedale Press, 1855), pp. 4-5.

50. Edith Roelker Curtis, A Season in Utopia (New York: Thomas Nelson & Sons, 1961), pp. 210-11.

51. "Reminiscences of Brook Farm," Old and New 4 (September 1871):349.

52. W. W. Dutcher, "True Marriage," Spiritual Reformer 2 (April 1861):95.

53. "The 'Higher Law' in Marriage," The Progressive Age 5 (October 1863):46.

54. "History and Constitution of the Icarian Community," trans. Thomas Teakle, Iowa Journal of History and Politics 15 (1917):249.

55. Moreau of Rice Institute, "Champ d'Aisle," trans. Thomas G. Rice, Houston, n. d. Ms. in the Barker Texas History Center, University of Texas at Austin.

56. Richardson, Stewart, and Simmonds, Organized Miracles, p. 146.

57. "Marriage and Communism," The Communist 4 (January 1877):22.

58. W. D. Sprague, Case Histories from the Communes (New York: Lancer Books, 1972), pp. 11-12.

59. John David Hawkins, "Utopian Values and Communal

Social Life." Unpublished Ph. D. dissertation, North-western University, 1975, p. 339.

60. The Kerista Village Handbook (San Francisco: n. p., n. d.), p. 6.

61. Richard Fairfield, Communes USA (Baltimore: Penguin Books, 1971), p. 298.

62. Ron E. Roberts, The New Communes: Coming Together in America (Englewood Cliffs, N. J.: Prentice-Hall, 1971), p. 42.

63. Robert Houriet, Getting Back Together (New York: Coward, McCann & Geoghegan, 1971), pp. 245-46.

64. Ibid., p. 256.

65. Hawkins, "Utopian Values," p. 341.

66. Quoted in Jonathan Beecher and Richard Bienvenu, eds., The Utopian Vision of Charles Fourier (Boston: Beacon, 1971), p. 339.

67. Charles Fourier, The Passions of the Human Soul, trans. Rev. John Reynell Morell, Vol. 1 (London: Hippolyte Bailliere, 1851), pp. 347-48.

68. Quoted in Beecher and Bienvenu, The Utopian Vision, p. 57.

69. Taylor Stoehr, Free Love in America: A Documentary History (New York: AMS Press, 1979), p. 15.

70. Quoted in Joan Elias, "The Wisconsin Phalanx: An Experiment in Association," Unpublished M. A. Thesis, University of Wisconsin, 1968, p. 174.

71. A. Brisbane, "The American Associationists," United States Magazine and Democratic Review 18 (February 1846):146.

72. Robert Owen, Lectures on the Marriage of the Priesthood of the Old Immoral World, 4th edition (Leeds, England: J. Hobson, 1840), p. 7.

73. Reported in The New Harmony Gazette, April 5, 1826, p. 252.

74. Stoehr, Free Love in America, p. 435.

75. Sprague, Case Histories, p. 55.

76. January Thaw (New York: Times Change Press, 1974), p. 19.

77. Ibid., p. 30.

78. Kathleen Kinkade, "Power and the Utopian Assumption," Journal of Applied Behavior Science 10 (No. 3, 1974): 413.

79. See: Home Free! (Occidental, Cal.: Friends of Morningstar Publications, 1978), pp. 39, 275; Sara Davidson, "Open Land: Getting Back to the Communal Garden," Harper's Magazine 240 (June 1970): 92-93; and Bennet M. Berger, The Survival of a Counterculture (Berkeley and Los Angeles: University of California Press, 1981), pp. 67-73.

80. Lani Wheeler Higgins, "Not Yet Utopia: A Study of Twin Oaks Community," Unpublished Ph. D. Dissertation, University of Virginia, 1979, p. 53.

81. Gordon Yaswen, "Sunrise Hill: A Postmortem." P. 147 in Jerry Richard, ed., The Good Life (New York: New American Library, 1973).

82. Zablocki, Alienation and Charisma, p. 122.

83. Constance Noyes Robertson, Oneida Community: An Autobiography, 1851-1876 (Syracuse, N.Y.: Syracuse University Press, 1970), pp. 277, 281-83.

84. John H. Noyes, "The Battle Axe Letter," The Witness 1 (January 23, 1839):49.

85. John Humphrey Noyes, Male Continence (New York: Arno Press, 1969; 1st publ. 1872), p. 8.

86. Ibid., p. 13.

87. Maren Lockwood Carden, Oneida: Utopian Community to Modern Corporation (New York: Harper Torchbooks, 1969), p. 51.

88. Ely Van De Warker, "A Gynecological Study of the Oneida Community," The American Journal of Obstetrics and Diseases of Women and Children 17 (August 1884):789.

89. Allan Estlake, The Oneida Community (London: George Redway, 1900), p. 87.

90. Robert Latou Dickinson and Dr. Hilda Noyes, "Interview, September, 1926." Ms. in the Oneida Community collection, Institute for Sex Research, Bloomington, Indiana.

91. Anita Newcomb McGee, "Interviews August, 1891, at Kenwood, New York with Herrick, Cragin and Hinds." Ms. in the Oneida Community collection, Institute for Sex Research, Bloomington, Indiana.

92. John Humphrey Noyes, "Message to the O.C., August 20, 1879," American Socialist 4 (September 4, 1879): 281.

4. LIVING IN THE SPIRIT:
IDEOLOGIES OF THE CELIBATES

As noted in the last chapter, the celibates never argued that it would be easy for people to follow a life of celibacy. As a prominent Shaker wrote in the latter part of the nineteenth century, "we must make no mistake" about the fact that men must deal with the feelings they have for women and women must deal with the feelings they have for men. We must, he said, each look into our own minds, for "that mind is one in ten thousand if it cannot distinguish within itself a feeling for man or for woman which is not only interest, not only kindness, not only friendship, but sex." [1] The difficulty of the celibate life was underscored by those groups that tried it and failed and by those that exalted it as the ideal even while virtually all of the members were getting married.

In addition to its admitted difficulty, many people have viewed celibacy as contrary to human nature and as a thwarting of the biological imperative that insures the continuation of the species. How, then, can celibacy be justified? Indeed, what kind of justification would lead numbers of people to accept the celibate life? Interestingly, there are a number of common themes in the ideologies of the celibates. These themes are all contained in the writings of Thomas Lake Harris, founder of the Brotherhood of the New Life. At first glance, Harris appears to be something of an enigma. He was obsessed with sex. His writings are laced through and through with sexual imagery. But he was a committed celibate and insisted on celibacy among his followers. We will examine his unusual ideology, identify the themes that he shares with others, and illustrate the common nature of the themes by the ideologies of other groups.

THOMAS LAKE HARRIS: PASSIONATE CELIBATE

William James once called him our "best-known mystic," but few Americans are familiar with Harris, who was born in England in 1823 and died in New York in 1906. Harris was not always a celibate; he had two sons by his first wife. At the time of his marriage, he was a Universalist minister in New York City. His restless mind was not at peace in the Universalist faith, however. He explored a variety of other systems of thought, including spiritualism, transcendentalism, socialism, Fourierism, and Swedenborgianism. The spiritualist and Swedenborgian influences remained dominant in his thought.

Swedenborg was an eighteenth century Swedish theologian, philosopher, and scientist who had an impact upon the thought of a number of the communitarian leaders. Two of Swedenborg's ideas that Harris picked up, elaborated upon, and made fundamental to his own ideology were the notions of "internal respiration" and "sexual counterparts." [2] Swedenborg had made brief reference to a kind of breathing that would put humans into harmony with the pulsations of the universe. Harris, in like manner, helped his followers achieve the kind of breathing pattern that enabled them to commune with God and to participate in the life of God. More germane to our purposes is Harris' doctrine of sexual counterparts, a doctrine that we must examine in the context of Harris' overall ideology of sexuality.

The Sexuality of All Being

Beginning with the "Passionate Divine," [3] Harris found sexuality in everything. Nature, he felt, is sexual. [4] The stars pair off into monogamous unions, have sex with each other, and give birth to new heavenly orbs (though it is not the material stars that we see, but their souls, that have such relationships). [5] And, of course, the angels engage in celestial nuptial unions. Harris claimed to communicate regularly with angels, often being transported to a different dimension of reality or different level of existence (that is, into the realm where the angels themselves abide). On such occasions, he learned of the exquisitely satisfying nature of celestial nuptial unions. Thus, of one pair that had been married for 500 years, he wrote that they were aware "at once of unity and duality, of sex in all the degrees of spirit, and thence in all the attributes of person; of eternal youth, of immortal vigour, of pure affection, translucent intelligence, and exquisite sensation. " [6]

At the same time, the celestial unions are not the same as an ideal marriage between two humans. The celestial beings experience the full pleasures of sex, yet it is a different experience from that of humans. Harris reported a conversation with the angel Amoleta, who talked about the mystery of sex:

> To be a wife is the golden end which the virgin looks forward to with the most exquisite and joyous auguries. I longed for marriage ... I had no sensations which you mortals call passions, nor have I now. I should seem coldness itself to inverted men upon your orb, and they would compare me to ice or marble. But I am tropical, with an intensity of affection which is like the blushing Spring, when, robing herself in bridal apparel, and wreathed in zones of flowers, she gives her hand to the Summer Bridegroom. [7])

Thus, we already see intimations of how Harris can write in thoroughly sensual terms and still insist on celibacy. The entire universe, he argued, is sexual in nature. But that sexuality is qualitatively different from ordinary human sexual intercourse, although it involves many of the same elements as ordinary human sexuality (union between male and female, offspring from the union, fulfillment through the union, etc.). Harris went even further; not only can we distinguish between different kinds of sexuality, we can label one kind as holy and another as unholy.

Holy and Unholy Sex

In a torrent of words, Harris proclaimed the exalted nature of sexuality. Spiced with metaphors, similes, and often with ambiguities and obscurities, his writings carry us passionately through all the realms of the sensual universe. An angel from the planet Saturn, says Harris, told him of the "ardency of lovers" on Saturn, which was "delightful to behold. " [8] Such love, like all celestial love, illustrates and exemplifies the holiness of sex. For sex is sacred. And all words pertaining to sex should generate within us an emotion of "supreme holiness. " [9] Sexual holiness "is the consummate flower and celestial crown of all holiness. " [10]

But, again, that holy sexuality must not be confused with ordinary human sexual relations. There is an unholy as well as a holy sex. And if sexual holiness is the supreme holiness of all, sexual profanation is the abyss of depravity. And what is sexual profanation? It is to think of sex in ordinary human terms as carnal relations between men and women. Such a way of thinking clearly shows human depravity. Indeed, to cast holy ideas about sex "upon the stream of the world's thought is like throwing a wreath of white lilies upon the black current of a sewer." [11]

Celestial sex differs so fundamentally from ordinary human sex that angel-husbands on Saturn have no sensuous notions of marriage. In fact, if a Saturnian husband came near to one of the harlots of earth, he would sense the harlot "as the fetid odor of a corpse in its utmost loathesomeness; and were a man of pleasure from this orb able ... so much as to touch the hand of a wife upon that planet, she would be affected by his sphere, as by the presence of a horror utterly infernal." [12]

As the above suggests, Harris had nothing good to say about human sexual relationships. In both his life and his work he insisted upon celibacy as the only way to spiritual growth. He did allow some marriages among his followers on the premise that only through marriage could certain individuals evolve into the better way. But even marriage did not mean that people had to engage in sexual intercourse. Harris himself entered into a celibate marriage with Emily Waters in 1855 (the new Mrs. Harris suffered insanity not long afterwards). And one of Harris' more prominent converts, Lawrence Oliphant, was allowed to marry his beloved Alice. The young couple, wrote their biographer, engaged in a "constant struggle to regard their love as an abstract and spiritual passion, and subdue the warm human sentiment which is perpetually bursting forth." [13]

In his writings, Harris justified such celibacy by speaking of human sexual relations in darkest terms. In fact, he often claimed that both men and women are corrupted by each other's presence, at least men and women who are still in the "natural" as opposed to the spiritual state. He advocated that the sexes should separate themselves from each other in order to overcome this mutually corrupting process. [14] To get rid of the "animal parasites" in her body, a woman will have to avoid any relationships with natural men. Natural men are impure, and one cannot evolve into spiritual fulfillment while associating with the impure.

On the other hand, Harris writes about women in terms that led some people to call him a misogynist. He denied the charge, but he clearly views women as more corrupting to men than vice versa:

> As a man, I charge, before most high God, that my sex, from immemorial ages, has been interiorly subjected by woman; and robbed by woman of its interior quality, by process of secret visitation, and violation. [15]

It is woman who is the real obstacle to forming a divine society. [16] It is woman who, in her natural state, exudes a quality that "eats into the flesh" of a man. [17] Woman is an "unfathomed mystery," a "hunter of man," a "form of artifice." [18] To sum it all up, a woman is

> a jest, a solicitude, a mystery and an adoration; a butterfly, a pastime, a fierce virago, a spoiled darling, a fury of hell; a tornado, a deluge, a kill-joy, an insane wild beast; a boundless, insatiable destroyer; an enticing lie; the subtlety of subtleties; an ulcer of proud flesh; an inane vacancy; the parasite of Nature; Nature's paragon; the animal quintessence; all things changeable, --glistening, --dissolving, --dying, --dead. [19]

In spite of such a passage, Harris insisted that he was not a misogynist. He was simply describing women in their natural state. Men were also corrupt in their natural state, though Harris never wrote about them in the same deprecating terms. At any rate, his main point is that ordinary relations between the sexes, including sexual intercourse, is corrupting. Natural sex is unholy sex. But in the new age there will no longer be such sex. Our sexual appetites will vanish and be replaced by the "rise of the bridal passion"; the "beast man" will be replaced by the "divine man." [20] Sex will not vanish; rather, unholy sex will be replaced by holy sex as each man and each woman enters into union with his or her sexual counterpart. We have now arrived at one of the more unusual aspects of Harris' teachings.

Sexual Counterparts: Holiness in Practice

The doctrine of sexual counterparts is rooted in Harris' ideas about the nature of God and of humans. First, the doctrine of sexual counterparts generally means chastity in ordinary human relationships. This follows from the nature of God, who is "Infinite Chastity." [21] Second, chastity does not mean a lack of fulfillment. God is chaste, but God is also complete. For God is both masculine and feminine-- "Heavenly King and Heavenly Queen, Father, Mother, two in one." [22] Just as, in traditional Christian theology, Christ is both fully human and fully divine, God is, in Harris' theology, fully Masculine and fully Feminine. Indeed, without both principles, God would not be God.

This same God created humans as bisexual creatures. "The unit of the race is not the individual homo or mulier, but the man-woman, two-in-one." [23] As a result of evil coming into the world, however, this complete man-woman was severed into two creatures, one male and one female. Redemption is the process of regaining the wholeness that was lost, or reuniting the separated female and male elements. Each individual must find his female or her male counterpart which will enable that individual to once again become a whole, godlike person. One of the basic principles of the Christian religion, wrote Harris, is that every person "is created with especial reference to an eternal conjugal union with his or her counterpart," and that there must be a reunion with one's counterpart "in indissoluble nuptial order" before it is possible to enter "into that holy state which is called Heaven." [24]

Thus, an essential element of the spiritual quest is the discovery of and reunion with one's counterpart. That being the case, however, how does one go about finding one's counterpart? And who is one's counterpart likely to be? And precisely what does it mean to enter into union with that counterpart? Unfortunately, these questions can not all be answered with certainty, but we have a number of indications in the writings of Harris and of some of his followers to make some general statements about counterparts.

In the first place, one's earthly spouse was very unlikely to be one's counterpart. God has allowed people to marry those other than their counterparts as "an accommodation to the disordered condition of mankind." [25] But rarely, if ever, is that spouse actually one's counterpart. Even a deep and fervent love for one's spouse (such as Laurence Oliphant had for Alice) is no evidence that the two are counterparts. It is not clear exactly how an individual was to discover a counterpart, nor even how one would know when he or she met the counterpart. Certainly, spiritual development was necessary, the kind of development that occurred through entrance into Harris' group and submission to Harris' will and direction. Harris would facilitate spiritual development by separating husbands and wives. This separation freed them to pursue their own spiritual quest as well as underscoring for them the fact that their first allegiance was to God and to Harris. Such separation undoubtedly made the celibate rule easier to maintain also.

At some point, members of the group apparently began to have the kind of visions and mystical experiences that Harris himself continually reported. They would interpret these experiences, or Harris would inform them that the experiences represented their contact with their counterparts. Apparently an individual's counterpart never turned out to be another living person. Harris told one of his female followers that her counterpart had died when he was four years old. Oliphant, in spite of his intense love for Alice, became convinced at one point that his wife was not his counterpart after all. Rather, he had become increasingly conscious of someone dead with whom he had been communicating. His counterpart inspired him with revelations in verse. His biographer reports hearing him read some of the verses:

> To see him produce these rhymed effusions, and read them with the strangest boyish pleasure and shyness, astonished at their cleverness, and pausing from time to time to assure me that of himself he could not produce a rhyme to save his life, was the most astonishing experience. If the reader should exclaim, as many have done, that this was sheer madness, I can only reply that a more sane person never existed, and that the verses in question, strange and bald as they were, and most unlike anything sent from heaven, were nevertheless as lucid as they were daring, and conveyed a trenchant attack upon social evils of all kinds, in something more like doggerel than poetry, but with much method and meaning, though little beauty. [26]

If Oliphant appeared misguided but sane in his experiences with his counterpart, some of Harris' other followers had experiences that today could be called psychotic episodes or symptoms of breakdown. One of the sisters reported strange sensations in her arms, as though her previously empty arms were being filled with something. She said that when her counterpart came to her she had a sensation of a hair on her hand, and that even thinking of him gave her chills from head to foot. She also said that her experiences left her totally exhausted so that at times she felt as if she could hardly endure it any longer. [27]

Ideally, when one discovered one's counterpart, the result would be an eternal conjugal union such as Harris enjoyed with his own counterpart, Queen Lily. This union had all of the elements of an earthly marriage. It was a companionate relationship, for one could converse with one's counterpart and share experiences like reading. The sister referred to above read a letter with her counterpart. The counterpart made various remarks during the course of the reading, remarks which the woman reported back to the writer of the letter. Harris had frequent conversations with Queen Lily. Oliphant received his rhymes from his counterpart. The individual who found his or her counterpart would never again lack companionship.

Furthermore, the relationship with one's counterpart was also sexual. Harris used erotic imagery in discussing the doctrine of counterparts. He called the union a nuptial one. He wrote about the individual entering into that union and both the individual and the counterpart "glow and vibrate in each other's ardency." [28] Some of Harris' followers described their experiences in erotic terms. To refer once again to the sister mentioned above, she described her experience on one occasion as similar to having someone inside her and all over her, especially around her mouth and tongue. On another occasion, she said her counterpart came to her through the "generative organs," and she thought that the experience was like sexual intercourse only more so. For every bit of her being had entered into union with every bit of the being of her counterpart. [29] Finally, the sexual nature of the relationship is illustrated by Harris' claim to have fathered two children in Heaven. Queen Lily was the mother.

All of the elements of what outsiders would consider an ideal earthly marriage are to be found in union with one's counterpart. And like an ideal earthly marriage, union with one's counterpart brings great satisfaction--"ineffable satisfaction in the bosoms of terrestrial wives and their beloved counterparts. " [30] Clearly, there is no need for sexual relationships between living humans. In fact, such relationships would be adulterous for the individual who has found and united with his or her counterpart. And the relationships would only be a hindrance to those still seeking their counterparts. Thus, Harris easily justified celibacy while he simultaneously exalted and pursued sexuality.

The Consequences of Holy Sex

One additional element in Harris' justification of celibacy caps his argument--the avoidance of unholy sex and the pursuit of holy sex have a number of desirable consequences. We have already noted one of them--personal satisfaction. Union with one's counterpart is "sexual communion of so exquisite a character, that even the minute atomic creations which exist within the celestial ichor, which corresponds to blood, are all intermarried. " [31]

A second consequence of holy sex is continued spiritual development. Indeed, that development is both a prerequisite to and a consequence of celibacy at the human level and holy sex with one's counterpart. The natural or unspiritual man is filled with lust, according to Harris. He tends to be polygamous in that he lusts after many women. Such lust precludes spiritual development. Marriage is a partial restraint on a man's lust, because it confines his sexual activity to one woman. Celibacy is an even greater constraint, setting the stage for finding one's counterpart. Thus, for some people marriage may be a necessary step to spiritual growth. Marriage may teach them something about the restraint of lust. They can then pursue their spiritual goal further by adopting celibacy, which they will do when they see the shame of their human carnal relationship. This entire process of spiritual evolution is evidence that God is at work in them and that they are following the leading of God's Spirit. [32]

Harris not only assured his followers that this was the way, but also insisted that there was no other way to heavenly bliss. For ordinary human sexual relations give rise to "all of the malformations of the species, its misery, its inverted religions, its apathy to the higher life; its grossness and vileness; its filth and shame. " [33] Indulgence in sexual relations even warps the thinking capacity of humans.

"Men cannot think as do the angels, whilst they cohabit and procreate as do the animals." [34] But once an individual is free of the contaminating effects of sexual relations, that individual can progress to the highest planes of spiritual development.

A final consequence of holy sex is social well-being. Sexual relationships corrupt not only the individuals who engage in them but the society in which those individuals exist. Harris does not give a rational account of just how unholy sex results in a deterioration of the social order except to argue that millions of men throughout the world, performing the act at the same time, pour "a perpetual torrent of passions and of passional and corrupted magnetisms into the nervous centres of humanity." These corrupted magnetisms divert the masses of people from seeking after eternal life, so that the earth "reeks with debauchery and cruelty, with every disease and every depravity." [35]

Harris also offers the peculiar argument that unholy sex is linked with individualism and selfishness, while holy sex involves social concern and altruism. Unholy sex characterizes Nature, which is selfishness. Holy sex characterizes "Arch-nature," which is unselfishness. In nature, animals and humans who engage in sexual relations are totally absorbed in each other, giving no thought to society. This is the "most undivine of all human performances: the slumber that follows is a drugged bestial torpor." [36] But in arch-nature, "the plants, the animals, the very minerals, instead of depleting each other for their own structure-building, are seen to exhibit a uniform tendency to yield themselves to the structure-building of others, and thus to support the series of organisms to which they affiliate." [37] The two who become one in arch-nature act as creative forces in society. Their sexual rapture results in social good, uniting them "by mysterious organic ways, to the great public body, of which they are a part." [38]

In the above argument, arch-nature refers to realms of existence beyond our earthly life. But humans can imitate the socially beneficial sexuality of arch-nature through their counterparts. And in so doing, they will inevitably enhance the well-being of their society as well as advance their own spiritual development.

In sum, Harris offered his followers an ideology of passion and celibacy. He taught them that sexuality pervades all existence. He promised them individual and social well-being. And he insisted upon celibacy as the only way to their own spiritual growth, the redemption of their society, and the exquisite sexual experiences to which their counterparts were calling them.

THE ELEMENTS OF CELIBATE IDEOLOGIES

In its particulars, Harris' ideology was unique among American celibate groups. In fact, each group had its own unique features, though none was quite as imaginative (some would prefer to say bizarre) as that of Harris. But there were a number of common elements that undergirded the unique directions taken by the differing ideologies. It is as though a limited number of reasons can be mustered in the defense of celibacy. The justifications, therefore, are variations on common themes, not idiosyncratic constructions that are completely diverse from each other. All of these themes are contained in Harris' ideology, which we elaborated above. We shall now abstract them, and show how the various other groups played upon them.

Sex Is a Baser Form of Human Activity

Of all the activities in which humans engage, sex, in the view of the celibates, is one of the most base. Harris viewed ordinary sexual activity, as we have seen, in terms of humans sinking to the level of the beasts. Sex is a mutually corrupting activity of men and women, condemning them to a life of wallowing in the muck of their own animal lusts. Among other groups, the extent to which sexual activity is condemned as base varies somewhat, but all agree that it is baser than other forms of behavior.

Why is sex so base? Essentially, the communitarians made a distinction between the spirit and the flesh, a distinction which is fairly common in the history of humankind. Flesh and spirit represent antithetical tendencies in humans, the tendency towards self-indulgence on the one hand and the nobler pursuits like altruism and development of the mind on the other hand. Plato made such a distinction when he described the human soul as a charioteer who must drive two horses, one of which is reason and the other of which is passion. Thus, there is a war within the human being, a war between the noble and the base.

The Jewish and Eastern religions also contained notions of an internal conflict between opposing tendencies.   In
Christian thought, the tendencies were given the names
"spirit" and "flesh. "   The spirit represents the individual's
striving for godliness.   The meaning of "flesh" is well expressed by a Christian theologian:

> No army can invade a country from the sea unless
> it can obtain a bridgehead.   Temptation would be
> powerless to affect men, unless there was some-
> thing already in man to respond to temptation.
> Sin could gain no foothold in a man's mind and
> heart and soul and life unless there was an enemy
> within the gates who was willing to open the door
> to sin.   The flesh is exactly the bridgehead through
> which sin invades the human personality.   The
> flesh is like the enemy within the gates who opens
> the way to the enemy who is pressing in through
> the gates. [39]

The theologian points out that "flesh" is not to be
equated with the human body.   But Christians have not always made that careful distinction.   Many of them, including the communitarians, equated "flesh" with indulgence in
bodily pleasure and, in particular, with sexual indulgence.
As such, there was a clear contradiction between sexual
activity and the striving after godliness.   Thus, Conrad
Beissel, the mystic leader of Ephrata, said that the only
value of marriage was to keep a man from fornication.
"Beyond that, and in spite of it, conjugal relations were
an abomination, revolting to God, and unworthy of anybody
who had a serious interest in religion. " [40]   The celibate
women's group that began in Belton, Texas, the Sanctificationists, made a clear distinction between sanctified and
unsanctified individuals, and insisted that a sanctified woman
could no longer live with an unsanctified husband.   Since
none of the husbands were sanctified, and since sex was
viewed as indulgence in the flesh in any case, the women
gradually left their husbands and lived together "in the
spirit" in their own home.

Thus, flesh and spirit were seen as antitheses.   One
could not simultaneously live in the spirit and continue to
indulge in the flesh.   There were a number of steps in the
argument which we will review here.   First, we should note
that a number of groups have practiced celibacy without a
Christian justification.   For instance, some contemporary

celibate communes base their practice on Eastern theology. But they share the belief in sex as a baser form of activity, consistent with some strands of Eastern thought. However, since most of the celibate groups have employed Christian ideas to justify their practice, we will confine our attention to the Christian argument.

The Christian argument began with the biblical teachings, including the example of Christ. In response to the question of whether all sexual activity is forbidden to humans, a Shaker writer vigorously affirmed the necessity of the celibate life. There is no doubt, said the writer, that sex is "positively forbidden as inconsistent with the purity of the Savior's life." The writer admitted that there was no express command in the Bible to that effect. "But still, to follow Christ in the regeneration, utterly forbids the gratification of 'fleshly lusts which war against the soul.'" [41]

The communitarians generally agreed that there was no explicit command in the Bible to cease sexual activity, but they found support for their position in a number of teachings that either exalted celibacy or logically implied that true spiritual living demands celibacy. They interpreted the Fall as the result of a sexual union between Adam and Eve. Adam walked with God, said a Shaker hymn, until he was deceived by Eve. Then, when "to his wife in lust had cleav'd, and of forbidden fruit receiv'd, he found himself rejected." [42]

Various other doctrines and scriptural passages lent additional support. The second coming of Christ, some said, demanded that Christians purify themselves in order to be ready to receive Him. Many pointed out the passage in the Book of Revelation where the 144,000 who were not "defiled with women" were exalted. They noted that Christ taught that there is no marriage in the Kingdom of Heaven. They quoted the Old Testament teaching that a woman was required to make a "sin offering" after she had borne a child. An imaginative Shaker writer even argued that the Old Testament practice of circumcision, which most Christians identified as a prefigurement of baptism, actually prefigured the "rejection of the works of the flesh under the gospel." After all, he said, there should be some resemblance to that which is prefigured. But what resemblance is there between immersion or sprinkling and cutting? Clearly, circumcision "prefigured that cross which should destroy the life of fleshly lust." [43]

The example of Christ and various biblical teachings, then, identify celibacy as the only way for those who wish to live in the spirit. Sexual activity is inherently incompatible with spiritual living. Sex is

> a mountain of darkness and death between our very existence and its fountain, and you might as well expect the sun to warm and enlighten the earth behind an eclipse of the moon. Lust is an iceberg between the mind and its fountain of life. But here we make the fundamental error when we consider these faculties were created for the insane paroxysms of gratification! [44]

Consequently, we must see sex not merely as an obstacle but as a dire sin. As Father Divine said, "any physical relationship between men and women is a black sin." [45] Even sex between husbands and wives is sinful, so that wives who agree to sexual relations with their husbands are sinning as much as if they were prostitutes. Father Divine was not the only leader to declare even marital sex the sin of adultery. A number of Shaker leaders also insisted that sexual activity is equivalent to sensuality, which is adultery, whether the couple is married or not. Some Shakers, particularly later in the nineteenth century and into the twentieth century, did acknowledge that sex for procreation was acceptable. But there must be no gratification involved. Otherwise, the sexual activity is "a debasing prostitution, and of the nature of whoredom." [46]

In line with this reasoning, writers declared that any sexual feelings were temptations from the devil. They tried to avoid all kinds of contact that might generate such feelings. One man said that he had never kissed a female nor been kissed by one, including his mother. When told by a listener that he had thereby missed a "world of pleasure," he told the other that he could add that he had also missed "a world of pain." [47] The communitarians agreed that they had sexual feelings, and that there was a certain pleasure involved in gratifying those feelings. But the pain outweighed the pleasure. The losses overbalanced the gains. After all, what does it profit one to gain a few fleeting moments of sensual pleasure and lose his or her eternal soul? Sex is clearly contrary to God's will for humans. It is clearly a violation of the spiritual quest for which we were created. Some evidence seems to support this argument, including such minor points as the fact that people engage in sex in darkness. Doesn't that prove that people know it is a shameful act that never came from God? [48] Even the way in which we engage in sex stands as a witness against indulgence.

The only rational course for humans, then, is to accept the way of the spirit, which is the way of self-denial. If there is a base way of life, there is also a noble way. And the noble way is the way of Christ, which alone can enable us to escape the clutches of sin. As Father Rapp put it:

> Of what use is it then to preach up morality, and to talk of performing duties, where the faculties for the performance are wanting; and besides this, the moral laws are not sufficient to keep the stimulated passions for luxury and sensuality under command: the religion of Jesus Christ only has the power to do it which teaches the perfect and decisive point: namely, Deny yourself. [49]

In the above quote, Rapp tersely summed up the communitarian response to the way of the flesh. It was to opt for the way of Christ, which meant to opt for self-denial. To live in the spirit is to conquer oneself, to deny oneself indulgence in the lusts of the flesh. This can only be achieved, of course, through the religion of Christ, who enabled individuals to conquer their fleshly lusts. Still, the conquest was one in which the human spirit could exult, for the individual had escaped the prison of the flesh to live in the free, life-giving realm of the spirit.

Sex Depletes One's Energy and Creative Powers

The celibates have assumed that people have a limited amount of energy. What is used for sex is unavailable for other and better pursuits. In their view, sexual activity never enhances an individual's outlook, never brings about the kind of tension release that can free an individual to pursue creative tasks with zest, and never contributes to an individual's physical and emotional well-being. Rather, sex depletes one's energy and stifles one's creative powers.

The notion that sexual activity diminishes one's energy for better and more creative tasks is found also in some strands of Eastern thought. Contemporary communes based

on Eastern philosophy encourage celibacy in order to avoid
such a waste of energy and to facilitate spiritual development. In this view, the individual simply does not have
sufficient energy and time to engage in sexual activity and
pursue the spiritual life simultaneously.

An individual must decide, therefore, whether to engage in the "weakening and wearisome" act of sex or to use
his or her energy for more constructive purposes. [50] As
Father Divine taught his followers, the choice is between
the destructiveness of self-indulgent sex and immersion in
constructive tasks of various kinds. Those who choose sex
are literally robbing themselves of physical and mental energy. [51]

Loss of energy means an impairment of one's abilities
as well as less energy with which to use those abilities.
For example, at Ephrata, where music was a fundamental
aspect of communal life, Beissel taught that sex and music
did not mix. He called music an "exalted art" which has
"a pure, chaste and virtuous spirit" and which consequently
"suffers no unclean, polluted and sinful love for woman,
which so inflames and agitates the blood of the young as
completely to undo them in mind, heart, voice, and soul." [52]
The Ephrata brethren were convinced that sex would make
their voices harsh and rough. They claimed that anyone
could easily tell a virgin from a matron by the tone of their
respective voices. [53]

Some of the communitarians went further yet. They
argued not only that sexual activity diminishes one's energy
for good pursuits, but that sexual activity can wreck one's
health and shorten one's life. We noted in chapter 1 that
many nineteenth century physicians accepted the notion of the
harmful nature of sex. Such views were not lost on the
communitarians, who used them to give scientific support
for the practice of celibacy. The great Shaker writer Frederick Evans pointed out that many of the "most enlightened
physiologists affirm that it is a violation of natural laws and
injurious to both the physical and intellectual faculties, to
use the reproductive powers for any other than procreative
purposes." [54] A physician who was a member of the
Skaneateles Community carried the argument to its final
conclusion and tried to convince his group that total abstinence from sex was the only rational course. He pointed out
that a "vast majority of all the disease, social and domestic
discord and misery" are rooted in sexual relations. He

buttressed his argument with a description of the physical changes accompanying orgasm, changes that should give us "some faint conception of the inward results upon the delicate tissues of the body." [55]

Thus, they argued that sex leads to disease, while celibacy leads to health; and sex shortens life, while celibacy prolongs it. What are the effects of abstinence? asked a Shaker. Freedom from the many diseases brought about by sexual relations, he answered. And what kinds of disorders arise from celibacy? None, he insisted. On the contrary, the celibate individual enjoys better health and a longer life than the non-celibate. [56]

Shakers used both analogies and empirical evidence to support their argument that celibacy enhanced their health and lengthened their lives. For instance, consider the plant kingdom. Many vegetables die in the process of producing their seed. And some fruit trees only bear every other year, "one off year being required to recruit the strength of the tree, after each bearing season, as a preparation for another." [57] The depletion and death that occur in plants cannot be avoided by humans. For it is a law of nature that sexual reproduction occurs only at the cost of the health and life of the reproducers.

Thomas Lake Harris promised his followers that the substitution of holy for unholy sex would lead to health and life. The Shakers not only made the promise but offered evidence from their records. For example, a report from the Society at Mt. Lebanon stated that over a ten year period the average age at death was over 86 years, and that there were still four people living in the community who had entered before they were 20 and who were now over 90. [58] Another report of a variety of societies in New York noted that average age at death was invariably over 70 years, and that there had been few cases of fever and, in some societies, not a single case of cancer in 40 years. [59] From their own records, from a number of analogies with nature, from scientific and medical opinion, and from their personal experiences the celibates confidently declared the superiority of total abstinence from sex for human well-being.

Celibacy Is Consistent with Divine and Human Natures

Critics charged that the way of the celibates was contrary to human nature and a violation of God's order (for God had commanded people to be fruitful and multiply). Not true, responded the celibates. It cannot violate God's order to live in a way that reflects the very nature of both God and humans.

In what sense is celibacy consistent with God's nature? Harris, influenced by Swedenborg, identified God as Infinite Chastity, as both Masculine and Feminine, as the complete Two-In-One. A number of other celibate groups, influenced by German mysticism, also accepted the dual sexual nature of God. God is a complete Person, both male and female, and has therefore no need of a sexual relationship. The celibates never argued for asexual being. They recognized the need for both male and female elements, without which nothing can be complete. Thus, the Shakers insisted on two Messiahs, Jesus the male Messiah and Ann Lee the female Messiah. Beissel, on the other hand, argued that Jesus combined within his own person the male and female elements. He came as a man, but he was female "in his constitution" because he was subject to God. [60] Being both male and female, Jesus was like God--he was complete within himself and had no need for a sexual relationship.

God's nature is the ideal. Initially, human nature was the same as God's nature. For God created Adam as a bisexual creature; Adam was both male and female. As it says in the book of Genesis 1:26-27: "And God said, Let us make man in our image, after our likeness ... So God created man in his own image, in the image of God created he him; male and female created he them." Jacob Boehme, one of the German mystics who was particularly influential in the thinking of the celibates, had even argued that Adam had "heavenly organs" instead of human genitals. [61] Had Adam remained in his perfect state, he would have reproduced the species through a spiritual process.

But Adam sinned. Adam developed sexual desire and was given reproductive organs like those of the animals. His female nature, Eve, was separated from him. A complete being became two people of different sexes. To the extent that sexual relationships reflect human nature, then, they reflect a fallen nature, a corrupted human. In the resurrection, individuals will once again be complete, male-female creatures. In the meantime, celibacy is a way to approximate the ideal nature. In language that reminds us of Harris' description of counterpartal union, Beissel wrote of the reunion of our male and female natures through a relationship with the divine:

> Virgin Sophia will assume no male-property burning in the fire into her chaste embraces, and if you want to be called a consecrated favorite of her, you must first indispensably become a priest ... and if a virgin desired the title, to be the wife of the priest Jesus, she must first be a virgin in body and Spirit ... for the everlasting virginity doth disanull all separation whatsoever, in order that also might germinate the Godly union, which was lost by the apostasy. [62]

Thus, celibacy is not contrary to human nature; in fact, it is the only way to restore human nature to what it was meant to be. To this argument, the Shakers added analogies from nature and evidence from history. The historical evidence is simply the continual outcropping of celibacy among various peoples throughout the world, from the Essenes among the Jews to the ascetics of the East. Such widespread practice suggests that "there is an element of continence in the human soul." [63] The analogies from nature include the laws of selective reproduction and progress. Selective reproduction refers to the fact that only a small proportion of the seeds produced are used for reproduction. There is no law that says that reproductive organs must be used simply because they exist. On the contrary, "the sacrifice of these organs to a higher use and nobler purpose is Nature's general law." [64] For Nature evidently intended the greater portion of vegetable seeds to be used for the support of animal life, thereby destroying their reproductive use in the service of a higher purpose. The law of progress is also superior to the law of reproduction. Seeds which are used for reproduction can do nothing more than propagate and die. They give up their life for their offspring, and do not enter a higher state of being. But those that give up the task of reproduction "enter into nobler uses and higher grades of life, forming blood, muscle, bone, nerve, brain, and thus subserving, if not actually constituting, the sublime mentality of human intellect." [65] To say that celibacy is contrary to the laws of nature is clearly wrong. Celibacy is analogous to the higher laws of nature.

Celibacy Is the Way to Spiritual Growth

If sex is a baser form of human activity and if celibacy is consistent with the nature of God and with the ideal nature of humans, it follows that celibacy is the only way to true spiritual growth. As Harris insisted, you can't think like the angels while living like the beasts. Many of the communities, of course, permitted marriage. But it was clear that those who followed the married way sacrificed their own quest for spiritual perfection. "It is difficult," wrote Father Rapp to his adopted son, Frederick, "to reform sensuous man into a moral being ... I have married several persons." [66] Father Rapp warned his followers about the lusts of marriage, which would be a snare to their souls. He married them if they insisted, but he would not grant them the same spiritual status as the unmarried. To encourage the quest for the perfection enjoyed by the original human, Adam, the Rappites printed copies of Jacob Boehme's work, Hirtenbrief, in 1855 and distributed them to every family. [67] The work contained the entire doctrine of human creation, fall, regeneration, and perfection, including the way in which we may return to our ideal bisexual state through a celibate life.

What is it about celibacy, other than a kind of return to our original, ideal nature, that facilitates spiritual growth? The celibates gave a number of answers to the question. First, celibacy represents a spiritual victory over lust. Many religions have taught their followers that the conquest of lust is one of the highest callings of the human. [68] There is something inherently good about subjugating one's desires, and especially one's bodily desires. Self-indulgence is the mark of the unregenerate; self-denial is the quality of godliness.

Second, celibacy enables an individual to have but one allegiance. Christ taught his followers that no one can serve two masters. The celibates accepted the teaching with a vengeance, insisting that even husbands and wives should cease all sexual relations in order to pursue holiness. As a Shaker sermon put it:

> They that are in the flesh cannot please God. Show me then the married man who is not emphatically in the flesh, and continually minding the things of the flesh. The man that thinks he is not, and lives in nature's works, must be blind indeed. [69]

As people who are married begin to grow spiritually, in fact, they will recognize this truth for themselves and voluntarily accept celibacy in order to pursue even greater growth. Frederick Rapp, in a letter to a newspaper publisher, said that the Harmonie Society contained some who had "so advanced in sanctification" and who had been "so ennobled in their virtue" by the power of Christ that they freely gave up "carnal intercourse and devote themselves fully to prepare for Christ and His Kingdom. " [70] The celibate individual, then, is able to give his or her whole self to godliness. The celibate individual is committed to a higher and more mature form of love. Young people forsake their parents for what they regard as the higher enjoyment and happier life of marriage. Even so, when a Christian becomes "wedded to Christ, " when a Christian experiences the love of Christ and the fellowship of other Christians, "he is weaned from all partial, sensual and lower loves, and gives his whole heart and all his faculties to the building up and support of this holy relation and institution. " [71]

Third, to be celibate is to imitate Christ. The imitation of Christ is an ideal that pervades Christian devotional literature throughout the ages. To imitate the ways of Christ is to attain the highest form of spiritual living. Shakers, according to a children's manual, are those who live the "angel life, " which means those who love all others and who live for the good of others. This, of course, is the way that Christ lived. [72]

It is important to note that celibacy per se is not sufficient for the spiritual life. Celibacy is important in its own right as a spiritual commitment, and it is essential for those who would strive towards perfection. But one can be a celibate and still not live in the spirit. For this reason, some Shakers emphasized the importance of what they called "virgin celibacy. " They argued that an individual can be celibate and yet lack the characteristics of a virgin character. A celibate might be "gross, natural, earthly, unspiritual" or simply single. But a virgin is, in addition, one who seeks after the highest spiritual attainments. [73] The virgin celibate seeks to imitate Christ in all things; his or her celibacy is more than a mere quirk of circumstances.

Celibacy Is the Basis for Social Well-Being

We noted Harris' argument that sexual relations lead

to a host of social ills. Other celibates agreed with that
assessment. It is not only the individual who will benefit
from the practice of celibacy but the entire social order.
Expressed negatively, this enhanced well-being is due to
stemming the flood of evil unleashed on the world by sexual
activity. Some celibates, such as Harris, believed that sexual activity released destructive energy into the world, leading to an increase in anti-social behavior. Others were
more concrete in their explanations. In particular, they
argued that indulgence in sexual activity represented a pattern of behavior that has dire social consequences. For sex
means gratification of the individual's passions, and he who
indulges in sex will also strive to satisfy all other passions:

> All contentions and wars have their origin in the
> selfishness of the flesh--for land, women, or else.
> Do away with the spirit of MINE, and the dawn of
> peace begins immediately; happier homes will re-
> sult, and grinders of the faces of the poor need not
> tremble because of so-called communists, who are
> only attempting to equalize the good things of this
> life unevenly shared by ungodly, unbrotherly
> monopolists. [74]

The individual who lives a life of self-indulgence,
then, is contributing to all of the misery of the world, from
marital quarrels to political corruption to wars between na-
tions. For all these problems are caused by people who
have never learned to control their passions. Sexual relations are but one manifestation of the self-focused life.
Furthermore, even if an individual did desire to bring about
good in the world, he or she would be unable to do so without adopting celibacy. For sex leads to "the dissipation of
those vital forces which give energy, strength of the will and
the power of self-denial, without which no reform can be accomplished in the individual or the community." [75] In other
words, even in those cases where sexual activity may not
represent a life of self-indulgence, the individual will be too
enervated to engage in the work of reform.

But does not sex enhance social well-being by becoming the foundation for a multitude of loving relationships
throughout the world? Absolutely not, said the celibates.
Ironically, sex leads to the very opposite of ideal love.
Love is indeed a crucial element of social well-being. As
a Shaker poem has it: "Life without love is like a sunless
sky, a night without its crown of glittering stars, an even-

tide without its golden bars. " [76] But the love that is analogous to a sun-filled sky is not sexual love. For sexual
love is too narrow, too demanding, too possessive, too prone
to violence when it is thwarted. Anyone who thinks that sex
can help create a loving relationship should look at the vast
amount of marital wreckage in the nation. All too often,
young people get married in anticipation of a life of bliss.
The bliss is elusive, but children come, bringing with them
cares and anxieties. The couple may decide against more
children. They abstain from sexual relations, and discover
how little they really care for each other. Even if they do
not take the route of abstinence, they are likely to feel "the
light of affection waning, and the flame of natural love grow
cold. " They gradually awaken to the fact that lust, not love,
brought them together and now rends them apart and thrusts
them into bitterness. [77]

Contrast this grim portrait of sexual love and its consequences with the bountiful benefits of celibacy. In the first
place, celibacy removes the cause of a good deal of dissension between individuals. The way is opened to the establishment of harmony in relationships. Father Rapp named his
first community Harmony, signifying his intent to restore the
universal harmony that had been lost at Eden, that is, harmony both between humans and God and between different individuals. [78]

The ideals of peace on earth and good will between
people seem to abide forever in the human heart, but continually elude the human grasp. It need no longer be so,
cry the celibates. People can live together in peace, enjoy-
ing each other as individuals in a great family. Abolish the
sexual evil, and the way to harmony and goodwill will be
opened. Moreover, said the Shaker leader Frederick Evans,
individuals who are part of this great family can be instrumental in bringing peace to the world, even though the world
has not adopted celibacy. Evans suggested that there should
be a "White Cross" class of intellectual celibates, men and
women who would be chosen to run the affairs of state.
Married people would remain at home, take care of their
families, and engage in business of various kinds (farming,
mechanical, mercantile). Once the White Cross celibates
were in control, they would put the "axe of reform" to the
root of all of our evils. They would also be peacemakers,
leading us away from the brink of war where we always
seem to hover. Like the celibate Jesus and the celibate
Ann, White Cross celibates will "bring from the Christ-
heavens the white-winged dove of peace. " [79]

Second, celibacy is the necessary foundation for social equality. Private property is the basis for marriage; celibacy is "the basis of and essential to a community of property, without which it cannot be supported." [80] Of course, all of the communitarian groups claimed to practice equality. The extent to which they actually achieved equality varied. But in general, there was more economic and sexual equality in the groups than in the rest of society. The Shakers, in particular, achieved a remarkable amount of sexual equality, and insisted that celibacy was the foundation upon which their community of equality rested. Women were freed from the control of men and the burdens of child-bearing and child-rearing. They were thereby able to participate with men equally in running the affairs of the communities. [81] Whether or not celibacy is a necessary ingredient in the construction of an order of equality, it is undeniable that women in many of the celibate communities used their freedom from sexual and maternal relationships to participate in the economic and political life of their groups.

Finally, celibacy is a rational form of birth control. Nineteenth-century Americans were very interested in limiting conception, primarily because of the physical, psychological, and economic strains of continual child-bearing. [82] A few advocated birth control for another reason. Still living in the shadow of the dire predictions of Thomas Malthus, they foresaw the time when the earth would be choked with multitudes of people. The birth rate must be lowered to avoid disaster. And what surer way to reduce the birth rate than by the adoption of celibacy? [83]

The point about birth control, however, raised a question that was repeatedly put to the celibates. What if everyone in the world adopted celibacy? That certainly could not enhance social well-being. On the contrary, it would mean the end of the human race. The questioners thought that they had backed the celibates into a corner from which the latter could not escape. But the celibates had no problem with the question. The Shakers shrugged it off as trivial. They said that the world would end sometime anyway. Besides, our main concern should be to do the will of God. The will of God is celibacy. How can we go wrong by following what God has willed?

Similarly, the Rappites saw no cause for alarm in the thought of universal celibacy. The way would only be more quickly prepared, they said, for the return of Christ and the establishment of a new heaven and a new earth. Indeed, that may be a part of God's design for humankind--that the race shall become extinct and that we shall all enjoy our existence in Heaven, which is infinitely more worthy of our concern than this earthly existence. [84] Father Divine had an even terser response: why fill the earth with even more misery? [85]

The celibates were unmoved by all of the arguments and objections put to them. They insisted that social well-being would be maximized in celibate communities. And they felt that if all the world should adopt celibacy, and if the human race should thereby perish from the earth, nothing would be lost. Indeed, people have nothing to lose, claimed the celibates, except their chains of lust and misery. And what do they gain? They are received into the bosom of the community, into the great family, where they share a life of equality, harmony, and good will. Why, then, would anyone cling to the chains?

1.   A. G. Hollister, Mission of Alethian Believers, Called Shakers (Mount Lebanon, New York: n. p. , 1892-99), p. 19.

2.   Joseph W. Slade, Historical Sketch of Thomas Lake Harris, Laurence Oliphant, and the Brotherhood of the New Life (manuscript in the Thomas Lake Harris collection, University of Nebraska at Omaha, n. d.), p. 6.

3.   Thomas Lake Harris, Battle Bells: Verse-Studies in Social Humanity (Fountaingrove, Cal. : n. p. , 1891), p. 44.

4.   Thomas Lake Harris, The Wedding Guest (n. p. , 1877), p. 14.

5.   Thomas Lake Harris, Marriage Mysteries (manuscript in the Thomas Lake Harris collection, University of Nebraska at Omaha, n. d.), p. 14.

6.   Thomas Lake Harris, The Breath of God with Man (New York: Brotherhood of the New Life, 1867), p. 94.

7. Thomas Lake Harris, "The Children of Hymen," The Herald of Light 2 (May 1858):7-8.

8. Thomas Lake Harris, "Conversation with Angels," The Herald of Light 1 (January 1858):393.

9. Thomas Lake Harris, Glimpses of Social and Sexual Order (manuscript in the Thomas Lake Harris collection, University of Nebraska at Omaha, n. d.), p. 5.

10. From a letter of Thomas Lake Harris to an Episcopalian priest. Quoted in Herbert W. Schneider and George Lawton, A Prophet and a Pilgrim (New York: Columbia University Press, 1942), p. 552.

11. Harris, The Breath of God with Man, p. 97.

12. Harris, "Conversation with Angels," pp. 392-93.

13. Margaret Oliphant W. Oliphant, Memoir of the Life of Lawrence Oliphant and of Alice Oliphant, His Wife, Vol. 2 (New York: Harper & Brothers, 1891), p. 96.

14. See Thomas Lake Harris, The Path into the New Life (1877), The Sexes Need for a Season a Monastic Separation, and A Sketch of Social Beginnings (manuscripts in the Thomas Lake Harris Collection, University of Nebraska at Omaha).

15. Thomas Lake Harris, The Golden Child, a Daily Chronicle, Vol. IV, Summaries and Conclusions (Fountaingrove, Cal.: n. p., 1878), p. 19.

16. Thomas Lake Harris, The Bridal Word (manuscript in the Thomas Lake Harris collection, University of Nebraska at Omaha, n. d.), p. 142.

17. Harris, The Sexes Need for a Season a Monastic Separation, p. 4.

18. Harris, The Golden Child, pp. 6-8.

19. Harris, The Wedding Guest, p. 67.

20. Harris, Glimpses of Social and Sexual Order, p. 6.

21. Harris, The Breath of God with Man, p. 100.

22. Ibid. , p. 96.

23. Harris, The Wedding Guest, p. 14.

24. Thomas Lake Harris, First Book of the Christian Religion (New York: New Church Publishing Association, 1858), p. 10.

25. Ibid. , p. 11.

26. Oliphant, Memoir of the Life, pp. 165-66.

27. Reported in Schneider and Lawton, A Prophet and a Pilgrim, pp. 523-32.

28. Harris, A Sketch of Social Beginnings, p. 6.

29. Schneider and Lawton, A Prophet and a Pilgrim, pp. 511, 516.

30. Harris, "The Children of Hymen," p. 4.

31. Ibid. , p. 8.

32. Harris, The Path into the New Life, pp. 35-36.

33. Thomas Lake Harris, A Voice from Heaven (privately printed, 1879), p. 5.

34. Ibid.

35. Ibid. , p. 12.

36. Ibid. , p. 10.

37. Ibid. , p. 8.

38. Ibid. , p. 10.

39. William Barclay, Flesh and Spirit (London: SCM Press, 1962), pp. 21-22.

40. Walter C. Klein, Johann Conrad Beissel: Mystic and Martinet (Philadelphia: University of Pennsylvania Press, 1942), p. 69.

41. Fayette Mace, Familiar Dialogues on Shakerism (Portland, Me. : Charles Day & Co. , 1838), pp. 37-8.

42. Quoted in Charles Nordhoff, The Communistic Societies of the United States (New York: Schocken Books, 1965; 1st published 1875), p. 123.

43. Mace, Familiar Dialogues, p. 48.

44. H. L. Eads, Shaker Sermons, 4th edition (South Union, Ky.: n. p., 1887), p. 52.

45. Quoted in Sara Harris, The Incredible Father Divine (London: W. H. Allen, 1954), p. 93.

46. A. G. Hollister, Mission of Alethian Believers, Called Shakers (Mount Lebanon, N. Y.: n. p., 1892-99), p. 5.

47. Eads, Shaker Sermons, pp. 313-14.

48. See Henri Desroche, The American Shakers (Amherst: The University of Massachusetts Press, 1971), p. 146.

49. George Rapp, Thoughts on the Destiny of Man (Harmony, Ind.: Harmony Society, 1824), p. 40. See also Alonzo G. Hollister, "Shakerism," The Manifesto 22 (October 1892):218.

50. James E. Ernst, Ephrata: A History (Allentown, Pa.: The Pennsylvania German Folklore Society, 1963), p. 16.

51. John Hoshor, God in a Rolls Royce: The Rise of Father Divine (New York: Hillman Curl, 1936), p. 112.

52. Julius Friedrich Sachse, The Music of the Ephrata Cloister (New York: AMS Press, 1903), pp. 67-68.

53. Klein, Johann Conrad Beissel, p. 146.

54. Frederick William Evans, Shaker Communism; Or Tests of Divine Inspiration (London: J. Burns, 1871), p. 80.

55. Dr. M. Dwight, "The Use and Abuse of Amativeness," The Communitist 1 (April 23, 1845):91.

56. Daniel Fraser, "Celibacy," The Shaker and Shakeress 3 (January 1873):4.

57. Hollister, Mission of Alethian Believers, p. 6.

58. Elder Richard Bushnell, "Celibacy and Longevity," The Shaker and Shakeress 3 (February 1873):12.

59. "Longevity of Virgin Celibates," Shaker Manifesto 12 (October 1882):218-19.

60. Johann Conrad Beissel, A Dissertation on Man's Fall (Ephrata, Pa.: n. p., 1765), p. 18.

61. Karl J. R. Arndt, George Rapp's Harmony Society (1785-1847) (Philadelphia: University of Pennsylvania Press, 1965), p. 98.

62. Beissel, A Dissertation, p. 19.

63. R. W. Pelham, A Shakers Answer to the Oft-Repeated Question "What Would Become of the World If All Should Become Shakers?" (East Canterbury, N. H.: n. p., n. d.), p. 7.

64. Ibid., p. 5.

65. Ibid., p. 10.

66. Karl J. R. Arndt, A Documentary History of the Indiana Decade of the Harmony Society, 1814-1824, Vol. 1 (Indianapolis: Indiana Historical Society, 1975), p. 399.

67. John Archibald Bole, The Harmony Society (Philadelphia: Americana Germanica Press, 1904), p. 52.

68. See Victor Francis Calverton, Where Angels Dared to Tread: Socialist and Communist Utopian Colonies in the United States (Freeport, N. Y.: Books for Libraries Press, 1941), p. 31.

69. Eads, Shaker Sermons, p. 49.

70. Arndt, A Documentary History, p. 775. See also Frank S. Beck, Christian Communists in America: A History of the Colony of Saint Nazianz, Wisconsin,

unpublished M. A. thesis, Saint Paul Seminary, 1959, p. 67.

71. R. W. Pelham, ed., Shakers: A Correspondence Between Mary F. C(arr) of Mt. Holly City and a Shaker Sister, Sarah L(ucas) (Union Village, Ohio: n. p., 1868), p. 7.

72. Lessons in Matters of Faith and Morality (manuscript in the Shaker collection, Western Reserve Historical Society Library, n. d.), p. 4. See also, "Editorial Notes," The Shaker 7 (January 1877):5.

73. Elijah Myrick, "Celibacy or Virginity, Which?" The Shaker Manifesto 10 (May 1880):104.

74. "Some Plain Answers," The Shaker Manifesto 9 (September 1878):223-24.

75. Fragrance from the Altar of Incense: Shaker Contributions to the Flaming Sword (n. p., n. d.), p. 11.

76. The North Family of Shakers, Mount Lebanon: Cedar Boughs (Buffalo: The Peter Paul Book Company, 1895), p. 131.

77. C. E. Sears, A Short Treatise on Marriage (Rochester, N. Y.: Daily Democrat Steam Printing House, 1867), p. 12; Hollister, Mission of Alethian Believers, pp. 21-22.

78. Donald E. Pitzer and Josephine M. Elliott, "New Harmony's First Utopians, 1814-1824," Indiana Magazine of History 75 (September 1979):249-50.

79. F. W. Evans, "White Cross Celibacy," The Manifesto 18 (July 1888):164.

80. Evans, Shaker Communism, p. 76. See also Wm. Leonard, A Discourse on the Order and Propriety of Divine Inspiration and Revelation (United Society: Harvard, 1853), pp. 85-86.

81. See Lawrence Foster, Religion and Sexuality (New York: Oxford University Press, 1981), p. 38.

82. See James Reed, From Private Vice to Public Virtue (New York: Basic Books, 1978), pp. 3-33.

83.   Pelham, A Shakers Answer, pp. 6-7.

84.   Aaron Williams, The Harmony Society (Pittsburg: W. S. Haven, 1866), p. 102; Karl J. R. Arndt, George Rapp's Successors and Material Heirs, 1847-1916 (Rutherford: Fairleigh Dickinson University Press, 1972), p. 150.

85.   Hoshor, God in a Rolls Royce, p. 111.

5. LIVING IN THE SPIRIT AND THE FLESH: IDEOLOGIES OF SEXUAL UNION

Unlike the celibates, those who advocated some kind of sexual union did not have a common set of themes in their ideologies. There are some common elements, but the differences are sufficiently great to demand that we treat separately three of the types we discussed in chapter 3: the traditionalists, the deviants, and the system of complex marriage at Oneida.

DEFENDERS OF MARRIAGE

As we pointed out in chapter 3, the traditionalists insisted upon marriage as the proper sphere for sexual activity. They accepted the conventional morality that sex should be confined to marriage, and that marriage is a kind of sacred relationship. There is little to their ideology of sex beyond a simple defense of the conventional morality, with the exception of the question of the importance of sex in human life.

Most of the traditionalists downplayed the importance of sex to people's well-being. In fact, most of them exhibited the attitudes and behavior described in chapter 1 regarding nineteenth-century Americans generally. That is, their sexual lives were characterized by ignorance, prudishness, a depreciation of sexuality, and a sense of moral alarm.

For the religious traditionalists, of course, there was a biblical or other doctrinal basis for their attitudes. At Hopedale, an editor began an article about sexual relations as follows:

> The sexual relation, in its general and God-designed character, is an ordination of Infinite Wisdom and Love, and being so, must possess in itself intrinsic

excellence, beauties and joys.... Everything in it evinces a Divine hand. There are the necessary organs, the necessary desires, the necessary instincts, prophesying the purpose of God and fulfilling by their own instrumentality the prophecy. [1]

The editor went on to argue that the conventional arrangements, including marriage, were all established by God for the purpose of perpetuating the race.

Similarly, Katherine Tingley, long the leader of the theosophical community at Point Loma, California (1898-1942), wrote about the "sacredness" of marriage. "When marriage is accepted as a sacred sanction, a sacred gift, and a sacred power, and it is entered into understandingly by both man and woman, we shall have no more divorces." [2] Various other groups agreed with the assertion that marriage is a divine institution, the divine setting for human sexual relationships.

At the same time, most of the traditionalists did not regard sexual activity in marriage to be of high priority for human fulfillment. Most have believed what we have seen at Hopedale and among the Hutterites--sex was given to us by God primarily for procreation. Hence, there was an ongoing sense of moral concern about sexual behavior and a tendency to disapprove of sexual excess or anything that smacked of romantic love or that might generate erotic feelings. At Shalam, Oahspe, the community's Bible, condemned uncontrolled sexual indulgence. [3] At Hopedale, they taught that there is a distinction between "true love" and "free love." Free love is characterized by sexual passion, and that passion demands a variety of partners for maximum enjoyment. True love, on the other hand, is founded upon exclusiveness. True love wants to totally possess the beloved, and will be satisfied with nothing less than such possession. [4] In other words, Hopedale members believed that sexual passion should be subservient to the creation of an exclusive, ongoing relationship. Sexual activity was not wrong, but the Christian was not to let it become a dominant concern. As an article addressed to young women in the community put it:

In the solemn and joyful name of humanity, and the angel world, we call upon you to listen to the Voice of Wisdom--you, especially, who are violating the laws of your physical health, and degrading your moral sense, by sexual excesses--whether Solitary or Social. The earthly end of that journey is sadly fearful; and few are the angel whispers of peace to the souls of unrest on their descending course! [5]

The "solitary" sexual excess referred to above is masturbation. The traditionalists shared the conventional morality about the horrors of masturbation. A writer in the Point Loma journal called it "the worst and most subtle foe," a practice that can grow until "the whole nature of the man or woman, including every cell of body and brain, every thought and habit, becomes warped and cast in a vicious mold, and the entire after-life is rendered a miserable failure." [6]

Some of the nonreligious traditionalists also warned about excessive sexuality. At Kaweah, the editor of the community's paper pointed out that those who are the slaves "of unnatural appetites and lusts cannot assist in socialistic progression." [7] On another occasion, the editor wrote that sensuality brings about all kinds of undesirable results: "It leads to crime, violence and outrage. It ruins reputations and it breaks hearts. It breeds drunkenness, lust, and kindred other horrors. [8]

Not all of the traditionalists downgraded the importance of sex to human well-being, however. The Icarians viewed sex and marriage as essential to human happiness. A similar view prevails at the modern commune, The Farm. In sexual relations, Gaskin teaches his followers, there is a life force, an "electricity," that passes between the two lovers. "Making love is a way in which you can feel the presence of the Holy Spirit. And if people can be open and trusting enough with one another when they're making love, they can move that energy around and they can heal themselves." [9] Gaskin also warns about the excesses of sexual activity, however. This generation, he writes, has been obsessed with sex because it was taught not to be. In an effort to correct the prudish restrictions of the past, this generation has gone to the other extreme. But people who keep pursuing sexuality may find themselves requiring greater and greater amounts of "sensation," so that they go into "sadism and masochism and violence." [10] The answer to the repression of the past is not promiscuous and/or sado-masochistic sex, but a loving relationship between a man and woman in which they share in each other's life-giving energy.

THE JUSTIFICATION OF SEXUAL DEVIANCE

Groups that have advocated group marriage, free love, or a laissez-faire arrangement tended to justify their sexual pattern on the basis of one or more of five themes, each of which can be expressed in positive or negative terms: sex is intrinsically good (celibacy is harmful); people grow more mature through sex (individual growth is stifled through improper sexual arrangements); all sexual relations should be based on love and affection (sex should not be based upon narrow legal or religious strictures); individuals should be free to choose their sex life (people should not be allowed to choose an exclusive sexual relationship); and proper sexual arrangements enhance group harmony and well-being (improper sexual arrangements erode group solidarity).

Sex Is Intrinsically Good

Expressed positvely, the deviants argued that sex itself is good. Expressed negatively, they asserted that celibacy is undesirable or even harmful for humans. Fourier grew lyrical in his praise of love:

> What are the other passions compared to love?
> Can any one of them be compared to it? Without
> love life would lose its charm. When love has
> gone man can only vegetate and seek distractions
> or illusions to hide the emptiness of his soul. [11]

God believes that love is supreme, according to Fourier, so that in God's ideal society there will be love for people even in their old age. Fourier also argued that love fares poorly in civilization because it is confined to marriage. This shows that so-called civilization is a social order that is contrary to the design of God. If people were to establish a divine social order, they would insure ample opportunities for the expression of love, the King and source of all other human passions.

Like Fourier, other sexual deviants stressed the fact that love, including sexual relations, between humans is a good in itself. They argued that sex is not merely a way to procreate, not a necessary evil, not a concession to the animal nature of males, but a form of behavior that is both desirable and beneficial. If there is a "good life," that life must include sexual relationships.

One way to underscore the goodness of sex is to contrast it with the undesirable nature of celibacy. Robert Owen had utter contempt for those who advocated celibacy as a permanent arrangement in a utopian community:

> Therefore, let it now be known to all, that when the mind of man shall be regenerated, and he shall enter upon the state of moral good, in an association of sufficient numbers to support and protect itself, and its rising generation, against the ignorance and consequent prejudices of moral evil; that CELIBACY ... will be known to be a great crime, necessarily leading to disease of body and mind, and to unnatural thoughts, feelings and conduct, and to every kind of falsification of our real impressions, sympathies and sensations. [12]

If the celibates could argue that sexual relations carry with them intrinsic evils and are therefore intrinsically wrong, the deviants could turn the argument on its head and insist that it is celibacy, not sex, that inherently generates evil among people. Hence, celibacy, not sex, is the demon that must be cast out of human society.

Sex Facilitates Individual Growth

One of the reasons that sex is intrinsically good is that it helps people to grow, to become more mature, more fulfilled individuals. Jacob Beilhart, who established the Spirit Fruit Society in Lisbon, Ohio in 1899, used an amalgam of spiritualist and theosophist teachings to exalt love as the foundation of his community. Love, including sexual love, was the supreme good for people. In one of his pamphlets, Beilhart wrote that he had only one message for his followers, "and that message is Love ... Love is the only Life that exists." [13] Beilhart said that the Spirit seeks to create through every individual, but that the Spirit can only accomplish that task as the individual gives way wholly to Love. Beilhart himself was extremely appealing to others, he pointed out, not because he was wiser or more attractive or more forceful, but because of his Love.

Beilhart linked love with freedom, particularly with the freedom of women. How can a woman become free? Beilhart answered the question by saying that it is not just her lack of property rights that enslaves woman, but her jealousy, fear, and doubt. The power to free woman from such chains is "the unselfish Love of Man." [14] His own joy in life, noted Beilhart, was to help men become men and women to become free and to gain their inheritance of love.

Similarly, the credo at Harrad West stated that the members had become better people through group marriage. They found that they were more affectionate, had deeper friendships, increased their capacity to be warm and understanding, and had richer lives as a result of their sexual arrangement. [15] These benefits of group marriage sound ironic in view of the tension and conflict that led to the demise of Harrad West (chapter 3). But the credo was probably written before the group developed the extreme tensions that seemed to characterize their final days. In any case, ideologies do not have to reflect reality. The point of the ideology is to state ideals, justify behavior, and convert others.

Ideally, then, sex results in more mature, more appealing individuals. But not every sexual arrangement yields the desired outcome. The deviants were careful to point out that the traditional sexual pairing through marriage does not make better people. Quite the opposite occurs. Marital sex is a cause of degeneration. People grow only when sex is freed from the bonds of an exclusive relationship. As Beilhart put the case:

> I saw that if I lived the Life of Love, it must be the Universal Love. It must mean freedom for me and freedom for all who enter Life. Freedom from what? ... freedom from jealousy, from doubt that Love will give them all they need ... Love is not limited nor can one take what is for another ... this universe is not a game of "grab and take," with the majority getting left, but love is bountiful in its blessings, and its delight is to give them all their real heart's desire. [16]

A female member of the Ruskin Commonwealth, a mother and a wife, wrote about the virtual necessity of having more than one sexual partner. In responding to a critic who wondered if any women believed in or practiced "variety" in sexual relationships at Ruskin, she exhibited neither qualms nor hesitation about affirming the importance of variety:

> I want to say Yes; most emphatically. My husband

and myself are in perfect harmony on this point;
and can see no more harm in having an exchange
of partners in the sex relation than in having variety in food, clothing, or friends. Who could be
happy in this world if only permitted to enjoy the
companionship of one individual? Who loves flowers? Does any one love but one kind of flowers?
Is any one healthy who is confined to a single article of food? ... then who can give a sensible reason why the sex relation should be confined without
variety? [17]

To put the matter negatively, the deviants pointed out
the perils of married life for individual well-being. Fourier
presented a list of twelve "misfortunes" attendant upon the
married life. [18] The first is the possibility of unhappiness
and anxiety as the individual anticipates marriage. The
marital union is, after all, indissoluble and lifelong, he
pointed out, and yet crucial to the individual's happiness.
An individual is taking a gamble with high risks to enter into
marriage. Once married, the couple soon discover that they
have somewhat disparate tastes and personalities. Compli-
cations inevitably arise either in the couple's relationship or
in the circumstances that circumscribe their lives. Various
other misfortunes include the financial problems of establishing a household, the tendency for monotony to plague the
wife, and the common problem of adultery.

Owen had, if anything, even harsher words for the
outcomes of marriage. The priests who bind two people together in an indissoluble union, he argued, are responsible
for all kinds of human misery, including prostitution, impure
and unchaste thoughts and desires in people, and the "almost
unimagined multiplied crimes and miseries of the married
life." [19] The priests have defined chastity as having sex
with only one other person in accord with "their most fan-
tastic whims and unnatural notions." The consequence of
this unnatural arrangement is a stifling of the individual's
pursuit of happiness. Owen was outraged: "What a sacri-
lege of the best and finest sympathies of our nature! What
ignorance of the organization of man and woman! What horrid sacrifice of the happiness of the human life!" [20]

The case made by many of the deviants, that marriage is evil because it involves an indissoluble union of only
two people, is not valid today. Many Americans practice
what has been called serial monogamy: many marital part-

ners during the course of one's life, but only one at a time.
The deviants would not have been satisfied with such an arrangement, however. They did not believe that sexual relationships should be confined to just two people for even a
few years. Rather, they insisted upon nothing less than the
next two points we shall discuss: love and affection as the
basis for sex, and the absolute right of individuals to choose
their own sexual arrangements.

Love and Affection Are the Basis for Sex

An individual might enter a sexual relationship for a
variety of reasons. As Victor points out, a person can use
sex to "obtain erotic pleasure, expressions of affection, relief from daily tensions, conception for childbearing, approval
from others, relief from loneliness, satisfaction of curiosity,
a sense of power over another person, or money." [21]
People also enter marriage for a variety of reasons, many
of which are similar to those given for sexual relations. In
a utopian community, according to the deviants, sexual relations should not be based upon such things as the need for
financial security, the need for approval from someone else,
or social pressures. In the laissez-faire groups, they argued that sex should be based only upon the reasons chosen
by individuals who are in the process of fulfilling themselves. Frequently, that meant that no one inquired into the
sexual practices of others in the community. As Kinkade
wrote about Twin Oaks, there isn't a great deal to be said
about love affairs because lovemaking is largely a private
matter. You can't tell whether two individuals holding hands
in public are lovers or not. "They may be and they may
not be. Nobody asks, and nobody much cares." [22]

This attitude of "let people do what they like in the
matter of sex" was also the ideal at Josiah Warren's communities (Equity, Utopia, and Modern Times). But the assumption at the laissez-faire communities was that people
will choose to enter sexual relationships because of their
love for the other. For example, Andreas Dietsch, the
founder of a short-lived group at New Helvetia, Missouri,
wrote a book about utopia in which he expressed his ideal. [23]
In the book, a man called "A" wants to settle in the community. He also wants to marry the founder's youngest
daughter, whom he loves. "A" discovers that the appropriate procedure is to go to the girl and request her hand in
marriage. The girl will then frankly tell him whether she

will accept him as a husband. There are no considerations of financial advantage attached to her decision. If she loves him but, for some reason, doesn't want to marry him, she can move into a house for unmarried women and give him the key to her room. He may then visit her as long as they both agree to the arrangement. Dietsch's account neatly expresses the essence of the deviants' view of sex and marriage. Neither sex nor marriage should be based on external considerations like financial need or advantage. Rather, love and affection will be the basis for the decision of each individual about his or her sex life and marriage plans, if any.

With the exception of a few modern communes, none of the utopian groups accepted the swinging concept of sex, the notion that sex is a casual, almost impersonal, act with a variety of others. The laissez-faire groups expected love and affection to be the basis for sexual decisions. Similarly, those that practiced group marriage expected each member to love equally every other member. Even though sex occurred with a variety of partners, each sexual encounter occurred (at least in theory) in the context of love and affection for the other.

Many groups made the point explicitly. Replying to a letter from a Shaker, Robert Owen argued that "true chastity consists in having no sexual intercourse except when God's affinity, or pure love and affection, exists at the time between the parties." [24] Owen distinguished between "promiscuous," "unnatural," and "natural" intercourse. [25] Promiscuous intercourse results in all sorts of personal and social disorders. It is the "intercourse of savages, without affection, sentiment, or refinement." [26] Owen would call swinging a form of promiscuous intercourse. "Unnatural" intercourse is that which occurs in the context of an indissoluble marriage of two people. "Natural" intercourse is "the intercourse of refinement, sentiment, and affection, between the parties; it cannot be purchased; the priesthood cannot give it." [27] Natural intercourse will occur only in the ideal society or "new moral world" as Owen called it. Owen was, of course, never able to establish that new moral world in his own experiments. But he argued that it would come one day, and when it did people would finally be able to experience the bliss of natural intercourse.

Sex Is a Matter of Free Choice

The deviants all argued that individuals should be free

to choose their own sexual arrangements, with one exception --some groups have explicitly or implicitly refused to acknowledge the validity of exclusive relationships. Of course, those that practiced group marriage, by definition, disallowed any exclusive relationships. Their argument was still that people should be free to choose. Hence, they maintained that those that prefer group marriage should be free to engage in it, while those that prefer some other option should be free to pursue it (though outside the group in which each one is married to all others). In some free love and laissez-faire communities, exclusivity was also disallowed or disapproved. In others, people could choose whatever sexual arrangement they liked, including a monogamous relationship.

For the anarchists, freedom to choose one's sexual life was an expression of the more basic freedom to make all of one's own decisions without the interference of church or state. Josiah Warren pointed out that the charge against his groups that they had "an unusual latitude" in marital relationships was unjust. He was not concerned to either abolish or maintain marriage, but to establish a community based on the principle of the sovereignty of the individual. Sovereign individuals might well opt to retain a traditional marriage. But it should in any case be their option rather than a decision imposed upon them. "I find no warrant in my 'sovereignty,'" wrote Warren, "for invading, disturbing, or offending other people, whatever may be their sentiments or modes of life, while they act only at their own Cost. " [28]

Other deviant groups also cherished the notion of individual freedom in the area of sexual relations. Some based this on the idea that there are individual differences in desires and needs. It is therefore unrealistic and detrimental to human well-being to impose a uniform system upon everyone. Fourier argued that humans are universally inclined to "polygamous" relations. [29] He noted that a good part of the world's people practice polygamy as a legal form, while a good part of the civilized world is composed of "clandestine polygamists." In other words, most of the people of the world, both males and females, have sexual relations with more than one partner. How, then, can supposedly wise people denounce a system which is practiced by the bulk of the world's population? "How can the savants disregard the secret insurrection of the human race against any form of legislation which requires perpetual fidelity in love?" [30]

Thus, in the eyes of the deviants, uniformity necessarily means a thwarting of individual growth and a stifling
of individual freedom--at least to the extent that the uniformity is imposed upon people rather than growing out of their
own decisions. In sexual matters, they argued, Americans
should have the same freedom that they hold as their right in
other matters, namely, the freedom of the individual to make
his or her own choice.

Proper Sexual Arrangements Enhance Social Well-Being

The deviant groups argued that appropriate sexual patterns not only facilitate individual growth, but also lead to
social well-being. Stated negatively, they insisted that inappropriate arrangements--such as a uniform pattern for the
entire society, sexual relations governed by law or religion,
or, in some cases, sexual exclusiveness--are socially detrimental because they erode group solidarity.

What kind of social well-being results from a correct
sexual system? Fourier said that the right kind of sexual
arrangement could foster both social harmony and economic
well-being. At Kerista Village, they stress the fact that they
have created intimate family units through their practice of
group marriage. They have, they claim, achieved what many
Americans consider the ideal for a family--participation in a
small, intimate group in which every member is important,
loved, and supported. Similarly, in his study of four modern communes Hawkins found that a number of the members
accepted the importance of sexual relations to the establishment of intimacy. One communard told him that if he could
relate to a woman every way but sexually, then the lack of
the sexual relation would keep them from "really being together." [31] As far as the deviant groups were concerned,
an imposed barrier to free sexual relations is, among other
things, also a barrier to intimacy. With the freeing of sexual
relations from the restrictions of law and religion, they insisted, intimacy was extended from a small group to the entire community. The community itself became a family.

If the right sexual arrangements enhance social well-
being, the wrong arrangements erode the social order. In
particular, the deviants insisted that improper sexual relations
threaten the solidarity of the group. Judson Jerome took the
argument a step farther. It is not possible, he asserted, to
maintain a communal living arrangement without "overcoming

embarrassment and squeamishness--and, most importantly, lustfulness and possessiveness in regard to sex. " [32] It is an interesting argument, for some social scientists have made the same point.

Lewis Coser has summarized the argument cogently in his analysis of greedy institutions. He says that those groups that set themselves off from the larger society must gain the total commitment of their members if they are to survive. Anything that gains a portion of that commitment is a threat to the group. Every individual has a limited capacity for emotional involvement with others. To the extent that an individual is committed to, emotionally involved with, one other person, that individual will have less of himself or herself to give to the group. As a result, many groups have been fearful of dyadic intimacy among their members.

The nub of the problem for the utopian groups, then, was not sex per se "but rather dyadic withdrawal into a private--hence, non-communal--world. " [33] Consequently, quite different sexual practices, including both celibacy and group marriage, performed the same social function, namely, the elimination of dyadic involvements that threaten group solidarity.

In sum, the contention of the deviant groups that the monogamous relationship is a threat to the group is supported by sociological argument. But the argument overlooks the empirical fact that a number of groups, such as Amana and the Hutterites, have survived for a number of generations while maintaining a traditional pattern of marriage and the family. Dyadic relations did not destroy those groups. Nor did the lack of dyadic relations maintain the solidarity of groups like Harrad West. We would argue, then, that the nub of the problem for the utopian groups was commitment to the group's ideology. After all, people who have strong dyadic involvements also have group attachments; few, if any, people exist in the private world of the dyad. Dyadic involvement, therefore, is only a threat if the group's ideology insists that it is a threat. In a sense, then, the deviant groups were correct in arguing that improper sexual arrangements threaten social well-being, for those people who flout the sexual norms will always be defined as a threat to the welfare of the group.

THE IDEOLOGY OF COMPLEX MARRIAGE

As noted in chapter 3, complex marriage at Oneida was a unique system among the utopian groups. It also had a unique ideology, though some of the themes discussed above are also found in the teachings of Noyes. We shall look first at the goals identified by Noyes for his utopian community, and then at the justification for the system of complex marriage and male continence whereby Noyes would achieve his goals.

Goals of the Oneida Community

The first and primary goal of Noyes was to establish a group rooted in the will of God. In the First Annual Report of the Oneida Association, Noyes set forth the religious basis for his community:

> The Oneida Association regards itself as a branch of the kingdom of heaven, the exponent of the principles, and servant of the spiritual will of that kingdom.... In the place of all formulas, it relies on inspiration, working through those who approve themselves as agents of God. [34]

Even the relationship between the sexes, as contrary as it was to traditional Christian practices and beliefs, was defined by Noyes as based on the will of God and the teachings of the Bible. The First Annual Report contained an extended justification entitled "Bible Argument; Defining the Relations of the Sexes in the Kingdom of Heaven." In the "Bible Argument" Noyes made the point that any plan must begin with reconciliation with God. It is important, he continued, to restore the "true relations between the sexes" and to reform the economic system. But first of all, there must be a "settlement with God."

A second goal of Noyes was to free women from the bondage of continual child-bearing and child care. Two years before he set up the community at Oneida, Noyes had written about "woman's slavery to children." [35] He noted that people generally accepted the proposition that a woman's most important duty is to care for her children, and that such care enables her to serve God more effectively than in any other way. But the proposition has resulted in much evil, Noyes contended:

> Doubtless, women may and do serve God acceptably
> in performing these offices. But we say that that
> absorbing and almost exclusive devotedness to wait-
> ing on their children, which is practised by so
> many mothers--inasmuch as it leaves them little
> or no time for their own spiritual and intellectual
> improvement--robs them of much that they owe to
> God and to themselves, and in fact unfits them for
> the office of true education, and thus defeats the
> very end (the best good of their children) which
> they seek to accomplish. [36]

Noyes went on to say that there are three claims on
a woman that supercede the claims of her children: the
claim of God; the woman's duty to herself; and the claim of
the husband. The claim of God is, of course, paramount.
We would expect that in a religious community. But Noyes
insisted on the validity of the other claims as well. A
woman who does not engage in her own personal development,
he said, neglects a God-given duty and, moreover, cannot
adequately mother her children. And a woman who neglects
her husband for her children chooses an inferior love for a
superior one:

> The love and care of children in parents should not
> supplant or interfere with their love as man and
> woman. Amativeness takes precedence of philo-
> progenitiveness, and parental feeling becomes a
> usurpation when it crowds out a passion which is
> relatively its superior. [37]

As a third goal, Noyes set himself to the task of freeing everyone from the bane of private property. All the ways
of getting property in the world, the First Annual Report
stated, are forms of a "grab-game," a game where the prizes
are doled out not according to wisdom or justice "but are
seized by the strongest and craftiest." [38] Such a system
is based on the false assumption that property is the rightful
possession of anyone who can get control of it. In actuality,
God holds the "original title" to all property. God, therefore, also holds the rights of distribution. What humans
gain, they hold in joint-ownership with God. As a result of
this line of reasoning, the report concluded, the Oneida
community does not hold an "ordinary platform of communism." Rather, the Oneida doctrine is that of

> community, not merely or chiefly with each other,

but with God; and for the security of individual rights they look, not to constitutions or compacts with each other, but to the wisdom and goodness of the Spirit of truth, which is above all. The idea of their system, stated in its simplest form, is that all believers constitute the family of God; that all valuables, whether persons or things, are family property; and that all the labors of the family are directed, judged and rewarded in the distribution of enjoyments by the Father. [39]

Note in the above quote that "persons" as well as "things" are included as family property. In Noyes view, marriage was a form of private property, with the man literally possessing the woman as his property (a view, incidentally, easily defended on the basis of the legal status of women in the nineteenth century). Furthermore, he claimed that the possessive feeling that an individual gets when he or she uses the pronoun "mine" is the same whether the "mine" refers to people or money or property. In the ideal community, the community rooted in the will of God, there will be no private property of any kind. It will be as it was in the days of the first church, when the believers had all things in common. Noyes admitted that the communism of the first Christians did not extend to family members, but he also argued that "the same spirit which abolished exclusiveness in regard to money, would abolish, if circumstances allowed full scope to it, exclusiveness in regard to women and children. [40] As evidence that God's will included the abolition of exclusiveness in family relations, Noyes quoted Paul's statement to the Corinthians that property in women and property in goods would both be abolished in the Kingdom of Heaven. At Oneida, therefore, people would be free of the bane of private property and follow God's will for nonexclusivity in all things.

Finally, Noyes had the goal of affirming a proper relationship between the sexes. In order to build an ideal society, he maintained, people must first be reconciled with God. And then those people must establish proper relationships between the sexes. Noyes put the problem of sexual arrangements ahead of such things as the economy and the polity. For he believed that the love between a man and a woman is one of the most important facets of human well-being. Sharing the agony of his wife when four of their children were stillborn, he considered emulating the Shakers for a time and establishing a celibate community. But he rejected that option as a denial of the intrinsic worth and manifest importance of sexual love.

Sexual love was so important to Noyes that he wanted, as Parker rightly points out, to make it both a sacrament and a science. [41] That is, sexual love would take place in a manner that was pleasing to God and in accord with the best knowledge of humans. Outsiders, of course, frequently viewed the Oneida system as nothing more than an expression of the worst kind of human depravity. They charged that complex marriage was simply a justification for the expression of animal lust. But Noyes carefully distinguished between lust and love. The community, in fact, was careful to weed out or reprimand those that they thought were motivated by lust rather than the love of God. One man, for example, proved a "very serious" case for the group:

> He is very insincere, unfaithful, superficial and
> pleasure-seeking--has sought acquaintance with one
> of the neighbors' girls, and once at least by his
> own admission has made an attempt to entice some
> of the other boys of his class into communication
> with some abandoned women in the neighborhood,
> although it appears he did not succeed. If he does
> not find out a way to become in earnest for salva-
> tion, and quit his develtries [sic], he will be ob-
> liged to leave the community. [42]

Similarly, a woman who lived in the community for a time on probation, then left for awhile, sent a letter requesting their prayers and seeking admission. But the people decided that the woman "will have to have the will and lusts of the flesh a little more quelled in her before she will be prepared for Community life." [43] The Oneidans had their own notions about what constituted lust, and they were no more tolerant of it than were outsiders about the so-called lusts of the community.

The Justification

The system of complex marriage and male continence, described in chapter 3, allowed the Oneidans to achieve the above goals. In a sense, the goals justified the means used to achieve them. But Noyes worked out a thorough justification for his means as well as for his goals.

Noyes began his "Bible argument" for complex marriage by pointing out that the Bible predicts the coming of the kingdom of heaven on earth. As we already noted, he further stated that the Oneida community was a branch of the kingdom on earth. As such, the laws attendant upon the people were God's laws, supplanting the laws of all human governments. Thus, the laws of the government established a system of monogamous marriage. But "the institution of marriage which assigns the exclusive possession of one woman to one man" does not exist in the kingdom of heaven. [44] For Christ taught us that in the resurrection people neither marry nor are they given in marriage. Moreover, Noyes pointed out, the death of Christ brought an end to the Jewish law. And while Paul did not expressly carry the principle of our freedom from the Jewish law to the realm of marriage, "it is perfectly clear that the same logic that would make an end of any part of the Jewish law, would make an end of marriage. " [45]

If marriage is abolished, what is the relationship between men and women? There are only two possibilities, according to Noyes, if we are to follow the biblical teachings --celibacy or "pantogamy. " People who follow celibacy interpret the lack of marriage in the kingdom of heaven to mean that there are no sexual relations. Those who opt for pantogamy, on the other hand, affirm the place of sex in God's kingdom. Pantogamy means that "the intimate union of life and interests, which in the world is limited to pairs, extends through the whole body of believers, i. e. complex marriage takes the place of simple. " [46] After all, Christ enjoined his followers to love one another. We are to do that "not by pairs, as in the world, but en masse. " [47]

Noyes maintained that experience as well as biblical teachings support the system of complex marriage. For example, he pointed out, second marriages are certainly contrary to the notion that an individual should love only one other person for life, yet second marriages are frequently the happiest marriages. And throughout the world, men and women have found that the gratification derived from love is not "burnt out" by one honeymoon or satisfied by a single lover. "On the contrary, the secret history of the human heart will bear out the assertion that it is capable of loving any number of times and any number of persons, and that the more it loves the more it can love. " [48]

Thus, one aspect of Noyes' justification of his system

was his defense of multilateral sexual relations on biblical and experiential grounds. A second aspect was his distinction between the amative and propagative sides of sexual relations. The Shakers, among others, insisted that sex is only justifiable for propagative purposes. Noyes took a contrary position: sex is primarily for social rather than propagative purposes. When he was wrestling with the problem of continued child-bearing, he wrote, he first "conceived the idea that the sexual organs have a social function which is distinct from the propagative function." [49] Moreover, he decided that the social function was of greater importance. For Eve was called Adam's "help-meet." She was created to be Adam's companion. In the Garden of Eden, amativeness preceded propagation. In fact, propagation did not occur during the period of innocence. It was not until after the fall from grace that God told Eve she would bear children in pain, "from which it is to be inferred that in the original state, conception would have been comparatively infrequent." [50] Noyes' logic appears strained here, for it is not clear why conception would be infrequent before the pain of childbirth appeared on the human scene. But lapses in logic seldom trouble ideologues, and in any case what is illogical to one person makes perfect sense to another. Presumably, Noyes found his argument quite cogent.

Noyes not only gave the amative priority over the propagative, but also argued that the amative enhances our well-being. Sex, quite apart from procreation, is good in itself (here, obviously, Noyes agreed with the other deviant groups). As Noyes rather poetically put it, "amativeness is to life, as sunshine to vegetation." [51] It was crucial to the well-being of people, therefore, not to forego amative relations. The "grand problem which must be solved before redemption can be carried forward to immortality," Noyes wrote, is how to obtain the benefits of amativeness and reduce the expenses of propagation "to such limits as life can afford." [52] The Shakers, he noted, focused on the latter part of the problem--reducing the expense. As a result, they shut off both the profits and the expense of sexual relations. Robert Dale Owen suggested a way to gain the benefits and minimize the expense in his book, Moral Physiology, namely the use of coitus interruptus. This, said Noyes, is unnatural, filthy, and a waste of life. Others have opted for abortion. But Noyes considered abortion a form of murder. There must be a satisfactory solution, he argued, and that solution will be one that is natural, healthy for both males and females, conducive to amativeness, and effective in con-

trolling conception. Thus, he laid out the foundation upon
which to erect his own system of male continence as the
grand answer to a grand problem.

In order to fully understand the reasonableness of
male continence, we must recognize that it is possible to
distinguish between the amative and propagative functions
not only in theory but also in practice. In fact, there are
three functions of the sex organs, each of which is theoreti-
cally and practically separable: the urinary, amative, and
propagative functions. Noyes strengthened his argument with
an analogy of the human mouth:

> The mouth has three distinct functions, viz., those
> of breathing, eating and speaking. Two of these,
> breathing and eating, are purely physical; and these
> we have in common with the brutes. The third
> function, that of speaking, is social, and subser-
> vient to the intellectual and spiritual. In this we
> rise above the brutes. They are destitute of it
> except in a very inferior degree. So the two pri-
> mary functions of the sexual organs--the urinary
> and reproductive--are physical, and we have them
> in common with the brutes. The third, viz. the
> amative, is social, and subservient to the spiritual.
> In this again we rise above the brutes. They have
> it only as a bait to the reproductive. As speech,
> the distinctive glory of man is the superior function
> of the mouth, so the amative office of the sexual
> organs is their superior function, and that which
> gives man a position above the brutes. [53]

People who are ignorant of the three functions of the
sexual organs, said Noyes, i.e., those who believe that the
organs only have urinary and propagative functions, and who
engage in sexual intercourse without intending to procreate,
are engaging in an act of masturbation. To be sure, such
sexual intercourse is not as likely to become "besotted and
ruinous" as is masturbation, because a woman is "less con-
venient than the ordinary means of masturbation." [54] On
the other hand, there is the "cruelty" of bringing about an
undesired conception in sexual relations which one does not
risk in masturbation. On balance, Noyes suggested, ordinary
sexual relations, carried on without the desire to conceive,
and masturbation are equivalent evils.

Male continence, then, was a way of recognizing the

three functions of the sexual organs and using those three
functions in accord with God's intentions. Male continence
had an additional purpose, however. It shifted the responsibility for birth control from the female to the male. Although the Oneidans sought to give women equal status with
men, they did not consider women equal to men in every
respect. In particular, they viewed women as the weaker
sex. It was, therefore, only right that men should assume
the responsibility for controlling conception:

> Nature and justice alike cry out against the wrong
> done to society and to woman, by imposing upon
> her weakness a task which man with all the ad-
> vantages of superior strength and superior position
> shrinks from assuming. The world is certainly
> upside down on this point.... Society places wom-
> an, the weaker member, in the front of the army
> and requires her to fight the battle, at her own
> cost and for both sexes. [55]

When the responsibility is shifted to the male, the courage
that has been spent in war will be spent on a new kind of
war--the conquest of the male's own "uncivilized passions."
Although the line of reasoning would not be acceptable to
present-day feminists, it is interesting to note that the
Oneidans achieved something that still eludes Americans--
having males assume the responsibility (or, indeed, even
share equally in the responsibility) for birth control.

If we grant Noyes all the benefits of male continence
discussed so far, one question still remains. Is the practice
really pleasurable and healthy for the male? We noted in
chapter 3 that Noyes insisted that the most gratifying part of
sexual intercourse is the union of the couple rather than the
orgasm. Ordinary sexual relations, he said, are a moment-
ary affair that leaves the couple with a feeling of exhaustion
and disgust. In contrast, when people make their sex organs
subservient to their spiritual natures, when the male abstains
from ejaculation, the couple can "enjoy the highest bliss of
sexual fellowship for any length of time, without satiety or
exhaustion; and thus marriage life may become permanently
sweeter than courtship or even the honey-moon." [56] Both
his own enjoyment and that of his wife increased after he
started the practice, he pointed out. Hence, his own experience verified his argument.

As far as the question of health was concerned, Noyes

made two points. First, he noted that many people objected
to the practice on the grounds that it was a difficult and injurious interruption of a natural act. But, he rejoined,
every time we engage in self-denial we are interrupting some
natural act. A lover who stops after a kiss is interrupting
a natural progression. There is nothing harmful about such
interruptions. Only brutes, in fact, tolerate no interruption
to natural acts. But "it is the glory of man to control himself, and the Kingdom of Heaven summons him to self-
control in ALL THINGS." [57] Second, Noyes accepted the
doctrine of spermatic economy that we discussed in chapter
1. "The propagative act, i. e. the emission of the seed," he
wrote, "is a drain on the life of the man, and when habitual,
produces disease." [58] Thus, it is not true that male continence is a threat to male health. Quite the contrary.
Male continence preserves male health by preventing the continual loss of semen.

There is one final aspect to Noyes' ideology that illustrates how he provided for every need, namely his theory
of ascending and descending fellowship. [59] We have already
pointed out that older men introduced young girls to sex, and
older women initiated young men until the latter learned the
practice of male continence. But why should older men initiate young females? And how could the group insure that
older men and women generally would have their share of
sexual experiences? The ideology of ascending and descending fellowship helped resolve the problem. Noyes encouraged
his followers to observe the principle of ascending fellowship
in their sexual choices. Basically, the principle involved a
ranking of people according to the extent to which they had
achieved spiritual perfection. Noyes believed that people
could improve their own spiritual state by associating with
those at a higher spiritual level. He applied the same notion to sexual relations. An individual, that is, should try
to grow spiritually by having sex with someone at a higher
spiritual level. The spiritually superior person would not be
harmed by the relationship, but the inferior individual would
be elevated. Since older members were invariably more
spiritually advanced than younger members, there was ideological pressure upon the younger members to have sexual
relations with the older, more perfect members. Hence, the
needs of all would be fulfilled.

In sum, Noyes clearly shared many of the themes of
the other deviant groups. He believed in the intrinsic goodness of sex. He agreed that people can grow more mature

through sex, particularly when having relations with someone more spiritually advanced. He accepted the premise that exclusiveness is an unacceptable threat to the community, and went beyond that in insisting that it is contrary to God's will. He agreed that sex should be based on love and affection, though he was careful to note that each member must love every other member equally. And he granted his followers at least a limited freedom in choosing their sex life. People at Oneida were under no constraint to engage in frequent sexual relations. And they could choose partners according to desire, as long as they continually changed partners and tried to attend to the principle of at least sometimes choosing those more spiritually advanced. Unlike the others, however, Noyes cast the whole in a theological mold. His first goal was always to create a branch of the kingdom of heaven on earth. His unique sexual system, he argued, was an integral part of achieving God's kingdom.

Notes

1. "The Sexual Relation and Its Abuses," Practical Christian, April 19, 1856, p. 2.

2. Katherine Tingley, The Travail of the Soul (Point Loma, Cal.: Woman's International Theosophical League, 1927), p. 233.

3. Oahspe: A New Bible in the Words of Jehovih and His Angel Embassadors (Boston: Oahspe Publishing Association, 1891), p. 512.

4. True Love Vs. Free Love: Testimony of a True Hearted Woman (Hopedale, Mass.: Hopedale Press, 1855).

5. "Voice to Young Women," Spiritual Reformer 2 (June 1860):1.

6. H. T. Edge, "The 'Sex-Hygiene' Fad," The Theosophical Path 8 (January 1915):44.

7. Kaweah Commonwealth, March 15, 1890.

8. Ibid.,

9. Stephen Gaskin, Hey, Beatnik! (Summertown, Tenn.: The Book Publishing Co., 1974), no page.

10. Ibid.

11. Quoted in Jonathan Beecher and Richard Bienvenu, eds., The Utopian Vision of Charles Fourier (Boston: Beacon Press, 1971), p. 332.

12. Robert Owen, Lectures on the Marriage of the Priesthood of the Old Immoral World, 4th edition (Leeds, England: J. Hobson, 1840), pp. 10-11.

13. Jacob Beilhart, Love Is the Fulfilling of the Law (Lisbon, Ohio: Spirit Fruit Society, 1904), no page.

14. Jacob Beilhart, Very Personal (Ingleside, Ill.: Spirit Fruit Society, 1908, p. 13.

15. Richard Fairfield, Communes, USA (Baltimore: Penguin Books, 1971), p. 298.

16. Beilhart, Very Personal, p. 13.

17. Quoted in Isaac Broome, The Last Days of the Ruskin Co-Operative Association (Chicago: Charles H. Kerr, 1902), p. 123.

18. In Beecher and Bienvenu, eds., The Utopian Vision, pp. 178-81.

19. Owen, Lectures on the Marriage of the Priesthood, p. 11.

20. Ibid., p. 12.

21. Jeffrey S. Victor, Human Sexuality (Englewood Cliffs, N.J.: Prentice-Hall, 1980), pp. 95-96.

22. Kathleen Kinkade, A Walden Two Experiment (New York: William Morrow, 1973), p. 167.

23. See George Schulz-Behrend, "Andreas Dietsch and Helvetia, Missouri," The Swiss Record 2 (March 1950):8-9.

24. Robert Owen, "Reply to Brother Evan's Letter to Me, On the Part of the Shakers' Communities in the United States," Millennial Gazette, May 1, 1856, p. 9.

25. Robert Owen on Marriage, Religion, and Private Property. A broadside, London, April 29, 1839.

26. Ibid.

27. Ibid.

28. In Taylor Stoehr, Free Love in America: A Documentary History (New York: AMS Press, 1979), p. 445.

29. See Beecher and Bienvenu, eds., The Utopian Vision, pp. 333-36.

30. Ibid., p. 334.

31. John David Hawkins, "Utopian Values and Communal Social Life." Unpublished Ph. D. dissertation, Northwestern University, 1975, pp. 339-40.

32. Judson Jerome, Families of Eden: Communes and the New Anarchism (New York: Seabury, 1974), p. 138.

33. Lewis A. Coser, Greedy Institutions: Patterns of Undivided Commitment (New York: Free Press, 1974), p. 139.

34. First Annual Report of the Oneida Association (Oneida: Leonard & Company, 1849), p. 12.

35. "Woman's Slavery to Children," The Spiritual Magazine 1 (September 15, 1846):109-10.

36. Ibid., p. 110.

37. From the Circular, January 29, 1863, in Constance Noyes Robertson, Oneida Community: An Autobiography, 1851-1876 (Syracuse: Syracuse University Press, 1970), p. 319.

38. First Annual Report, p. 14.

39. Ibid., p. 15.

40. John Humphrey Noyes, Strange Cults & Utopias of 19th-Century America (New York: Dover, 1966; 1st publ. 1870), p. 625.

41. Robert Allenton Parker, A Yankee Saint: John Humphrey Noyes and the Oneida Community (New York: G. P. Putnam's Sons, 1935), p. 184.

42. Oneida: Record of Current Events, April 18, 1863.

43. Ibid., June 18, 1863.

44. First Annual Report, p. 19.

45. From the Circular, January 1, 1853, in Robertson, Oneida Community, p. 280.

46. First Annual Report, p. 19.

47. Ibid., p. 21.

48. Ibid., p. 24.

49. John Humphrey Noyes, Male Continence (New York: Arno Press, 1969; 1st publ. 1872), p. 11.

50. First Annual Report, p. 28.

51. Ibid.

52. Ibid., p. 30.

53. Ibid., p. 32.

54. Ibid., p. 33.

55. From the Circular, April 18, 1870, in Robertson, Oneida Community, p. 283.

56. Noyes, Male Continence, p. 14.

57. Ibid., pp. 9-10.

58. First Annual Report, p. 30.

59. Maren Lockwood Carden, Oneida: Utopian Community to Modern Corporation (New York: Harper Torchbooks, 1969), pp. 52-53.

6. KEEPING THE FAITH: MECHANISMS OF CONTROL

The English philosopher, Thomas Hobbes, raised a question in the seventeenth century that has intrigued social thinkers ever since: how is society possible if humans are basically creatures that pursue their own self-interests? How can a mass of such creatures live together in a reasonably harmonious social order? For Hobbes, the answer was a strong, central authority that would enforce rules and regulations.

Obviously, there are other answers to the question of how society is possible, how people can band together in a relatively peaceful, cooperative group. In fact, the utopians had to face the question directly. In their attempt to construct an ideal society, they not only had to build new institutions but also devise ways to insure that people would abide by the new norms and the new ways of thinking and feeling.

Order is the essence of social life, even in utopia. But order did not come naturally or easily to the utopians. For instance, in the counter-culture communes he studied, Hawkins found that daily life often was "chaotic" as the members attempted to establish some kind of routine. [1] The members soon realized that they would have to be explicit about certain rules. As one communard put it, the group cannot survive without rules because "it's too much of a hassle" to try to do everything that is necessary each day without a more-or-less set pattern to follow. For instance, they had to be explicit about how many hours each individual was expected to work and who was to do what task. When they began, the counter-culture communes were ideologically opposed to explicit rules. But they all developed rules in time in order to deal with the chaos of everyday living.

Certainly chaos occurred in sexual relations as well as in other areas. All of the counter-culture communities, therefore, developed rules about sexual behavior, even if the rule was that each one was free to do his or her own thing within the bounds of respect for others' rights and desires. Most of the groups had rules that narrowed the scope of sexual behavior. And since sex is such a powerful part of human life, they had to employ a great many other mechanisms of control in order to insure conformity to the rules.

Rules, then, are only one of the ways of exerting social control. In this chapter, we will look at the full range of mechanisms of control. There are various ways of categorizing such mechanisms. On the basis of the actual kinds used in the utopian communities, we have developed a fourfold categorization: spatio-temporal structuring, interaction patterns and experiences, cognitive input, and coercive measures.

SPATIO-TEMPORAL STRUCTURING

One way the utopians attempted to insure conformity to preferred sexual patterns was to impose a spatio-temporal structure upon all members. That structure had three elements: separation from the larger society, certain spatial arrangements within the community, and the structuring of members' time.

Separation from the World

By definition, a utopian community is separated from the larger society. But the extent of the separation can vary considerably. A community can allow visitors to come and go freely, or can allow its own members to come and go freely, and also freely interact with outsiders. Or various kinds of restrictions can be placed on interaction with outsiders, including restrictions about marriage. At Zoar, for example, during the time when marriage was permitted, the young couple had to secure approval from the trustees. There was a rule against marriage to outsiders, and the trustees were generally successful in preventing such matches.

Location affects the extent of separation. The contemporary urban commune, whose members work in various jobs in the city, has far less separation than the isolated rural commune, whose members seldom interact with outsiders other than visitors to the commune. In some cases,

leaders apparently felt it necessary to isolate members deliberately from contacts with outsiders. The Hutterites, for
example, typically built their communities in relatively isolated areas.

The "world" from which various groups thought it necessary to separate themselves frequently included family
members as well as other outsiders. The Shakers sang
hymns about the beauty of their relationships with each other
and the awfulness of their former relationships with their
kin. As one Shaker preacher put it, the "lust of holding to
worldly kin, or blood kin, within the household, is like Lot's
wife looking back to Sodom, it will petrify the soul." [2]
Undoubtedly, however, the extent to which members remained
isolated from their families varied. One young Shaker at
Pleasant Hill, Kentucky, maintained a warm relationship
with his father through the mails. [3] On one occasion, he
wrote that he always valued his father's favor, that he had
no peace of mind when he felt that his father was displeased
with him for any reason. Such a relationship would appear
to contradict the Shakers' views about ties with one's kin.
However, his father was favorably inclined towards the Shakers, was content to have his son a member of the group,
and even encouraged his son to turn over his property to the
Shakers and become a full, permanent member of the Pleasant Hill community. Understandably, the Shakers would not
object to a young man retaining a close bond with such a
parent.

Separation from the world was easier to achieve in
the nineteenth century when a rural commune, in truth, could
be a voice in the wilderness. Modern communes that want
to maintain separation, however, have greater problems.
The modern technology of transportation and communication
makes isolation difficult. One way to deal with the problem
is to cut members off from the mass media. Thus, among
the Sons of Levi, a Missouri religious community, there are
no telephones, no radios, and no television. [4] And at the
New Age commune in New Mexico, the leader told one young
member who had subscribed to the New York Times that he
never wanted to see copies of the newspaper in the dining
room. At the New Age commune, as Veysey found, members give up the outside world for another reason: they are
taught that isolation is necessary for their well-being. As
one member told Veysey: "I'm here because out there is
death. " Thus:

As one stays within the group and observes small revelations of unconscious attitudes, one sees that the members curtain themselves off from the world even more deeply than they like to admit. The ranch is their only home, and their life on it the only reality. They have to force themselves to go outside, to talk to strangers ... their true hunger is for isolation and apartness. [5]

In addition to cutting members off from the mass media, and teaching them about the hazards of having contact with outsiders, groups have effected separation through rules about interaction with outsiders. We already noted the stricture against marriage to outsiders employed by Zoar (and some others). Groups have also had rules about the comings and goings of members. At the Bruderhof, ordinary members are required to get permission before leaving the grounds. Most ventures outside the community are made by groups rather than individuals. The Shakers also required members to get permission from the elders before going outside the community. If the reasons for leaving were judged insufficient, the elders refused. Those allowed to leave had to give a full accounting of their activities when they returned.

The effect of separation from the world was to make the members emotionally dependent upon the community. And to the extent that members were emotionally dependent, they remained committed to the values of the community. Even the most difficult sexual norms, such as the norm of celibacy, were easier to enforce among those who needed to maintain the respect and approval of the group for their own psychic well-being.

Spatial Arrangements

Fourier underscored the importance of spatial arrangements for a utopian community by laying out an elaborate plan for the building in which the members would live. The building, or phalanstery as he called it, was supposed to be six stories high, having a main body, two wings, and a symmetrical, rectangular shape. Fourier also specified the size and nature of each of the rooms in the phalanstery. [6] The American Fourierists always compromised with the ideal, but they, like the other utopians, were sensitive to the importance of spatial arrangements to the success of the community.

Some of the more elaborate spatial arrangements were undertaken by the celibates. Basically, their communities were arranged to provide for as much segregation of the sexes as feasible. At various communities, the sexes might have separate buildings, or separate wings, separate dining facilities, and separate work areas. A visitor to the Labadists, a group that flourished in the late seventeenth and early eighteenth centuries, wondered after supping with them if they had no women in their midst. Yes, was the reply, but the women and men eat separately. [7] After a number of hours in the community, the man had not yet even seen a woman!

At Ephrata and St. Nazianz, they had separate cloisters for the brothers and sisters. But the most detailed separation occurred among the Shakers. The Shakers not only had separate rooms for men and women but, in many of the communities, segregated stairs leading to upper floors and segregated doors for entering church. Some of the Shaker cemeteries even had segregated burial areas. In addition, the Shakers minimized privacy. Members slept two to six in a room (similarly, at the House of David there were typically two members of the same sex in each room). Work was normally done in groups and segregated by sex. One man who left the Shakers and investigated Oneida, wrote a letter to Elder F. W. Evans, reaffirming his faith in Shakerism and requesting readmission to the community. But he and his wife did not want to be separated. They could be celibate, he insisted, while remaining together. But the Shakers could not relax their rule on sexual segregation. Elder Evans responded to the man that the Shakers had no desire to separate him from his wife, but the man's request was unthinkable: "That you request to be admitted into a society, the fundamental principle of which is celibacy, making a proviso that you room with a woman, evidences your destitution of the simplest element of Shaker faith." [8] To become a Christian, Evans continued, a man must be willing to forsake father, mother, wife, and children.

Thus, spatial arrangements helped enforce sexual norms. At Oneida, where each member was to have sexual access to every other member of the opposite sex, members had private quarters. Where sex was confined to marriage, the groups tended to have separate houses or specific rooms for married couples. And where sex was considered undesirable or unacceptable, various kinds of spatial arrangements were made to keep males and females (including children) as separate as practical.

Temporal Structuring

Some psychologists argue that one of the basic needs
of humans is a restructuring of their time. If so, the need
was more than fulfilled in the utopian communities. Most of
the communities have had a fairly rigorous schedule of activities for each day. For the celibates and those who depreciated sex, a full daily schedule meant minimal time for
erotic behavior and, hopefully, erotic thoughts. Thoughts,
of course, cannot be controlled, but given a sufficient amount
of activity throughout the day an individual might have little
energy for the erotic. A Shaker hymn made the point explicitly:

> For while I am faithful to do what is right,
> And have not a moment to spare;
> I'm guarded about by the angels of light,
> And Satan can never come there.
>
> O what a great privilege I do enjoy!
> Good Elders to teach what is just,
> And always a plenty of righteous employ,
> Sufficient to mortify lust. [9]

It seems that most of the celibates agreed with the
need for a full complement of activities during the day. At
Ephrata, the entire day was structured and included no more
than three hours for sleep at a time. For example, the
daily schedule of the Sisters, beginning at six in the evening,
was as follows:

> 6 P.M. to 7, chief meal of the day.
> 7 to 9, instruction (Schulübung).
> 9 to 12 N., sleep.
> 12 N. to 2 A.M., religious services.
> 2 A.M. to 5, sleep.
> 5 to 6, awaking, ablution and prayer.
> 6 to 9, labor.
> 9 to 10, refreshment and prayer.
> 10 A.M. to 5 P.M., labor.
> 5 to 6, spiritual contemplation. [10]

The two-hour religious services at midnight were initially
four hours long, "so that from this severe spiritual exercise
one had to go at once to one's physical work, which was a
sore crucifixion of the flesh." [11] Such a daily regimen allowed little time or energy for any kind of sexual thoughts or
behavior.

As illustrated by the schedule at Ephrata, work and religious activity comprised the bulk of the daily activities of the celibates. At St. Nazianz, members arose at 4:45 a. m. and retired at 9:30 p. m. The only free time in the daily schedule was a half hour at noon. A visitor to the Rappites noted that the people went to religious services three times every day and that they were "never seen in idle groups; all is moving industry; no kind of idling; no time for it." [12]

Temporal structuring not only consumed people's time and energy, but was also used to strengthen commitment to the group and, therefore, to its sexual norms. For the time spent in religious activity both symbolized and reinforced the member's acceptance of the group's ideology. Consequently, groups that preferred celibacy and those that insisted on confining sex to marriage also had highly structured daily schedules that included a good deal of religious activity. At Point Loma, the day began at 5 a. m. with various household and gardening tasks performed in silence. At 6:30 a. m. , the first devotional service was held. At 8:00, as they commenced their daily work, they listened to a spiritual reading. Before sitting down to the evening meal, they recited together an affirmation of theosophical thought. Before retiring, they had two minutes silent meditation and a closing spiritual thought that they recited in unison. [13]

Finally, the commitment function of temporal structuring also was used by the sexual deviants. At Oneida, the day began with breakfast at six a. m. At 6:45 a. m. , the members listened to a reading from the Bible. After supper, they conducted business and various kinds of classes, followed by a general reading or a lecture at 7 p. m. One woman logged one of her days as follows:

> Arose when the bell rang. Dressed and put my bed to air--took breakfast, then studied Bible lessons; knitted while the Bible exercises were attended to. Went to my chamber to put the room in order, then attended to ironing until about 11 o'clock. Wrote about half an hour, then studied next Bible lesson until dinner. Gave a lesson on the piano from 1 o'clock until 2, another from 2 o'clock until 3; then practiced myself from 3 o'clock until 4. Then read in "Plurality of Worlds," took the evening repast, worked a short time; read a Home Talk on keeping accounts. Listened to a lecture on

grammar ... attended evening meeting; worked a little at knitting, then retired, grateful for being permitted to enjoy the benefits of this school. Awoke early on Thursday, exclaiming with joyful spirit, "Blessed art thou among women!" [14]

Obviously, the woman's day was well structured with activities, including a certain amount of ideological indoctrination. Just as obviously, the day's schedule reinforced her commitment to the community.

INTERACTION PATTERNS AND EXPERIENCES

While separable for purposes of analysis, the varied mechanisms of control overlap in reality. For instance, we have already seen how interaction patterns were structured to some extent by spatial arrangements. Among the celibates, spatial arrangements typically minimized interaction between the sexes. In other groups, spatial arrangements facilitated that interaction. Other kinds of interaction patterns and experiences, however, were not affected by the spatial arrangements but by the rules or customs of the communities. We shall examine six types of patterns and experiences that helped control sexual activity: expectations about demeanor and decorum; unifying rituals; the practice of confession; small-group experiences of criticism and examination; the pressure of collective opinion; and tension-reduction experiences. Every group used one or more of these mechanisms.

Expectations About Demeanor and Decorum

Factors such as dress, demeanor, and appropriate behavior are important determinants of the interaction that occurs between people. The utopians were aware of this fact and made their expectations consistent with their sexual norms.

Among the celibates, people were expected to look and act like asexual creatures. The dress of the celibates certainly contributed to the goal. At Ephrata, they dressed like Capuchin monks. Apart from the beards on the men, the sexes were almost indistinguishable. The dress of the Shakers, Rappites, and other celibate groups was plain, minimizing the outline of, and virtually covering, the body. Thus, the celibates generally approved of a sober demeanor to accompany their plain garb. Some groups had strict rules against gossip or levity. For example, one of the rules of discipline of the Ephrata sisters stated:

> What then further concerns our intercourse with and toward one another is this: It is to be striven in all seriousness and diligence, that our life be modest, quiet, tranquil and retired, so that each becomes an example for the other, and exemplifies the secret course of life and communion with God. All levity and needless gossip with one another, or light laughter, is not to be thought of, nor shall it occur in this spiritual society. [15]

The extent to which the celibates tried to make their lives asexual is illustrated by the fact that the Shakers and Zoarites even despised kissing between parents and their children. When one Shaker was asked whether he had ever, in the eighty years of his life, kissed, or been kissed by, a woman, he replied: "Never; neither the one nor the other; and if my sainted and consecrated mother ever kissed me I am wholly ignorant of the fact." [16]

The traditionalists also had rules of decorum governing interaction between the sexes, though they were not quite as restrictive as the celibates. At Point Loma, there was a rule of silence in children's classrooms, at mealtimes, and whenever two members passed each other on the grounds. Promiscuous visiting between members was also considered inappropriate. The need for conversing with others could be fulfilled in evening socials where "conversation might be directed along desired channels." [17] Such regulations helped maintain the group's view of the sanctity of marriage. For two people could hardly have any kind of romantic encounter without breaking a norm of the group. A different rule, but with the same consequence, was effected at The Farm. Farm members are expected to maintain total openness in their relationships. It is a norm of the community for each member to tell others "where it's at," to tell the truth without fear. There is no privacy on The Farm. As Gaskin wrote, Farm members don't believe in the kind of privacy that enables anyone to "cover up" anything. "We say that we're like a mental nudist colony, and you have to take off your head clothes." [18] The rule of openness facilitates the maintenance of monogamous relationships.

The deviants' expectations about demeanor and decorum were, as one would expect, the least restrictive in the sense of traditional restrictions. But the deviants had their own rules, and they expected their members to conform to them. Basically, the expectations of the deviants were that all rules of demeanor and decorum should facilitate meaningful interaction between the sexes. In the manner of dress, for example, the deviants preferred female outfits that expressed the sexual equality they advocated. The fashions for nineteenth-century American women virtually guaranteed their subservience to men, and threatened their health and well-being in the process. [19] At many of the communities, including Oneida, New Harmony, the North American Phalanx, Modern Times, and the Ruskin Commonwealth, some or most of the women wore a Bloomer-type costume that gave them the freedom to function like men. Some of the women loved the new costume and some of them disliked it. Those who disliked it did not always have the opportunity to discard it. Some of the deviant groups were as firm in their rules as the traditionalists and celibates. For styles of dress and demeanor express a group's ideology. At the Sunrise Hill commune, which advocated free sex, the members adopted group nudity for a time. The practice proved valuable, wrote a former member, in helping members become familiar and warm towards each other. In addition, it was "a symbolic act of communion with and trust in each other and helped to cement us together." [20]

Unifying Rituals

As noted above, anything that promotes solidarity in the group also promotes conformity to norms. There were various rituals in the communities that tended to enhance group solidarity. We use "ritual" here in the broadest sense. For in some communities, the ritual was a business meeting in which all members were expected to participate and vote. Collective decision-making was one important way of unifying the group. At Oneida, even the names of new babies were decided collectively.

In addition to group decision-making, there were certain periodic rituals that enhanced solidarity. The religious groups, of course, had their regular worship services. Most of the groups had communal meals. The Shakers had an annual "feast," held in an isolated area such as a mountain top. The members would each receive an imaginary

many-colored outfit, and take imaginary food and drink to
their feast location. They would bathe in an imaginary fountain and sing as a part of their feast. And Father Divine,
whose followers were primarily the poor and dispossessed,
had real feasts. During the Great Depression, he served
sumptuous meals for fifteen cents. The feast was more than
a mere meal, however:

> His banquets were punctuated by the confession of
> sins, by rolling and throbbing, jerking and moan-
> ing, cries of "Father, I love you," "Ain't it won-
> derful?," "He is my lover," and songs like "Fath-
> er's on the Mainline, Now Tell Him Just What You
> Want." These feasts were reminiscent of Shaker
> rituals with a little jive thrown in. [21]

Holidays were also a way of cementing group solidarity. In any group, the calendar of events expresses ideology
and builds commitment to the group. National holidays re-
mind the people of a nation of their collective history and
renew a sense of allegiance and patriotism. The same consequences flow from the observance of holidays in a smaller
group. Among the Rappites, for instance, holidays were
viewed as a way to reaffirm their collective covenant with
God. In addition to Christmas, Pentecost, and Easter, the
Rappites enjoyed a number of other holidays. The "Har-
moniefest" was a religious holiday on February 15 to cele-
brate the founding of the group. The Harvest Festival was
celebrated each fall, and was a holiday of relative gaiety.
The Lord's Supper was observed annually, and included an
entire meal rather than just bread and wine. Finally, they
celebrated July 4, though not just as an American holiday.
The Rappites arrived in Baltimore on July 4, 1804, and considered America their promised land. They celebrated the
day by inviting neighbors in for food and drink, listening to
a speech by a politician, and then sitting down to their own
love feast while their guests were drinking beer and having
fun. [22]

The Practice of Confession

A number of the religious groups had mandatory or
voluntary confession. The practice of confession had a number of functions. It reminded members of their need to be
sexually pure. It legitimated the authority of the community
to govern sexual norms. And it motivated members to follow

the norms. For the very existence of the confessional meant that members faced a dilemma if they broke a sexual norm. Either they had to confess their sin, openly acknowledging that they had violated the utopian ideal, or they had to hide their sin and face the judgment of God. The latter option meant the possibility of eternal condemnation.

The practice of confession varied from group to group. Some, such as the Rappites and St. Nazianz, had regular times for confession. In others, confession was a matter of individual choice. Sometimes, the confessional was used in an extremely coercive way. At Bethel, confession was mandatory. Dr. Keil, the leader, had unmarried individuals visit him alone and married people come as couples. He then questioned them, rather than letting them simply volunteer any confession of sins. Furthermore, he questioned them closely about their sex lives, and then used the information in his sermons in order to discipline them. [23] The confessional was also coercive at the House of David, according to one former member. [24] A new member had to write out and sign a complete confession of everything wrong that he or she had done prior to coming to the community. The written confession was filed for future reference. In addition, members wrote out monthly confessions of sins and turned them in to the leaders. According to the member, when some of the young men in the celibate group confessed to masturbation, the confessions were read aloud to other members, including young girls, who were then ordered to shun the sinner.

Whether the actual practice of confession was voluntary or mandatory, all agreed that it was valuable. Moreover, all agreed that confession should be made to another person, not simply to God alone. As a Shaker editor wrote, "Mother Ann Lee taught that the first step in obedience to spiritual light, was an honest confession of our sins to God, before a witness." [25] Of course, if the confession is not "before a witness" it loses much of its value as a mechanism of social control.

Small-Group Experiences of Criticism and Examination

A good deal of sociopsychological research has shown that small group experiences can be remarkably effective in shaping behavior. Particularly when the individual is isolated from outside influences, intense interaction in a small group

can radically alter an individual's personality. A number of
the utopians used the small-group experience to shape members' behavior. They used two basic methods: total openness and honesty about feelings and thoughts, and thorough
criticism of the character and behavior of particular members.

The scheduling and practice of small-group experiences varied from community to community. At Ephrata,
they had a quasi-group practice called the "Lectiones."
Members were required weekly to examine themselves while
alone, then hand a written statement of spiritual condition to
the Superintendent. These statements were called the Lectiones. They were read at the Saturday worship service and
hundreds were published. [26] Thus, the entire group heard
the statements, though they did not respond directly to them
as a group.

A truer small-group experience was held at Amana in
their yearly examination (called the Unterredung) of members.
Every man, woman, and child had to participate. The Elders
in each of the seven villages of Amana were examined by Elders from the other villages. Members of each village were
examined in the presence of their own Elders. Each member
was to make a public confession of his or her spiritual condition, and each was questioned in detail by a village leader.
The leader would then exhort the member to a holier mode
of life. For instance, one leader told a woman: "Oh, weep
over your ill-spent squandered time! Esteem the grace of
your God more highly and go out of yourself.... Strive for
your salvation. Oh, make better use of your time; go forward with careful step and seek with tears for thy lost
grace." [27]

At Oneida, the group practiced "mutual criticism."
Individuals applied to the committee on criticism when they
wished to advance spiritually. They could use the committee, or other members, or the entire community as critics.
At the session, each critic in turn specified those matters
about the individual that were objectionable. "In this way
the person criticised had the advantage of a many-sided mir-
ror in viewing himself, or perhaps it may be said was placed
in the focus of a spiritual lens composed of all the judgments
of the Association." [28] The subject could not respond to
any of the statements at the session unless there was some
obvious error of fact. The critics were expected to be loving and respectful, but quite frank.

Mutual criticism sessions at Oneida were designed to correct the faults of members, including any flaws in the art of love-making. For example, Noyes once criticized a man for being too intellectual and too fond of food. It is a proverb, Noyes said, "that a book-worm is awkward in love-- slow to be smitten, and likely to behave foolish when he is." And as for the man's love of food: "Epicures and drunkards extinguish at last the sexual attraction.... As in religion, sensuality of appetite is a hindrance to spirituality, so it is equally an enemy to love, and the development of the highest power of fellowship between the sexes." [29]

Various other groups also used mutual criticism sessions to deal with interpersonal, including sexual, relationships. The practices differed somewhat from the Oneida pattern. At the Friendship Community, near Buffalo, Missouri, the Articles of Agreement specified regular sessions:

> A social meeting of the community shall be held weekly for free criticism and the mutual instruction and improvement of the members, in which every member shall be free to make any remarks which shall be for the general interest and welfare of the members. The disposition, habits and conduct of any member ... may be commended or reproved, and any suggestions may be given for correcting any faults that may have been observed or for devising any better plans in reference to the affairs of the community. [30]

Not all of the communities carried on their small-group experiences in a way that enhanced either the well-being of members or group solidarity. At the New Age commune, one "confrontation" session began when the leader asked a young woman to publicly answer the question, "Who do you hate?" [31] She proceeded to give her list and her reasons. The end result of her confession, unfortunately, was greater divisiveness rather than increased unity. At the Progressive Community in Kansas, there were to be no secrets; each member confessed in weekly meetings to all of his or her thoughts about the others. The result was "mutual irritation." [32] Some of the utopians used the small-group experience successfully, in terms of enhancing their control of members' behavior. Others, however, simply added to their problems.

The Pressure of Collective Opinion

In every community, the pressure of collective opinion was an important factor in controlling behavior. A straying member knew the opinion of others by explicit statement or demeanor. For those who wished to remain a part of the community, collective opinion was an exceptionally powerful means of control.

For instance, in one modern commune a young woman pointed out that even those who preferred to have sex with a particular partner had to participate when everyone got high and started a group-sex party. The researcher asked her what she meant when she said that "you just knew you had to" participate. The young woman responded that anyone who refused would cause the others to get uptight. "They'd sort of close you out for a couple of days. It would be like they were saying you weren't doing your share." [33] The researcher pointed out that the commune was based on the principle of allowing every individual to do his or her own thing. Didn't such coerced participation contradict the principle of freedom? The young woman acknowledged the contradiction, but said that a commune also requires cooperation in order to pursue the common good.

Whether the pressure is towards sexual activity or celibacy, collective opinion is one of the more forceful mechanisms of control for commitment to the group. A member might resist the demands of a strong leader and possibly remain in a community. But no one can long withstand the force of collective opinion.

Tension-Release Mechanisms

Contradictions between individual desires and social constraints are inevitable in any group, including the utopian community. One way to retain control in the face of those contradictions is to provide people with some kind of tension-release mechanism. Such tension-release mechanisms would be particularly important among the celibates and groups with many restrictions.

The most common type of tension-release mechanism was some kind of religious ritual. The Shakers, for example, were noted for their orgiastic worship services. One visitor to a Shaker service described the ritualistic dance of the 130 worshippers. The Shakers lined up with rows of men at one end of the hall and rows of women at the other. Then:

> Two singers, from each sex, now took their stands at the head of their columns. A signal being given, the singers commenced, and the columns got into motion. They gently advanced and receded for some minutes, when on a sudden, they reversed fronts, quickened their motions, and dance in similar manner: suddenly, they wheeled to their former positions, increasing in the violence of their actions, as they were warmed by the spirit, and animated by the singing. By one impulse they now broke the order in which they stood, and each column whirled within its own limits, in vertical commotion, throwing their heads, hands, and legs in wild disorder, occasionally leaping up and uttering a horrid yell. During this time each individual had chimed in with the singers, who had themselves fallen in their columns, and were all singing with stunning violence ... the motions which were before violent, became furious, and the noise, before stunning, was appalling. Shrieks and yells followed in alternate succession, till by their violence, and the incessant fury of their dancing, the worshippers were exhausted. Some sunk on the floor, while others were scarcely able to get to their seats. The worship closed, and I left the house with feelings of horror which you can better imagine than I can describe. [34]

Certainly, a good deal of sexual energy was dissipated by such services.

At Amana, they had the Bezeugungen, testimonies given under inspiration and accompanied by a violent shaking of the body. Interestingly, only the charismatic leaders, who were more likely than anyone else in Amana to be celibate, experienced the Bezeugungen. Among Father Divine's followers, there was the phenomenon of "vibrating," a jerking of the body accompanied by shouts of praise and love for Father. In some modern communes, chanting is a milder form of tension release available to members.

Tension release was also provided in many groups by the exigencies of carving out a new community on the frontier.

The tasks were arduous, the work day was long, and the food was spartan. There was frequently little energy left over for illicit sexual liaisons. The social control of sexual behavior is not so problematic when the energies of the people are consumed with the work of survival.

COGNITIVE INPUT

A third mechanism of control was cognitive input. Various ideas and information were given to members that legitimated the particular ways of each group. We have already covered the content of the cognitive input in our discussion of group ideologies. Here we want to look at the various ways in which the ideologies were communicated to people. One aspect of the communication was touched upon above--the control of information coming into the community through censorship of reading materials. A number of the communities employed this mechanism. On the positive side of the communication, the communities used three major channels to communicate the ideologies: music, educational programs, and explicit norms.

Music

Music has been an important part of most social movements. Music gives people a symbolic expression of their unity. It encourages them in difficult times. It is a way of reaffirming determination and commitment to a cause. And it also expresses the ideology to which people are committed. In the utopian communities, music was used for all these purposes.

The religious communities were especially prone to use music. For many of them, standard Christian hymns reinforced their morality. For others, particular hymns were written to express their particular sexual ideas. For example, at Ephrata many of the hymns (which were all in German) exalted virginity. The Shakers also sang of the glories of the celibate life. They wrote such hymns as "The Virgin Spouse," and "Resolution Against a Carnal Nature." [35] One early Shaker hymn, entitled "The Believers Will," illustrates the explicit way in which they sang about the virtues of celibacy and the wickedness of sex:

I'll leave the world behind, I will

Their filthy carnal lives
Their husbands and their wives
I'll leave them all behind I will
Now we may all inherit
Relation in the spirit
If we'll be strong to travel on
And leave the world behind us.

I'll hate my carnal ways I will
I'll quit my ugly ways
In love I'll spend my days
I'll quit my carnal ways I will
In carnal words and actions
There is no satisfaction
And these will shun and forward run
And be a Godly people. [36]

On the other hand, the Oneida community song stressed the loving relationships between members, calling the community the "Eden of heart-love," a place where there was "one home" and "one family relation" and "true love shall dwell in peace and joy forever." [37] The groups that used music did not waste the opportunity to include something of their ideology.

Educational Programs

Educational programs were of various kinds in the communities. Most groups set up an educational system for children, recognizing the importance of early training in order to produce good members of the community for the future. Most also had specific programs of education or indoctrination for new adult members.

Educational systems for children generally provided the basics of reading, writing, and so forth. But most groups also eliminated certain topics from children's education and added a certain amount (sometimes a considerable amount) of ideological training. In the religious communities, the children's education tended to be extremely detailed. For instance, some of the rules of living in the children's catechism at Amana were:

1. Dear Child: As soon as you are awakened in the morning, get up. In fact, regulate yourself to awaken without being called and do not dawdle in

getting up and out of your bed.
2. Let your first thoughts be of God ...
3. Next, greet your parents and brothers and sisters and others in the house with "good morning" not only out of habit but in true feeling ...
9. When you say grace at the table, don't let your hands hang to the floor. Don't lean on the table. Don't gawk around but be reverent before the holy majesty of God ...
14. Cut your food into small pieces. Grasp the knife and spoon daintily and be careful not to soil your clothes or the tablecloth. Don't slurp your soup, etc., or make any other noise with your mouth. [38]

Note that rule 14 still focusses on breakfast table behavior. In fact, the first 30 rules applied to the time between waking and finishing breakfast!

The Shakers also had detailed instructions that they used to train children. As with the Amanaites, their instructions covered virtually the whole of life, and frequently made implicit or explicit references to the need for celibacy and behavior that would facilitate celibacy. For example, one "juvenile guide" had the following rules listed under the category of "modesty":

5. All lustful, lascivious or wanton feelings, thoughts, words or actions, towards the opposite sex, are absolutely immodest. When in company, to be scratching the body is immodest.
6. All obscene or wanton stories are immodest. Wanton songs are extremely so. [39]

Whether dealing with sexual matters or with other kinds of behavior, the religious groups gave their children what they considered a Christian, moral education. Children only needed to learn certain matters--those things that would help them to be good Christians and good members of the community. Thus, the Shakers, while generally providing the children with good schools and a good education, saw no need for such subjects as philosophy.

Other religious groups followed the same principles as Amana and the Shakers in educating their children. That is, children's education was limited to what the group considered the essentials, and always had a moral emphasis.

As the catalog of the Hopedale school put it, "particular and watchful consideration" was given to the moral and religious influence of the school on the children, who would be trained to "habits of neatness, order, propriety, and purity; to a reverence for truth, justice, and mercy; to a love of God as the universal Father and of man as the common Brother; to a watchful observance of the divine principles and practical duties of Christianity." [40] Nor did they wait until the children began formal education. In communal nurseries or in the homes of parents, children learned from infancy the ways of the community. By the time a Hutterite child entered school, Hostetler and Huntington found, he or she had learned four things: the group has priority over the individual; the individual has little control over the environment; patterns of living do not change; and the individual must respond positively to every other Hutterite. [41]

Nonreligious groups also had educational programs for children. The one at New Harmony was outstanding. The educational system became a model for other systems. The children entered a Pestalozzian school at the age of five. As with the religious groups, the emphasis at New Harmony was on those subjects that would make the children good members of the community. But the notions of the Owenites on the matter of what was needed to produce good community members differed from the ideas of the religious groups. All boys learned a trade. They also learned math, natural history, geography, and various other matters associated with an English education.

Apart from the subject matter, the mechanics of the educational systems tended to bring about commitment and conformity to the community. At New Harmony, for example, children entered the infant school at the age of two, when they became the property of the total community. The educational system, like the other institutions, underscored the communal nature of the individual's existence.

Adults also had educational programs, some of which were mandatory indoctrination programs. A number of the groups, like Oneida and Brook Farm, had regular classes or sessions for adults at which various topics were discussed. Some of the religious groups, like the Rappites, used their worship services for lengthy indoctrination sessions. At other communities, like Llano, the charismatic leader would periodically or regularly gather the members together for a discourse. Most of the communities recognized that adults, like children, needed instruction in the ways of utopia.

Explicit Norms

There were two ways in which a new member could determine the norms of the community: implicitly, through watching the behavior of others, and explicitly, through verbal or written instructions. None of the communities depended purely on implicit learning. Nearly all had written statements for new members to read and accept.

The Constitution of Hopedale, to which each new member had to "deliberately and cordially assent," illustrates the kind of explicit statement of norms used by the communities. The new member agreed to be bound by the "holy requirements" of the New Testament, which meant:

> never, under any pretext whatsoever, to kill, assault, beat, torture, enslave, rob, oppress, persecute, defraud, corrupt, slander, revile, injure, envy, or hate any human being, even my worst enemy; never in any manner to violate the dictates of pure chastity; never to take or administer an oath; never to manufacture, buy, sell, deal out, or use any intoxicating liquor as a beverage; never to serve in the army, navy, or militia of any nation, state, or chieftain; never to bring an action of law, hold office, vote, join a legal posse, petition a legislature, or ask any governmental interposition...; never to indulge self-will, bigotry, love of preeminence, covetousness, deceit, profanity, idleness, or an unruly tongue; never to participate in lotteries, games of chance, betting, or pernicious amusements; never to resent reproof nor justify myself in a known wrong; never to aid, alert, or approve others in anything sinful;--but through divine assistance, always to recommend and promote, with my entire influence, the holiness and happiness of all mankind. [42]

Note that both sexual and general moral matters are covered in the document. "Chastity," of course, meant sex only in marriage at Hopedale. All of the communities had norms about sexual behavior, and those norms were either written or made quite explicit to members. The norms included more than just the question of who can have sex with whom. They also included the frequency of sex (at the Maharaj Ashram, the unmarried could have sex once a month and married couples could indulge twice a month [43]); endogamous regulations (in many of the communities they were only permitted to marry within the membership); male-female interaction rules (dating was prohibited in the Christ Communal Organization; males and females were not allowed to pass each other on stairways among the Shakers); and miscellaneous rules designed to maintain the sexual morality of the group (at Point Loma, the children's hands were bound at night to prevent masturbation [44]).

The nonsexual norms helped reinforce sexual norms by securing the individual's commitment to the community. As illustrated by the Hopedale Constitution, nonsexual norms could cover an enormous range of behavior and generally included a number of prohibitions as well as prescriptions. Many of the communities had prohibitions on alcohol, drugs (including tobacco), certain kinds of foods, unseemly language, gossip, and various kinds of amusements. At Amana, for example, there was no instrumental music and no recreation except group singing. At the Progressive Community, coffee, tea, sugar, and salt were not allowed. The "conditions of admission" to the Icarian community at Nauvoo had, as the 32nd provision, the observance of decency in language: "Obscenity is entirely useless and more worthy a brute than a man." [45]

Kanter has discussed such regulations, along with various practices in the communities, as mechanisms for gaining commitment to the communities. [46] She argues that the difference between the successful and unsuccessful groups (she defines success as at least 25 years of existence) was the extent to which they could build commitment. Six processes were involved in commitment-building, including the process of transcendence in which members gain a sense of being a part of something that is greater than their individual existence.

This process of transcendence included the development of "institutionalized awe," a sense of the charismatic nature of the entire community. Charismatic leaders and ideologies helped develop the sense. It then became normative to follow the dictates of the leader or leaders without question. For example, all formal control at Amana was in the hands of the Elders. Those who rebelled against the authority of the Elders were rebuked openly in a general meeting and could be expelled from the community. In many communities, the charismatic leader (often, the founder) had virtually total control over members' lives, including their sex lives. John Humphrey Noyes well illustrates the power of charisma. He set the norms for the Oneida community, and when the cognitive input was the words of Noyes the result was likely to be unquestioning obedience. Noyes established the system of complex marriage. One of the norms he set forth to maintain the system was the banning of dolls for girls. The problem with dolls, according to a report in the Circular, was that they encouraged "philoprogenitiveness," the love of one's progeny, and that the "doll-spirit" seduced girls away from a community spirit and from focusing on their own self-development. [47] All of the dolls in the community at the time that Noyes made his pronouncement, therefore, were discarded.

Of course, not every leader had the charisma of Noyes and not every community could create the institutional awe of Amana. Many of the communities, therefore, were not able to gain consensus on the norms, and were unable to build the necessary commitment. The more successful they were, however, the deeper the commitment of the members and the more the members conformed to the sexual morality of the group.

COERCIVE MEASURES

A variety of coercive measures were the final mechanism of control. One such coercive measure was threat, a measure particularly useful in the religious communities. For members of the religious groups who deviated from the norms were defined not only as betraying the community but also as violating the will of God. Thus, they faced the possibility of eternal damnation. In Father Divine's community, they also faced the possibility of earthly retribution. Stories circulated in the group about those who had become ill or disabled or who had suddenly died after criticizing Father Divine. In addition to threats, there were two basic types of coercive measures in the communities: surveillance and punishment.

Surveillance

It is ironic that utopia should require ongoing surveillance. But a number of the communities--mainly the religious groups--used surveillance to keep members in line. One method of surveillance was the reading and censoring of all incoming and outgoing mail by leaders. This was done at the Bruderhof and among the Shakers. The practice not only enabled the groups to keep undesirable information away from their members, but also allowed them to check on the spiritual progress of their members.

A second method of surveillance was some kind of check list that gave the location of each member during the day. There was a board at Oneida to tell where each member was located. The Shakers were convinced that it was necessary for someone to know where everyone in the community was at all times. The job fell to the Elders, and every member was obligated to keep his or her Elder informed of his whereabouts throughout the day. At Oneida, such a system made it difficult for a couple to have an exclusive relationship. Among the Shakers, the practice made it difficult for a couple even to meet.

A third method of surveillance was the use of members to spy on each other and inform the leaders about any transgressions. The Shakers felt obligated to inform the Elders about any sins that they witnessed. Indeed, if a Shaker did not inform the Elders, he or she was as guilty of the sin as the one who committed it. Acting as an informant was a godly act, not a sneaky one. At Zoar, according to a former member, Baumeler encouraged husbands and wives to watch each other. If, for example, a woman reported to Baumeler that her husband had uttered disrespectful words against the leader, Baumeler would praise the woman and punish the man. [48]

Some of the nonreligious communities also used members to spy and inform on each other. Cabet encouraged such behavior among the Icarians at Nauvoo. And at the Fourierist colony of La Réunion, one member complained, the people did not even have the freedom to read. When a member was reported by another member as having read to one of his friends a libel written against the leaders, the member was called to task. The man explained that it was a book about work and idleness, not libel. But the leader responded that "Phalansterians should not read a work of this sort. " [49] It is one of the dilemmas of the utopian quest that the groups frequently felt constrained to shackle their members with restrictions in the name of freedom and progress.

Punishment

Punishment, the most coercive measure of all, was meted out in virtually all of the communities. There were five ways that straying members were punished: revoking privileges; loss of status; public rebuke and ridicule; isolation and separation; and expulsion.

The revocation of privileges might appear, on the surface, to be the mildest form of punishment used. But it could be viewed as extremely coercive and threatening by those punished. At Zoar and Amana, for instance, those who strayed might not be allowed to attend church. In a religious community, this is a severe form of punishment. Four boys who played baseball on Sunday at Amana were forbidden to attend church for two Sundays. A newspaperman who interviewed the boys' leader pointed out that this was not punishment where he lived. The Amanaite man responded with a smile:

> It is different here. Church to us is everything.
> It was so with our fathers. It is so with our sons
> and daughters, and it is so with our grandsons and
> granddaughters. To bar the children from church
> --that is the worst punishment. [50]

Whether the sin is sexual or nonsexual, revocation of privileges in a small, integrated community is a harsh form of punishment.

Similarly, the loss of status is extremely punitive in a communal society. Members were demoted in status by formal or informal means. One way to achieve a formal demotion was by dividing the membership into ranks in some visible way. For example, at Amana there were three ranks, based on the amount of spiritual progress the individual had made. The ranks were clearly visible because members sat in church according to rank. One who transgressed could be demoted by being required to sit in a lower rank. As one Amanaite recalled: "To be demoted in church was a severe form of disgrace.... We all tried to conduct ourselves so that we would not be demoted." [51] One of the more common causes of demotion was marriage. A newly married couple sat behind the children (who generally comprised the bulk of those in the third rank) in church to show in a conspicuous way that they had given in to the temptations of the flesh. A couple was also demoted upon the birth of each child. As a result, some couples spent most of their early years of marriage in the third rank. The congregation thereby was continually reminded of the spiritually inferior nature of the sexual relationship. Other groups, such as Koreshan Unity and some modern communes, also have had formalized ranks for their members. Those who fell short of the norms suffered the embarrassment of public demotion.

Loss of status can also occur in an informal way, as the members show their disdain or disappointment with the straying member. Among the Rappites, for example, there was no formal sanction imposed upon those who failed to live up to the ideal of celibacy. But, as Karl Arndt pointed out:

> ... those who succumbed to nature's temptation soon began to feel uncomfortable and were subjected to a feeling of inferiority, which usually resulted in their "voluntary" withdrawal from the society. Celibacy had become the social custom of the members in good standing, and the persons who did not live the celibate life felt like the wedding guest who appeared without a wedding garment, even though the invitation did not specify that a "wedding garment" should be worn. [52]

A third form of punishment was public rebuke and ridicule. Public ridicule occurred in the group criticism or examination sessions of some communities. Frequently, it took the form of the leader or leaders publicly identifying individuals and their deviation from the community's standards. In some religious communities, the straying individual was identified and condemned in a worship service. Preachers among the Hutterites sometimes told the congregation about the sins of particular individuals. At Zoar, in the early days, all those who broke the norms, whether young or old and whether the norm was a major or minor one, had to sit in the front row of the church. Then "the sermon was given according to the sins represented by the persons in this pew. Following the sermon, all the offenses were mentioned and the names of the offenders given." [53] Rebuke and ridicule also was given in a less collective, though still public, setting. Among the Shakers, for example, a member might openly rebuke another member by pointing a finger at the offending member and crying "Woe! woe!"

Public rebuke and ridicule necessarily mean a loss of status as well for the offending member. Sometimes, the loss of status was made explicit, particularly for grave offenses. A Shaker man who left his community to pursue a former sister with whom he had strong feelings, returned within twenty-four hours. With tears in his eyes, he begged to be taken back into the community. An eyewitness described the scene that occurred in the public assembly that was called to deal with the case:

> The poor brother, looking haggard and wild, was called forth to be publicly humiliated. Elder Freedom, with pointing finger, thundered out denunciations, and heaped up texts like these: "Depart from me into everlasting torment;" "There the worm dieth not and the fire is not quenched." "Hear the awful sentence," he said, "against unfaithful souls," and he depicted a frightful hell upon earth, and an infinitely worse hell hereafter.
>
> Then the crying brother confessed before the congregation, and after thanking the assembled ministry for their unbounded charity in giving him another opportunity of becoming a Believer, hands were raised to signify whether he might return. Dear old Sister Mercy put up both hands and arms high over her head, and Brother Eben was the only dissentient.

The brother was disgraced from the first to the foot of the fourth rank, behind and below the smallest child. [54]

One other way in which the Shakers made the loss of status explicit along with a public condemnation occurred at South Union, Kentucky, where the record keepers frequently put their own titles at the head of the list of those who had left the community. Among the titles were: "Backwards they go"; "Wormed out"; "Off the hinges"; "Off to Babylon"; and "Fleshed Off." [55] Thus, the record keepers' evaluation of the apostates was left for all future generations to see.

Isolation and separation was the fourth coercive form of punishment. Separation was used to break up couples in those communities where the dyadic bond was viewed as wrong. When a young man and young woman among the Shakers seemed to be developing romantic inclinations toward each other, one of them was often carted off to a different community. Similarly, at Oneida, where exclusive love was regarded as being as wrong as celibacy, suspect couples were separated by sending one of them off to the branch at Wallingford. Separation also occurred within a community. Thomas Lake Harris separated husbands from wives and also parents from their children in order to facilitate their spiritual growth.

Isolation, a harsher version of separation, was used by a number of religious communities. In isolation, the individual was not merely physically separated from another person, but was psychologically severed from the community. Among the Rappites and Hutterites, "shunning" was a punishment used for the graver sins. The individual who was shunned was not allowed to communicate with anyone else in the community, including his or her own spouse. The shunned individual was virtually treated as nonexistent, except that the individual still had to perform his or her work. Among the Hutterites, the individual had to eat alone in the community dining room, and if he or she attended church, had to sit at the back, separated from the other members. "When he is thus constantly surrounded by a disapproving, but not hostile, group, shunning as a punishment takes effect and becomes more and more oppressive with time." [56] Indeed, shunning is an extremely harsh form of punishment. As William James once observed, there is nothing more cruel, including physical torture, than to be treated as though you are nonexistent.

A somewhat milder form of isolation was practiced in a modern commune. Four teenagers had violated the rules of the "colony-in-Christ." Two had walked alone in the woods one afternoon; the other two had held hands and the girl had tickled the boy while they were working. The violations were announced at the worship service and the leader spoke solemnly:

> You all know the penalty. Each of them will be required to spend an entire week in an isolation hut. They will be allowed to eat only sparingly. They must spend their time meditating and praying. Let them now come forward. [57]

The four walked down the aisle, heads bowed in shame, prepared to endure their isolation. But at least their isolation had a fixed time limit, and they experienced no further public humiliation. Among the Hutterites, the shunning was open-ended, depending upon the transgressor's willingness to confess publicly and ask for the community's forgiveness.

The final form of punishment, the one that the people of the communities themselves considered the most severe of all, was expulsion. All of the communities had rules for expulsion, though it was rarely used. At Oneida, for example, only one man was expelled in the community's 33-year history. The grounds for, and the mechanics of, expulsion varied from one community to another. At Zoar, the Constitution did not state the specific violations for which a member could be expelled. It simply stated that the trustees were to maintain peace and order. In practice, the trustees acted along with a standing committee to handle the few cases of expulsion that occurred. In other communities the membership itself had to vote on expulsion. At Communia, Iowa, members were expelled for failing to observe the rules and for immorality. Two-thirds of the members had to approve the expulsion.

Expulsion was a traumatic experience for at least two reasons. First, the fact that the community had to expel someone indicated that the individual preferred to stay within the community. The individual obviously had made some kind of psychological and/or financial commitment, which was forcibly rejected by the community. Most of the groups had provision for returning money and property, or at least some portion of it, to those who left or were expelled. But the Rappites burned the records of contributions, so that anyone who left or was expelled had no way to reclaim the total original investment. Quite apart from any financial loss, however, was the severing of the individual's intimate relationships against his or her will. Those cast out had to experience the same trauma as one whose most intimate relations all die at the same time. Secondly, in the religious communities the expelled individual was not merely cast out of the community but, so they typically claimed, out of the grace of God. To leave the community was virtually to walk into the fires of hell. In any case, expulsion was a reenactment of the fate of Adam and Eve in the Garden of Eden-- the expelled individual was cast out of paradise, or what was in the process of becoming paradise. Clearly, it was far better to conform than to suffer wretchedness in this life and damnation in eternity.

Notes

1. John David Hawkins, "Utopian Values and Communal
   Social Life." Unpublished Ph. D. dissertation, North-
   western University, 1975, pp. 259ff.

2. H. L. Eads, Shaker Sermons, 4th edition (South Union, Ky.: n. p., 1887), p. 224.

3. See the letters of William Byrd, Byrd Manuscripts,
   Lilly Library, Indiana University.

4. See Robert Wolf, "The Sons of Levi," The Modern
   Utopian 1 (July/August, 1967):3-6.

5. Laurence Veysey, The Communal Experience: Anarchist and Mystical Countercultures in America (New
   York: Harper & Row, 1973), pp. 376-77.

6. Nicholas V. Riasanovsky, The Teaching of Charles
   Fourier (Berkeley: University of California Press,
   1969), pp. 46-48.

7. Victor Francis Calverton, Where Angels Dared to
   Tread (Freeport, N. Y.: Books for Libraries Press,
   1941), p. 35.

8. Marywebb Gibson, Shakerism in Kentucky (Cynthiana,
   Ky.: The Hobson Press, 1942), pp. 128-29.

9. Quoted in John McKelvie Whitworth, God's Blueprints:
   A Sociological Study of Three Utopian Sects (London:
   Routledge & Kegan Paul, 1975), p. 36.

10. Julius Friedrich Sachse, The German Sectarians of
    Pennsylvania, Vol. II (Philadelphia: n. p., 1899), p.
    186.

11. Lamech and Agrippa, Chronicon Ephratense, trans. J.
    J. Max Hark (New York: Burt Franklin, 1786), pp.
    77-78.

12. Reuben Gold Thwaites, Early Western Travels, 1784-
    1846 (New York: AMS Press, 1966), pp. 249-50.

13. Helen Harris, Katherine Tingley: Theosophical Lead-
    er and Teacher (n. p., n. d.), pp. 6-10.

14. The Circular, February 22, 1855.

15. Sachse, The German Sectarians, p. 196.

16. Eads, Shaker Sermons, p. 313.

17. Emmett A. Greenwalt, The Point Loma Community in California, 1897-1942 (Berkeley and Los Angeles: University of California Press, 1955), pp. 86-87.

18. Stephen Gaskin, Hey, Beatnik! (Summertown, Tenn.: The Book Publishing Co., 1974), no page.

19. Jeanette C. Lauer and Robert H. Lauer, Fashion Power: The Meaning of Fashion in American Society (Englewood Cliffs, N.J.: Prentice-Hall, 1981), pp. 208-14.

20. Gordon Yaswen, "The Rise and Fall of a Modern Commune," in J. Richard, ed., The Good Life (New York: New American Library, 1973), p. 147.

21. Donna Lawson, Brothers and Sisters All Over This Land: America's First Communes (New York: Praeger, 1972), p. 125.

22. The holidays are described in Daniel B. Reibel, Selected Reprints from The Harmonie Herald, 1966-1979 (Ambridge, Pa.: Pennsylvania Historical and Museum Collection, 1980), pp. 227-29.

23. William Godfrey Bek, "A German Communistic Society in Missouri," Missouri Historical Review 3 (October 1908):61.

24. Mrs. Isabella Pritchard and Mrs. Harry Achterberg, with R. Leonard Jackson, The Truth About the House of David as Related by Former Members (Benton Harbor, Mich.: House of Antarrah, 1927), pp. 13-14.

25. "Confession," The Manifesto 18 (September 1888):210.

26. Lamech and Agrippa, Chronicon Ephratense, p. 81.

27. Bertha M. H. Shambaugh, Amana: The Community of True Inspiration (Iowa City: The State Historical Society of Iowa, 1908), p. 286.

28. Mutual Criticism (Syracuse: Syracuse University Press, 1975; originally publ. 1876), p. 17.

29. Robert Allerton Parker, A Yankee Saint: John Humphrey Noyes and the Oneida Community (New York: G. P. Putnam's Sons, 1935), pp. 216-17.

30. "Articles of Agreement," The Communist 2 (April 1872):67.

31. Veysey, The Communal Experience, p. 313.

32. Avrahm Yarmolinsky, A Russian American Dream (Lawrence, Kan.: University of Kansas Press, 1965), p. 46.

33. W. D. Sprague, Case Histories from the Communes (New York: Lancer Books, 1972), p. 70.

34. "The Shakers," The Telescope 2 (June 11, 1825):6.

35. Edward Deming Andrews, The Gift to Be Simple: Songs, Dances and Rituals of the American Shakers (New York: Dover, 1940), p. 16.

36. Quoted in Daryl Chase, "The Early Shakers: An Experiment in Communism." Unpublished Ph. D. dissertation, University of Chicago, 1936, p. 67.

37. Constance Noyes Robertson, Oneida Community: An Autobiography, 1851-1876 (Syracuse: Syracuse University Press, 1970), p. 1.

38. Barbara S. Yambura, A Change and a Parting: My Story of Amana (Ames, Iowa: Iowa State University Press, 1960), pp. 74-5.

39. A Juvenile Guide; Or Manual of Good Manners (Canterbury, N. H.: United Society, 1844), p. 52.

40. Catalogue: Teachers and Pupils of the Hopedale Home School (Boston: John Wilson and Son, 1859), p. 18.

41. John A. Hostetler and Gertrude Enders Huntington, "Communal Socialization Patterns in Hutterite Society," Ethnology 7 (October 1968):337.

42. Adin Ballou, History of the Hopedale Community (Lowell, Mass.: Thompson & Hill, 1897), p. 28.

43. Hugh Gardner, The Children of Prosperity (New York: St. Martin's Press, 1978), p. 126.

44. Greenwalt, The Point Loma Community, pp. 62-63.

45. Icarian Community: Conditions of Admission (Nauvoo, Ill.: Icaria Printing Establishment, 1854), p. 22.

46. Rosabeth Moss Kanter, Commitment and Community (Cambridge, Mass.: Harvard University Press, 1972), pp. 75-125.

47. The Circular, October 19, 1874.

48. Goesele vs. Bimiler, U.S. Supreme Court Record, Brief 209, p. 11 in the Nixon Family Papers, 1816-1936, Ohio Historical Society.

49. The Fulfillment! Or Twelve Years Afterwards, Paris, June, 1858 to Texas!! Occasional Publication No. 2 of the DeGolyer Foundation Library, Dallas, Texas, 1963.

50. "An Iowan Utopia." The Literary Digest 52 (April 1, 1916):922.

51. Yambura, A Change and a Parting, pp. 136-37.

52. Karl J. R. Arndt, George Rapp's Harmony Society (1785-1847) (Philadelphia: University of Pennsylvania Press, 1965), p. 358.

53. Hilda Dischinger Morhurt, The Zoar Story (Dover, Ohio: Seibert Printing Co., 1967), p. 88.

54. "Fifteen Years a Shakeress," Galaxy 13 (1872):461.

55. Julia Neal, By Their Fruits: The Story of Shakerism in South Union, Kentucky (Philadelphia: Porcupine Press, 1975), p. 74.

56. Victor Peters, All Things Common: The Hutterian

Way of Life (Minneapolis: University of Minnesota
Press, 1965), p. 159.

57.   Sprague, Case Histories from the Communes, p. 13.

7. DREAM AND REALITY:
EXPERIENCES OF PARTICIPANTS

The pursuit of an ideal is the zest of life. Some observers of the human scene even argue that it is only the pursuit, and not the attainment, that gives life zest. The utopians, however, were never satisfied with mere pursuit. They were determined to achieve their dream. For them, it was only the attainment that would give fullness to life. Their thirst for attainment raises the question: to what extent did they succeed in their quest? To what extent did the reality of their lives express the dreams they had pursued? More particularly, for our purposes, to what extent did sexual arrangements yield the quality of life they sought in their utopian communities?

The question is not easy to answer because we have no surveys of members' attitudes. But there are a number of ways to get some indication of their feelings. One is in the writings of members, including both the faithful and the apostates. Another is through the writings of visitors to the communities. And a third source of information is found in the records of events in the communities, including incidents of celebration or conflict. Through these various sources, we get a general sense of the experiences of the participants. As one would expect, those experiences were quite varied.

THE CELIBATES

Can happiness be found in the celibate life? Was the reality of life in the celibate communities as enriching and fulfilling as their ideologies indicated? In his conclusions about the various communal societies, including the celibates, Nordhoff noted that the communal life would appear at first to be "inexorably dull and dreary." But "the surprise was the greater to a visitor like myself to find the people everywhere cheerful, merry in their quiet way, and with a suffi-

cient number and variety of healthful interests in life." [1]
Nordhoff's generalization is interesting because of his first-
hand knowledge of many of the communities. But the experiences of members were considerably more complex than he
suggested. There were, indeed, merry, cheerful, and healthy
members in the communities. Some of the celibates were
ecstatic in their praise of their way of life. But others had
different experiences. We will look first at some of the
positive evaluations by members and outsiders, and then at
evidence of problems.

In Praise of Celibacy

Among others, the Shakers were effusive in their
praise of the celibate life. They claimed that it increased
the length and also the fullness of life. Celibacy, they insisted, was not a sacrifice of present pleasure for future
bliss, a way of appeasing God now in order to secure heavenly reward. Quite the contrary:

> Shakers do not believe in the propriety of making
> themselves unhappy and miserable in this world
> for the sake of being happy in the next. A good
> Shaker is the most thoroughly happy being in ex-
> istence. Why not? The world, the flesh and the
> devil have no attractions for him; he is at peace
> with God, himself and his neighbor.... [2]

If one can believe Shaker writings, the above quote
encapsulated the experience of most Shakers. Again and
again, individual writers exulted in the virtues of celibacy
and the glory of the Shaker way of life. When one was asked
whether he found Shaker life monotonous, he replied: "Nay.
It is peaceful and we are bound together by brotherly and
sisterly love. This is an earthly heaven. I could live here
forever." [3] A 73-year-old Shaker interviewed by Nordhoff
agreed that his life had been a success: "I have been living
out the highest aspirations my mind was capable of. The
best I knew has been realized for and around me here....
Here I found my place and my work, and have been happy
and content, seeing the realization of the highest I had
dreamed of." [4] A sister who had spent more than 67 years
among the Shakers said that they were years richly blessed
by association with "loved teachers and true friends." "I
have never regretted my choice," she affirmed, "and from
the many activities of education and responsibility that have

absorbed my interest I find my Shaker life has been richly rewarding. " [5]

The Shakers pointed out that they were not really deprived by abstaining from sex. As one sister put it:

> Dearly do I love the virgin life for its purity and sweetness. I have never bewailed my virginity, nay never. O that thousands who are this day suffering under yokes of bondage, and are slaves unto sin, could realize the happiness so real which I enjoy. [6]

A brother claimed that he had found peace and comfort, such that he had no desire for sexual relations. On the contrary, he had come to regard any sexual inclination as "odious and loathsome to every feeling of my soul. " [7]

Thus, the Shakers provided an abundance of testimonies to the fulfillment of their dreams. Members of other celibate groups were not as prone as the Shakers to express their joy in writing, though some of them did record their feelings of fulfillment. In addition, visitors and researchers commented on the apparent state of well-being of the people. They frequently agreed with Nordhoff that the people indeed seemed to be happy and content. According to an early historian of the Ephrata cloister, the sisters "lived contented; ambition or politics did not disturb them; vice entered not into their lowly and humble dwellings.... Christianity and brotherly love united them together. " [8] A physician who had been associated with the community pointed out that those women who left the cloister to be married invariably regretted their decision, while those who remained "continued steadfast in their state of single blessedness. " [9] A Rappite agreed with a German visitor who said that there was more happiness and less vice in the community than anywhere else. " [10] A visitor to Zoar pointed out that "a bright and cheerful tone" prevailed everywhere in the community: "The people are affable, polite, obliging and always ready to jest. In the workshop, they sing and laugh and the old separatists, who officiate there as overseers, are the jolliest. " [11] The Sanctificationists, who were an all-female group by the time they moved to Washington, D. C. near the end of the nineteenth century, "demonstrated that they can live a perfect life without the aid of men" according to a newspaper account. [12] The writer said that the women allowed each other perfect liberty (there were no written rules) and that all of them were happy. Nor were they a group of "cranks." Rather, the members were described as "ladies" who were "irreproachable as to character." They simply lived together, shared all things in common, adhered to the celibate life, and minded their own business. Finally, a member of the Bethel community, where celibacy was preferred and sometimes imposed, called his group "an ideal settlement, happy and prosperous and bound together by a community of interests." [13]

Clearly, then, there is abundant evidence that many of the celibates found their dream fulfilled. According to their own statements and the corroborated observations of visitors, they attained peace, contentment, and fulfillment. For them, utopia had been realized. As some of them pointed out, it did not come immediately. They had to struggle, sometimes for years, before they achieved their dream. But eventually they reached their goal, and they agreed that it could not have been reached anywhere but in the community where they lived. As we shall see below, however, the experiences of the fulfilled members were not shared by all of the utopians.

Celibacy As a Problem

Those quoted above regarded celibacy as part of the solution to the utopian quest. For others, celibacy was part of the problem rather than the solution. Some members (it is impossible to specify what proportion) clearly found celibacy a continual psychological, physical, and spiritual battle. Even some of the Shakers openly admitted that sex bothered them, that they still had to wrestle with sexual desires. Not all of them found the very thought of sex as odious and loathsome to their being as the brother quoted above. Individual members of other communities also found celibacy more of a struggle than a solution. At Bishop Hill, the effort to enforce celibacy sharply divided the community and eventually was a major factor in its demise.

Thus, celibacy was not a royal road to utopia for all individuals nor for all of the communities that tried to adopt it. We noted in chapter 3 that, on balance, the evidence indicates that most of the members of the celibate communities kept the rule while they were in the community. Some were aided in their efforts by alternative outlets such as masturbation or, in the case of men, wet dreams. The various mechanisms of social control also helped members maintain the rule of celibacy. Still, a number found it an impossible ideal. In spite of the ideologies and the varied forms of social control, some members succumbed to temptation and engaged in sexual relations. Those who succumbed were not necessarily the happier for the experience, however. A Frenchman by the name of John Reignier joined the Ephrata community and advocated extreme asceticism. [14] The Superintendent had the brethren build a hut for Reignier where he could live alone in his self-imposed deprivation. Shortly thereafter, Reignier "lost his reason" and was expelled from the community. Eventually he joined the Moravian Brethren and was married. He returned after some time with his wife and asked to be taken into Ephrata again. The Superintendent put his wife into the Sisters' Convent and allowed Reignier to enter the Brothers' Convent. The wife was unhappy with the arrangement, insisting upon being returned to her husband. He reluctantly agreed and "lost his reason" a second time. When he regained his reason, he began making slanderous statements about the Superintendent and was again ejected from the community. He left with his wife; "at length he ended his restless life in Savannah in Georgia. God be merciful to him on the day of judgment!" [15] John Reignier illustrates the kind of trauma that could be experienced by those trying valiantly to live a celibate life but unable to attain their ideal.

For Reignier and some others, the effort to remain celibate brought pain, but the failure to do so brought even more pain. They remained true to the ideology of the group even though they could not maintain the ideal. Their indiscretion, therefore, was not a delectable morsel stolen in secret but a bitter experience that left them in even greater turmoil. Not all who broke the rule of celibacy suffered so. Some rejected the ideology and left the group. Some were able, according to the ideology, to pursue an acceptable, though inferior, pathway--sex in marriage. But those who continued to believe in an ideology that made sex unacceptable under any circumstances were sometimes caught between the Charybdis of their impulses and the Scylla of group rejection.

In addition to being a problem for individuals, celibacy proved to be a problem for the groups. Three types of problems afflicted the celibate groups--recruitment and retention of members, outside criticism and opposition, and internal dissension. With regard to recruitment and retention, the only way that the celibate groups could maintain themselves (apart from illicit pregnancies) was to convert outsiders and retain those already converted. But even in the nineteenth century, when the common American view of sex was laced with prudery and depreciation, it was difficult to recruit people to a celibate group. The history of the Rappites illustrates the problem. [16] The first Rappites all came from Germany. They came in waves, with later waves being friends of those who had come earlier or those who had been members of Father Rapp's congregation in Germany but who had not come with the first wave. But the last of the Germans came in 1819. Over time, the number of applications to the group declined. The Rappites had no more new members from Germany and fewer and fewer applications from Americans. Furthermore, younger members were not as committed to the ideal of celibacy. Many of them opted to leave the community in order to be married. The group declined rapidly during the second half of the nineteenth century, as the following membership figures show:

Year	Members
1814	421
1827	522
1834	403
1844	385
1864	170
1879	70
1888	34
1897	10
1903	4 [17]

Of course, the celibate groups declined for reasons other than their celibacy. But celibacy was one of the problems, for it required them to convert outsiders and, at the same time, made conversion an unattractive option for most outsiders. Indeed, even the later generations of members all too frequently decided that the celibate life was not for them. Among the Shakers, the bulk of children reared in the community (whether orphans or unwanted children taken in, or the children of married converts) left when they matured. Hinds reported one Elder at North Union who said that they had "taken in young people enough to make a continuous line half a mile long: and I alone remain"; and a man who had left the Hancock community said that he was the only one of eighty boys with whom he had gone to school who stayed in the community until the age of twenty. [18] The records of the Shakers show that these observations were

not far out of line. The Boy's Journal of Work at Mount
Lebanon records 144 boys who were taken into the community between November, 1821 and July, 1864. Of that total,
eight died, ten were "carried away," two were sent away,
twenty-two became full members, and "102 went to the
world." [19]

A second way in which celibacy caused problems for
the groups was that it drew criticism and opposition from
outsiders. One might expect an adverse reaction to the
groups engaged in deviant sex, but why did outsiders harass
the celibates? There were three bases for outside opposition. One was the problem of the unconverted spouse. What
happened when a husband or a wife was converted to a celibate group? What would be the fate of the unconverted
spouse and of any unconverted or small children? The question was not easily answered. The kind of turmoil that such
a situation could generate is seen in the case of Eunice
Chapman, whose husband was converted by the Shakers. [20]
Upon his conversion, James Chapman, who had earlier de-
serted his wife and three children, wrote to the family that
he had found the "City of God" and would soon bring them
out from under the power of the Antichrist. James did not
find a receptive wife waiting for him. But eventually Eunice
agreed to visit a Shaker community. After an overnight
stay, she decided that she was unsuited to the Shaker way
of life. She returned with the children to her home. After
more than a year of conflict, James used an occasion when
Eunice was not at home to take the three children back with
him to the Shaker community at Watervliet. Eunice pursued
them, but the Shakers would not give the children back to
her. She stayed in the community for a few weeks in an attempt to work out some solution. They were not happy
weeks. According to Eunice, the Shakers castigated her for
being a mother:

> "The Shakers presented me with an old gown and a
> pair of old stockings, they at the same time said,
> 'Eunice you are a nasty dirty good-for-nothing ___
> ___ ; and you are worse than the brutes for being
> the mother of children. Confess your dirty sins,
> and travel out of your carnal nature, and walk in
> the way of God.'" [21]

For three years, Eunice continued her battle with the Shakers
over the control of her children. She pursued every legal
avenue open to her. She got a number of depositions from

witnesses who supported her or who said they saw how unhappy her children were with the Shakers. Finally, in 1814,
the New York Legislature, after a long debate, passed a
special bill that stated that when a man joined the Shakers,
the children would remain with the wife. The bill also dissolved the Chapman's marriage. It was the only time in
New York history that a divorce was directly voted by the
state legislature. Eunice won her case, but only after a
prolonged battle and some cops-and-robbers kind of antics,
including one time when Eunice found her son hidden away
in a haystack. She carted him away with the aid of a hired
bodyguard while another man shot a gun near the Shaker village to distract the brethren. Eunice, incidentally, had the
support of many people in the area surrounding the Shaker
village. The Shakers generally had the respect of outsiders,
but such incidents as the Chapman case did not help their
cause.

The unconverted or uncommitted spouse was a problem in a number of the celibate communities. It was not a
major problem but, as in the case of the Chapmans, it could
cause serious trouble at times. At Ephrata, for example,
Conrad Beissel found his very life threatened by frustrated
and outraged husbands. [22] On one occasion, he persuaded
the wife of one of the married couples in the community to
enter the solitary life. The woman became quite enchanted
with her new, higher spiritual status and spent much time
with Beissel learning the ways of God. Her husband became
increasingly angry over her behavior, and finally forbade her
to see Beissel any more. She continued to visit her spiritual
mentor, however. Finally, the man burst into Beissel's
cabin one day, and dragged Conrad by the neck-cloth toward
the door, almost choking him to death. Beissel was rescued
by other members of the community, who tied the attacker's
hands and sent him and his wife to their home. Subsequent-
ly, the woman was ordered by the church to remain at home
with her husband.

A second basis for outside criticism of and opposition
to the celibates was the suspicion that the leaders of the
group were outwardly pious but secretly lecherous and adulterous. We have noted the accusation against Father Rapp
that he fell in love with a young woman, the charges of sexual immorality against Thomas Lake Harris, the suspicion
that Beissel practiced "whoremongering" and had fathered an
illegitimate child, and the charges and lawsuit brought against
King Ben of the House of David. A lawsuit was also brought

against Cyrus Teed, founder of Koreshan Unity. [23] In 1892, Sidney Miller, a Chicago publisher, brought suit against Teed for alienation of affection. Miller said that Teed had taught his wife that her body was her own, that she should disavow sexual love, and that she should leave her husband and join Teed's community of celibates. In reality, Miller contended, Teed was keeping Mrs. Miller for "a vile, unlawful and wicked purpose." Three days after Miller began his action, another Chicago husband filed the same kind of suit against Teed. There was no evidence that Teed had engaged in any kind of illicit relationships with the women. The cases were eventually dropped. But people do not dismiss cases as easily as do courts. Suspicions continue on the part of outsiders that, though there is insufficient legal evidence to convict a leader, the charges are undoubtedly true. "Where there is smoke, there is fire," is a saying quickly called up to defend one's suspicions.

The third basis for criticism and opposition from outsiders was the suspicion that not merely the leaders but the entire community was engaging in illicit sexual relations. Early in their history, the Shakers were accused of secret sexual orgies, of dancing naked at night and then extinguishing the candles and engaging in promiscuous sexual relations. People claimed that the children born as a result of these orgies were killed to hide the evidence. The result was a certain amount of rejection and persecution of the Shakers. For example, in 1810 a mob of 500 men, uniformed and armed, appeared at the meeting house of a Shaker community in Ohio and "demanded of us that we should renounce our faith and practice, our public preaching and mode of worship, or quit the country." [24] The mob also demanded that the Shakers release some children who were presumably being held against their will. The mob action was apparently stimulated by some apostate Shakers, who claimed that the children were severely beaten, the Elder kept all the money and had total control (like a pope), and the men and women engaged in sexual relationships. The Shakers invited the leaders of the mob to inspect the village. The inspection satisfied the men that there was nothing horrendous going on in the community. But mobs returned in 1812, 1813, and 1817. The Shakers were also, at times, physically assaulted when they tried to convert others, and in some instances their property was destroyed by fire. Similarly, some outsiders believed that the brothers and sisters at Ephrata were engaging in illicit sex, as evidenced by the fact that the men and women lived so close together. And as with the Shakers, there were rumors of infanticide being used to cover up the evidence of sexual activity. When Beissel and his followers first tried to establish their community, some nearby residents attempted to burn them out. The fire only destroyed a barn, however.

Obviously, outsiders could react against utopian communities on the basis of very little evidence. The utopians were like foreigners, strange people who practiced strange ways. It did not take much to generate suspicion and rumors, nor to stimulate people to action against those strangers. Even when the "strangers" were related to them, outsiders could be moved to violence. The Sanctificationists, for instance, were a celibate group who originated in Belton, Texas in the 1870s and later relocated in Washington, D. C. During their decades of existence, their membership was primarily female. Mrs. Martha McWhirter was the founder of the group. After the death of a brother and two of her children (she had twelve in all), she had a profound religious experience of "sanctification." [25] To Mrs. McWhirter, sanctification meant, among other things, celibacy. She continued to live with her husband until his death, but no longer shared his bed. A group of women gradually gathered around her, and her home became the home of the group after her husband's death. Some of the women converts remained in the homes of their unsanctified husbands, but refused sexual relations. Others left their husbands and moved into the McWhirter house. The men of Belton tolerated the strange ways of the women until 1880. But two Scotsmen, David and Thomas Dow, had moved onto small farms near Belton in 1879. They had been members of a sanctificationist group in Scotland, and requested membership in the McWhirter group. There was nothing in the ideology of Mrs. McWhirter that prohibited males from being members. The Dow brothers were accepted. The men of Belton could live with the queer ways of the sanctified women, but their frustration could no longer be contained with the addition of two males into the group. In February, 1880, a mob took the Dow brothers from their houses, severely beat them, and ordered them to leave the country. When the Dows refused to leave, they were pronounced lunatics and ordered into the state asylum at Austin. The authorities at the asylum realized that the brothers were sane, and released them upon their promise not to return to Belton. Thus, even when most of the members of a group were well known to the surrounding residents, suspicion and rumors could make life hazardous for some of the members.

The third type of group problem caused by celibacy was internal dissension. We have already noted that the effort to impose celibacy was one of the reasons for the demise of Bishop Hill. Other groups also had internal dissension. Three brothers who entered the Ephrata Cloister in the first part of the eighteenth century greatly aided the economic development of the community. But they placed too great an emphasis on economic matters and also challenged Beissel's views on celibacy and marriage. The brothers of the Cloister finally rose up in defense of Beissel, burned the writings of one of the brothers, and drove the trio from the community.

The Rappites also had a number of members who rebelled against the celibate rule. A number of them, including Rapp's son, Johannes (born before the celibacy rule went into effect), brought suit against Father Rapp to gain their independence from the community (some brought suit to get back the money they had given when they joined). The Rappites suffered a major division in their ranks in 1831 with the appearance of Bernhard Muller, who called himself Count Maximilian de Leon. Count de Leon claimed to possess the Philosopher's Stone; he had, that is, the secret of making gold. He also began to preach new doctrines, including marriage and a "livelier life." [26] The community was soon divided. After much conflict, they decided to take a vote to see who was for Count de Leon and who was for Father Rapp. The man who kept the tally reported:

> I was in the utmost anxiety as I made out the two lists; at last they were complete; all the names had been called; we counted and found that five hundred were for Father Rapp, and two hundred and fifty for Count Leon. Father Rapp, when I told him the numbers, with his usual ready wit, quoted from the book of Revelation, 'And the trale of the serpent drew the third part of the stars of heaven, and did cast them to the earth.' [27]

The outcome was that a third of the community left with the Count to found a new community. According to one observer, the schism "was no doubt not a misfortune for the society, inasmuch as it rid them of their worst members." [28] Nevertheless, as we noted above, it was difficult enough for the celibate communities to secure and retain members without enduring a schism that took away a third of the group. Internal dissension and schism may not have brought immediate harm to the group, but it did little to stay the rapid decline that occurred throughout the latter half of the nineteenth century.

THE TRADITIONALISTS

As with the celibates, the traditionalists had members who reported great satisfaction with the arrangements. However, even though they followed the normative American pattern for sexual relations--sex in marriage--the traditionalists were not able to escape a number of problematic situations.

Not many of the members of the traditionalist communities wrote specifically of their experiences with marriage, but at Hopedale a number of the members published glowing accounts of traditional marriage. One woman wrote that she hardly felt competent to discuss the marriage relation because it was so important. Nevertheless, she said she had no bitter experiences to relate. In fact, in a time when women generally were enslaved to men, she could only speak of the "happiness of my own peaceful home" and the "largest freedom of thought, opinion and action" which she enjoyed. [29]

The strong affirmation of marriage at Hopedale was partly a reaction to the case of free love which had occurred in the community. In other traditionalist communities, there may not have been actual cases of free love, but there were rumors and threats by outsiders. In spite of their commitment to the traditional form of marriage, the communities did not escape the charge of being sexual deviants. At Brook Farm, for example, rumors circulated that the young people were accepting Fourier's ideas on sex. George Bradford and Ralph Waldo Emerson met to discuss the situation. According to Bradford, "Plain dealing is the best defence of manners and morals between the sexes." But Emerson thought to himself that "the danger arises whenever bodily familiarity grows up without Spiritual Intimacy." [30] The young people at Brook Farm did enjoy considerable freedom in relating to each, in "bodily familiarity." But there is no evidence that any of them ever experimented with free love or even with anything beyond the kind of flirtations which might have been considered highly inappropriate to proper Bostonians but totally innocuous to others.

Of course, rumors do not depend upon solid evidence. They grow out of situations of ambiguity. Humans are not comfortable with ambiguous situations; we always try to make sense out of them. One of the ways to make sense is to construct some statement that is reasonable in the light of the evidence we have. Thus, it makes more sense that the brethren and sisters at Ephrata were engaging in secret sex than that they lived so close together in the unnatural state of celibacy. It made more sense to the New Englanders around Brook Farm that the young people were experimenting with illicit sex than it did that young people could frolic freely together without supervision and still remain chaste. It made more sense to the residents around Shalam that the members there, in spite of their condemnation of sexual license, their insistence upon either celibacy or marriage, and their concern for homeless children, were actually "perpetuating slavery, engaging in connubial irregularities, mistreating their ill, and forbidding their members to eat salt." [31] After all, the people of Shalam did have their own peculiar Bible, which taught them to be pacifists, vegetarians, and spiritualists. People who practice strange ways and advocate strange writings are capable of anything, are they not? Thus, even if a utopian group practiced a traditional marriage, they were sufficiently different in other ways to suffer the same suspicions and threats from outsiders as the celibates.

The threats were generally quite explicit. The Friendship Community, near Buffalo, Missouri, was forced to relocate because of the threat of mob action. The following letter was delivered to Alcander Longley, leader of the group, in April, 1877:

> We the undersined Has taking this method of asking you to stop the way you air doing and if you dont their air some of you that will look up a lim Before you air two months older. We dont approve of such Doctern and it Shant Be alloud in our country. And if you want to live in this country you haf to quit advocating such Doctern.... We mean what we say take warning Before it is everlasting to late A word to the wise is sufficient. [32]

Neighbors who were sympathetic to the community agreed that the threat was real and would be carried out. Longley noted that it has been the fate of virtually every new or unusual movement to be charged by outsiders with licentiousness and all manner of immorality. Though the charges were untrue, Longley decided that it would be wise to move on.

The problem of real or rumored sexual deviancy was a matter of ongoing concern in the traditional communities. Most of the members of the communities seemed satisfied with the traditional arrangement. There were only a few cases recorded of any deviancy or even of any suggestion by members that the group experiment with nontraditional forms. Nevertheless, outsiders frequently refused to believe that the utopians were truly monogamous. Like the celibates, the traditionalists experienced problems both within and without because of their sexual arrangement.

THE NON-TRADITIONALISTS

We would expect the members of the non-traditionalist groups to be plagued by opposition from outside the community. And they were, although they had their share of internal problems as well. Outsiders gave the communities mixed reactions also. Some found them to be pits of sin, while others--sometimes reluctantly--said that the communities appeared to function well for the members. One of the more vigorously and widely discussed groups was that of Oneida. We will begin by looking at Oneida as seen through the eyes of outsiders.

Complex Marriage--the Views of Outsiders

Outsiders who accepted the nineteenth-century view of the deleterious effects of excessive sexual activity came to Oneida expecting to find a group of people who bore the marks of overindulgence in their own bodies. Proponents of the contemporary sexual morality expected to find, in addition, a group of people who were clearly degenerate. And some indeed found what they were looking for. Moralists found the system nothing less than heinous, and at least some found the people to be physically as well as morally degenerate.

One of the vociferous critics, John B. Ellis, wrote that the system was "so curious and monstrous that I almost shrink from the task of explaining it to the reader." [33] Noyes, argued Ellis, was blasphemous and adulterous. He

had distorted the Word of God and made it appear to justify
an adulterous system. Not only did the members of Oneida
practice adultery, but they openly talked about sex in their
community (an unthinkable habit in the extremely prudish
day):

> The filthiness of the conversation these women are
> required to engage in passes description. Nothing
> is considered too impure for general discussion in
> the family-hall. Topics which outrage all decency
> are discussed by the sexes without reserve. Noth-
> ing is too gross, too impure; and the women ex-
> hibit, in their discussion, an adeptness--a profundity,
> I might almost say--which is simply appalling.
> There is not a first-class brothel in the land where
> such conversations would be allowed. Yet it is
> proper and popular here. Doubtless it is an es-
> sential part of the system of moral degradation to
> which these women are subjected. [34]

Ellis felt that the horrid system had its effects even
upon the physical appearance of the members. The women,
he said, appeared to him to be coarse, lacking in refinement, and having an "air of unhealthiness." Even a casual
glance at them, he said, would convince a physician that they
were unhealthy. For the signs of sexual excess were written
in their faces and in the faces of the men as well:

> The eyes were heavy and dull, the expression of
> the entire face was one of fatigue, and there was a
> sensual, gross look about the mouth. Never have
> I seen lustfulness written so plainly on the human
> face as at this community.... You may go into
> any of the better-class houses of prostitution in
> our great cities, and find women of far more at-
> tractiveness, of greater outward modesty, and of
> higher mental culture. [35]

Ellis' comparison of "first-class" and "better-class" houses
of prostitution with the group at Oneida is interesting. Nineteenth-century moralists considered prostitution a wicked
practice. Yet Ellis was so passionate in his denunciation of
Oneida (and other groups of "free lovers") that he could write
of prostitutes as almost virtuous people.

A number of other critics were also severe in their
denunciation of the system of complex marriage. A minister

wrote about the "utter impiety and solemn mockery" of Noyes
in trying to "couple his gross licentiousness with the sublime
mysteries of Christianity." "Never," the minister affirmed,
"was the grace of God more completely turned into lascivious-
ness! Never was the demon of darkness more effectually
transformed into an angel of light." [36] Still another critic
said that not even the beasts of the field behaved sexually as
did the people at Oneida. If the community persisted in their
"inbreeding," he argued, they would be trying to reverse the
"law of animal production." [37]

But some outsiders found a completely different Oneida,
including some who visited the community expecting to see the
scars of sin in the bodies of the members. As Parker
pointed out in his biography of Noyes, many intelligent visitors who came to the community expecting to find gross immorality and the effects of that immorality in the appearance
of the people, left with an entirely different perspective.
They went away with praise rather than condemnation. Parker quotes a reporter who wrote that, to be perfectly honest,
he had to admit that he had "looked in vain for the visible
signs of either the suffering or the sin. The Community
makes an impression utterly unlike that left by the pallid
joylessness of the Shakers, or the stupid sensualism which
impressed me in the few Mormon households I have seen." [38]
The reporter went on to point out the fact that children who
grew up in the community rarely wanted to leave it. Even
those who had been sent away to school would return "eagerly
and devote their lives to the Community." [39]

One striking testimony from an outsider to the state
of well-being of community women came from a physician,
Dr. Ely Van De Warker, who was called in to examine the
women when some concerns arose about the effects of complex marriage upon health. The doctor examined 42 of the
women in 1877, nearly three decades after the founding of
the community at Oneida, and published his findings in a
medical journal. [40] Near the end of the article he pointed
out that he was not defending the system of complex marriage; on the contrary, he agreed that "evasions" of the
"legitimate, physiological sexual relation" were both "physically and morally wrong." Nevertheless, he found the women
at Oneida to be remarkably well. Hysteria was a common
affliction of nineteenth-century American women, but at Oneida
hysteria was "remarkably absent." Women who had passed
through menopause reported that they had "passed this trying
period without any unpleasant effects." Dr. Van De Warker

tabulated and discussed a number of characteristics of the women's physical well-being. Finally, he concluded that the evidence, in spite of the fact that gynecologists of the day were attributing uterine disabilities to sexual deviance of various kinds, pointed to one fact--there was nothing but "negative evidence" on the effects of complex marriage upon health. Thus, there were no physical problems resulting from early and frequent sexual relations by the women of the community. There was also no evidence that the men had adverse reactions.

Complex Marriage--Views of Insiders

How did those who practiced complex marriage and male continence experience the system? We no longer believe that frequent sexual activity is physically debilitating to people, but many people, like the contemporaries of the Oneidans, would assume that male continence was not very satisfying to the men. In fact, the authors heard a professional speaker at a conference in the 1980s label male continence as a kind of feminist system that may have enhanced the pleasure of the women but gave minimal enjoyment to the male. We cannot know with certainty, but all of the evidence we have suggests that both males and females derived satisfaction from the practice. Dr. Van De Warker reported that some of the women he examined said that the practice of male continence was popular among them and was easily followed by all but a few of the men. Noyes himself testified that his own sexual enjoyment and his wife's sexual satisfaction increased after he started the practice of male continence (recall that he argued that the most pleasurable part of sex is the presence of the male organ in the female, not the orgasm). Havelock Ellis, on the basis of correspondence with a former member of the community, wrote that the women experienced orgasm and the men not only had no emission but after prolonged union "felt no need of emission." [41]

Testimonies of members, published in the First Annual Report, support the conclusion that males as well as females found male continence sexually satisfying. [42] The theory of Noyes, according to one member, "has delivered me from the bondage of an insubordinate amativeness, which had been the torment of my life. It has brought me into a positive purity of feeling, that I am confident could come from no source but God." Another spoke of the way that he had been invigorated with life and refined in character. A

third testified that his respect for love had been increased
and that he was now able to look upon sexual love not as
"low, sensual passion," but as "holy and noble." In these
testimonies, the religious devotion and self-discipline of the
Christian disciple readily appear. That is, the Oneidans
were aided by their religious commitment. The experience
of sex is rarely, if ever, a purely physical phenomenon.
The meaning of sexual experiences is defined in terms learned
from social relationships, not merely in terms of the pure
physical reaction. The Oneidans defined that meaning in
terms of their religious beliefs. In other words, the fact
that they found the experience of male continence pleasurable
does not mean that others, who do not share their religious
commitment, would also find it so.

But there seems little doubt about the Oneidans' experience. There was never any rebellion against the system
of male continence. Members who recalled their experiences
at Oneida years after the breakup invariably spoke in positive
terms. A sociologist who interviewed a number of aged sur-
vivors reported some of their positive recollections. [43]
One said: "We all love the old place ... so many of the
people who move away seem to come back.... It's because
they had such good times and such happy memories." Another
said: "I was a child in the old Community and I can tell you
that they were a happy group ... my dominant memory is
one of contentment and happiness." A third was too young
when the community broke up to remember much, but said
that "as I grew older and asked my relatives about the Community days, their faces would light up."

In spite of such glowing reports, Oneida was not paradise. There were problems and conflict. For example, love
affairs between two people frequently caused problems. Some
members were unable to avoid the sin of "special love" for
one other person. And while there was never a rebellion
against male continence, there was conflict and growing dissatisfaction with the system of complex marriage in the last
years of the community. According to an informant of Dr.
Van De Warker, a woman who had left the community, young
females complained a good deal in the last years of the community about the high frequency with which they were expected
to engage in sex relations. "Ten years before," the informant said, "they felt just the same, but partly in bondage to
their religious beliefs about it, and partly from fear of criticism and the knowledge the relation with a loved one would
be broken up, they were quiet, and submitted. [44] An in-

formant of Anita McGee, the anthropologist who studied the community, said that there was "growing dissatisfaction" with complex marriage in the last years of the community, especially among the younger women. They said that it was a "man's plan, not a woman's." [45] The informant did not explain the basis for this statement. It may have reflected the women's desire for a more traditional monogamous relationship and family life, or it may have reflected their feeling that too many sexual demands were placed upon them. In any case, there were at least some men and women at Oneida who found the system less than utopian. They appear not to have been in the majority, perhaps not even a significant minority. Even when the community was breaking up and there was considerable conflict about certain details such as who should initiate young females into the system, the general sentiment was in favor of retaining complex marriage in some form. [46] Yet when Noyes, who had fled to Canada to avoid legal or other troubles from outraged citizens in the area, wrote to the community and suggested that complex marriage be abandoned, the leaders accepted the suggestion in spite of the general sentiment. Apparently some of the members were more than willing to abandon complex marriage.

The Perils of Deviant Sex

At Oneida and at other communities where some form of deviant sex was practiced, there were problems of various kinds from within and without. The deviant sexual arrangements did not bring about the utopia that was expected, at least not for all of the members. Specifically, there are five kinds of problems that have afflicted the deviants: lack of fulfillment, sexual excesses, desire for exclusiveness, lack of consensus over the arrangements, and outside opposition.

Lack of Fulfillment

As with the various other arrangements, some people did not find sexual fulfillment in the deviant communities. A young woman at a modern commune, Blue Mountain Ranch, wrote that as she was discovering her "sexual self" and "playing it out," she made love with many men. But "I realize that it was not totally fulfilling. I was living for the love I could receive from a certain man at a certain time.

Again my life was being man-defined, although I thought I
was being free." [47] The meaning of her life up to that
point had been defined by the men she fell in love with, but
free sex neither changed her male-defined life nor fully
satisfied her sexual needs.

Other members of Blue Mountain Ranch also appeared
to have problems finding fulfillment in the free sex arrangement. Accounts by members reflect a good deal of restlessness and searching. One young woman wrote that in her
sexual odyssey she had a child by one man, lived with another
man for a year, lived celibately with a third man, experimented with a lesbian relationship, returned to celibacy
again, and finally decided to try to fulfill herself sexually
through lesbian relationships. At the time of her writing,
she was still searching. A young man in the community
had a sexual relationship with two female members. He
found this satisfying to some extent, but "I also felt oppressed by it. There was the nightly scene of waiting around
to see whom I would sleep with. There was the feeling of
rushing back and forth, putting out fires.... I was just too
overextended." [48]

Visitors to other communes report a similar sense of
restlessness and searching among some members rather than
a joyous fulfillment in open relationships. [49] In some
cases, individuals who feel that openness is the answer to
their own needs have difficulty with other members who do
not share their feelings. For example, a married male
member of Morning Star, a modern commune, fell in love
with a single woman and decided that he would like to have
two wives. Any kind of sexual arrangement was acceptable
at Morning Star, so the young man brought the single woman
home one night. "For me it was great," he said, but the
two females did not get along. His wife said that by the end
of the night the bed "smelled like a gymnasium." The outcome was a dissolution of the man's marriage and despair:
"My own married life could be described as a battleground
in which ex-wives and children abound. The love syndrome
has left me exhausted and baffled." [50]

One could argue, of course, that given a sufficient
amount of time those in the free love communities would
find fulfillment. They were reared in a society where
monogamy is the norm and free love is viewed as immoral.
And people do not quickly and easily sever themselves and
their values from the past. Even when they can do so in-

tellectually, they may find it difficult to do so emotionally. Over time, however, they may gradually resolve their feelings and acquire a sense of well-being in conjunction with the deviant arrangements. Unfortunately, the free love communities have tended to be too short-lived to test the thesis.

Sexual Excesses

A second type of problem to afflict the deviants, oddly enough, is sexual excesses. Some communities have had difficulties because either certain members or the leaders have had an excessively strong sexual preoccupation. Contrary to what many outsiders believed, the communities were not established primarily as havens for sexual orgies. Utopia is not achieved merely by changing sexual patterns. Sexual arrangements, therefore, were always only one of the changed ways of life initiated by the utopians. Furthermore, they believed that it was important for members to accept the total way, to believe in all of the changes, to be as committed to the new economy, for example, as to the new sexual setup. None of the communities wanted new members who came only to enjoy a sexual adventure.

We have already noted the man at Oneida who presented a "serious case" to the community, and who was so engrossed in his own pleasure-seeking that he made advances to the neighbor's girls and even tried to get some of the community's boys into a sexual relationship with "some abandoned women." [51] But it was not only at Oneida that the problem arose. Virtually every community had some notion of "excesses," and all insisted that members not venture into that realm of excess. In one modern urban commune, two members were "gradually being banished from the group" because both communicated a sexuality that was "too much." "Their sensuality may have been too great a threat to our social order, to the covenants of restraint among us. Our household was powered by intellectualization--and by a suppression of sensuality." [52] The sexual excesses of leaders also caused some problems. One of the points of dispute at Oneida was the right of Noyes to first access to virgins. To some members, Noyes exceeded the bounds of his authority in this matter. In one modern commune, the leader announced that in order to get the members out of "a rut" in their interpersonal relations, he would have sexual relations with each female in turn. That would bring them all closer together, he said, though no other member followed the same procedure. [53] Again, some of the members considered this excessive.

Desire for Exclusiveness

As John Humphrey Noyes discovered, it is virtually impossible to prevent any dyadic attachments from developing. In spite of their ideology, and in spite of every effort to maintain group rather than dyadic commitments, "special love" between two people was a frequent problem at Oneida. Modern communes that cleave to an ideology of nonexclusive relationships have discovered the same fact. For example, at the commune he studied over a period of years, Bennett Berger pointed out that exclusive sexual access was "ideologically disavowed: coupling does not carry with it exclusive property rights for one to the other's body." [54] Nevertheless, Berger found that jealousy was a problem. Tensions arose in the group when individuals who were ideologically committed to nonexclusive relationships found their feelings on a different track from their beliefs.

Again and again, coupling emerged in modern communes in the face of ideological opposition. In one commune, a member noted, the members found themselves re-creating the kinds of things they hated in the larger society. They were falling short of a utopia. Among other things, even though they talked openly of their dislike of "closed, monogamous relationships," they suddenly found a "monogamous couple in our midst." [55] In some cases, individuals who were willing to try, and even ideologically committed to, open relationships found that they could not handle the arrangement. In one rural commune, two teen-aged females, one middle-aged man, and two married couples formed a group marriage. The group marriage ended abruptly when one of the married men saw his wife with another man in the group. He "pulled a knife, and dragged her away, yelling, 'Forget this shit. She belongs to me.'" [56]

The problems with trying to maintain nonexclusive relationships are so severe that some groups have given up and returned to monogamous arrangements. As one member of a rural commune described his experience:

> Concerning our sexual relationships, we are monogamous. We just can't accept the sexual sharing bit. We tried it to some extent earlier, but it

created too many problems, too much jealousy.
Two couples split as a result. It sounds OK on
paper, but it didn't work. [57]

One of the reasons for establishing open sexual relationships is to enhance group solidarity. The young man
quoted above said that in his commune the people were drawn
closer together by working together. Communal physical
labor, he said, was one of the main things that created a
family feeling in his commune. His observation could be
set forth as a general principle. Certainly, in our review
of the communities we have found no case in which the attempt to enforce nonexclusiveness was easily carried out.
Where nonexclusiveness has been the norm (rather than one
of the options), problems have invariably arisen. In some
cases, those problems threatened the survival of the group.
In all cases, there were members who endured a great deal
of personal trauma and interpersonal tensions because of the
expectation of nonexclusiveness. If the main point is to enhance group solidarity, communal work may be a better way
than nonexclusive sexual relationships.

Lack of Consensus Over the Arrangements

The fourth kind of problem in the deviant groups was
lack of consensus over sexual arrangements. One would
think that an individual would not enter a deviant group unless he or she were committed to the sexual arrangements
advocated by the group. But changes occurred in the groups
over time, and, in some cases, a new generation came with
somewhat different views. We have already noted that some
of the women at Oneida expressed dissatisfaction with the
system of complex marriage in the later days of the community's existence. In addition, one of the changes that occurred that caused problems was Noyes' eugenic experiment,
which he called "stirpiculture." Male continence had been
remarkably successful as a birth control mechanism. But
utopia does not mean the abolition of procreation. Noyes
had long been committed to the notion of scientific procreation. His stirpiculture experiment fulfilled that commitment.
Believing in the inheritance of acquired characteristics, he
decided that the most spiritually advanced members should
be the parents of children. Later in the experiment, Noyes
gave up some of his control of the experiment to others, and
physical appearance became one of the factors in mating. A
couple that desired to produce a child would apply to the

stirpiculture committee. They might or might not be allowed to procreate, depending upon their spiritual and physical condition. In addition, the committee suggested a number of couples as good candidates. Initially, both the men and women of the community signed a resolution stating that they were fully committed to God and to Noyes and would obey his decisions in the experiment. Later on, however, some of the women became dissatisfied with the arrangement whereby a committee decided whether or not they could bear a child.

At Reunion Community in Missouri, problems arose when a group of new members came in because of their commitment to communistic living. All of the new members except one couple had unconventional notions about marriage. Perhaps they expected a communistic community to share their notions. But the leader of the group was quite conventional in his own views of marriage and sex. Unfortunately, he "had framed his views in the Reunion constitution in an obfuscatory manner." [58] The new members proposed that the community abolish the traditional marriage system. The result was a vote and a split in the group. The majority, favoring unconventional arrangements, moved to Kansas. The minority remained in Missouri, but soon had other problems and disbanded.

A similar fate befell the Ruskin Co-operative Association in Tennessee. That is, members came in who were presumably committed to the socialist doctrine of the group. But an incident occurred that revealed significant differences of opinion, including differences on what marriage and sexual arrangements were desirable. According to one ex-member, the community disbanded because of internal dissension resulting from these differences. [59] One important point of difference was that some of the members openly advocated free love, while others were virtually horrified by the notion. The problem began when a man who worked as a printer in the community (though he was not a member) posted a notice soliciting funds to defend the "Fire Brand," an anarchist and free love newspaper. [60] Quickly a controversy erupted between those who labeled themselves as basically Socialists and those who agreed with the Anarchists and Free Lovers. The Socialists claimed that anarchy was and always had been the "great obstacle" to socialistic movements. The two systems "are diametrically opposite. Socialism claims evolution and perfection through the law. Anarchy claims its perfection in the abrogation of all law." [61] The Anarchists,

on the other hand, argued for voluntary cooperation in all
things, including sexual matters. Any individual, they insisted, should have the right to have sexual relations with
any other individual as long as both desired the relationship.
One of the Socialists, embittered by the experience, wrote
later that the real trouble turned out to be women:

> Well, like the Garden of Eden, the women brought
> on the trouble. If we had not had any women we
> would not have had any trouble. One trouble was
> brought on by eating the apples. The other was
> brought on by trying to give them votes. Both had
> the same effect. The apples smashed up the
> Garden of Eden, the votes smashed up Ruskin.
> At least that was the ostensible reason. If women
> had not been in the question we would have had no
> Free Love schism, either. [62]

Of course, Ruskin would not have been a trouble-free community if there had been no women. There were differences
other than those along the lines of sex and marriage. But
the sex and marriage difference became a focal point around
which the conflict crystallized and, ultimately, broke the
community apart.

Outside Opposition

The final problem is one that we would expect in a
deviant community--opposition from incensed outsiders.
Even where there was little or no practice of deviant sex,
the mere fact that unconventional arrangements were discussed or approved was enough to generate opposition. The
people of New Harmony were castigated for being promiscuous because of Robert Owen's unorthodox views on marriage.
The real purpose of the Owenites' views on private property
and religion, according to one critic, was to get rid of the
one thing they really detested--marriage. The Owenites'
anti-religious and communistic ideas were not based on any
inherent evils in the existing institutions; rather

> they were sensible of the fact, that, so long as the
> people retained any respect for religion, or kept
> up any of the distinctions created by wealth, their
> ultimate object, the destruction of the institution of
> marriage, could not be obtained. [63]

There were other communities where there were more
accusations of free love than actual practice. At Silkville,
Kansas, the leader, Ernest V. de Boissiere, was said to be
an infidel who believed in free love. Rumor had it that the
people engaged in sex orgies and ejected anyone who practiced
either religion or marriage. [64] Boissiere did try to follow
the teachings of Fourier in his community. But there was
no evidence that deviant sex was practiced at the community,
and we know that marriage was not abolished because at
least one marriage was performed and recorded. [65] Similar charges of free love, and similar lack of evidence of
any practice of free love, occurred at other Fourier groups.

Some communities, of course, did practice free love
or some other kind of unconventional sexual arrangement.
Outsiders reacted with hostility. That hostility found expression in local newspaper editorials, overt contempt on the
part of nearby residents, occasional threats, and in some
cases mob action or legal action. The Spirit Fruit Society,
for example, started by Jacob Beilhart in Ohio in 1899, had
the explicit purpose of teaching people how to apply the
truths of Christ. At first, the group had good relationships
with their neighbors. But Beilhart had some unusual teachings about love, or at least some unusual ways of expressing
his obsession with love. In an autobiographical account, he
wrote about his awakening to love, which occurred when he
healed a 24-year-old woman who had only two or three weeks
to live. One day she took a pencil at his request, and to
her surprise it began to write rapidly. A spirit was at
work within her, expressing through her the "ideal of woman-
hood." When the spirit was at work within her, he found
himself "alive with love" for her. She left for the West,
ending the love affair. "But love was begun. I had seen
an Ideal that was like the ideal within myself. To create,
to draw forth by the power, to create by Love, was now my
work." [66]

Beilhart taught about love in terms certain to arouse
suspicion on the part of outsiders. He said that only the unselfish love of man could free woman. He wrote that love
has no set rules of right and wrong: "Anything that Love
directs is lawful." [67] Within a couple of years after its
founding, rumors circulated that the Spirit Fruit Colony was
a nest of free-lovers. The birth of an illegitimate child
confirmed the suspicions and led to legal action. About the
same time, the wife of a Chicago physician joined the community. The doctor claimed that she had been abducted and

also brought legal action. The woman returned to her husband, but the local citizenry was outraged. They circulated a "warning" in nearby Lisbon:

> Wanted--Fifty good women, over twenty and under fifty years of age; also fifty good honest-hearted men with families, to meet upon the Square when called upon, and go to the Spirit Fruit farm and tell them to take their departure at once or take the consequences, as tar is cheap and feathers plentiful. [68]

The threat was sufficient to persuade Beilhart and his followers to move to Chicago.

Modern communes have also been opposed by outsiders with everything from threats to violence and legal action. For example, the members of Cold Mountain Farm preferred nudity in the warm weather. But the neighbors objected and let it be known to the members that "people were talking." Local people began to define members as hippies. The police started stopping the members whenever they went into town. A gas station attendant told some of them that the highway patrol had also been asked to keep watch on them. As a result: "It was easy to be paranoid, to imagine their trying to take our kids away for nudity. It was terrible to compromise, but most of us began to wear clothes again. That was a great loss." [69]

DREAM OR REALITY?

To return to our original question, to what extent did reality square with the dream? If there is one conclusion that is obvious, it is that no single arrangement is guaranteed to fulfill the needs of every individual. Most of the celibates apparently found their lives richly satisfying, but some of them could not measure up to the ideal and experienced far more trauma than gratification. Most of those in the traditionalist groups also appear to have found the arrangement fulfilling. But, again, some found traditional marriage too constraining. The evidence suggests that members of deviant groups, with the exception of Oneida, had more difficulties adapting to arrangements than members of the other two types of groups. Even some of those ideologically committed to free love found themselves unable to adapt to it in practice. For sexual and marital arrangements cannot be separated from cultural values and social institutions. A successful utopian arrangement, therefore, must include alternatives for people and must be congruent with the overall sociocultural system.

Notes

1. Charles Nordhoff, The Communistic Societies of the United States (New York: Schocken Books, 1965; 1st publ. 1875), p. 405.

2. Louis Basting, "Reply," The Manifesto 17 (September 1887):203.

3. "Among the Shakers. No. 2," The Manifesto 16 (April 1886):91.

4. Nordhoff, The Communistic Societies, p. 164.

5. Sister Aida Elam, History of the Shakers (Canterbury, N. H.: n. p., n. d.), p. 11.

6. Anna Hurd, "A Voice From Maine," The Shaker 7 (July 1877):54.

7. Testimonies Concerning the Character and Ministry of Mother Ann Lee (Albany: Packard and Van Benthuysen, 1827), p. 23.

8. Redmond Conyngham, "An Account of the Settlement of the Dunkers at Ephrata, in Lancaster County, Pennsylvania," Memoirs of the Historical Society of Pennsylvania 2 (1827):137.

9. William M. Fahnestock, "An Historical Sketch of Ephrata; together with a Concise Account of the Seventh Day Baptist Society of Pennsylvania," in F. Reichmann and E. E. Dollieds, eds., "Ephrata as Seen by Contemporaries," The Pennsylvania German Folklore Society 17 (1952):177.

10. Quoted in Karl J. R. Arndt, A Documentary History of the Indiana Decade of the Harmony Society, 1814-1824, Vol. II (Indianapolis: Indiana Historical Society, 1978), p. 886.

11. Karl Knortz, "The Portfolio of a German-American: Matters Godly and Ungodly." Translation of an 1893 pamphlet in the archives of the Ohio Historical Society.

12. "A Happy Home Without Husbands," syndicated story distributed to Hearst newspapers, August 24, 1901. Copy in the Eugene C. Barker Texas History Center, University of Texas, Austin.

13. Quoted in Harold Dailey, "The Old Communistic Colony at Bethel," Pennsylvania Magazine of History and Biography 52 (1928):164.

14. Reignier's experience is related in Lamech and Agrippa, Chronicon Ephratense, trans. J. Max Hark (New York: Burt Franklin, 1786), pp. 67-8.

15. Ibid., p. 68.

16. John Archibald Bole, The Harmony Society (Philadelphia: Americana Germanica Press, 1904), pp. 34-5.

17. Ibid., pp. 33-4.

18. William Alfred Hinds, American Communities (Oneida, N.Y.: Office of the American Socialist, 1878), p. 106.

19. Daryl Chase, "The Early Shakers: An Experiment in Religious Communism." Unpublished Ph.D. Dissertation, University of Chicago, 1936, p. 120.

20. Nelson M. Blake, "Eunice Against the Shakers," New York History 41 (October 1960):359-78.

21. Eunice Chapman, An Account of the Conduct of the Shakers (Lebanon, Ohio: Van Vleet & Camron, 1818), p. 20.

22. James E. Ernst, "Ephrata: A History," The Pennsylvania German Folklore Society 25 (1961):84-86.

23. Howard D. Fine, "The Koreshan Unity: The Chicago Years of a Utopian Community," Journal of the Illinois State Historical Society 68 (June 1975):213-27.

24. Benjamin Seth Youngs, "An Expedition Against the Shakers," document dated August 31, 1810, Ohio Archeological and Historical Society Publications 21 (1912):403.

25. George P. Garrison, "A Woman's Community in Texas," The Charities Review 3 (November 1893):20.

26. Nordhoff, The Communistic Societies, p. 79.

27. Ibid., p. 80.

28. "The Colony of Economy and the Harmonist Sect: Extract of a Letter from M. Louis Cortambert," trans. Mrs. Max W. Meyer, Missouri Historical Society Bulletin 28 (October 1971):45.

29. Spiritual Reformer 2 (April 1861):95.

30. Edith Roelker Curtis, A Season in Utopia: The Story of Brook Farm (New York: Thomas Nelson & Sons, 1961), pp. 209-10.

31. Daniel Simundson, "Strangers in the Valley: The Rio Grande Republican and Shalam, 1884-1891," New Mexico Historical Review 45 (July 1970):200.

32. The Communist 4 (May 1877):38.

33. John B. Ellis, Free Love and Its Votaries (New York and Cincinnati: United States Publishing Co., 1870), p. 162.

34. Ibid., p. 214.

35. Ibid., p. 211.

36. Rev. Hubbard Eastman, Noyesism Unveiled (Brattleboro, Vt.: n.p., 1849), pp. 35-36.

37. A. L. Slawson, Behind the Scenes; Or, an Expose of Oneida Community (Oneida: A. L. Slawson, 1875), p. 63.

38. Robert Allerton Parker, A Yankee Saint (New York: G. P. Putnam's Sons, 1935), p. 243.

39. Ibid.

40. Ely Van De Warker, "A Gynecological Study of the
     Oneida Community," The American Journal of Ob-
     stetrics and Diseases of Women and Children 17 (Au-
     gust 1884):785-809.

41. See Maren Lockwood Carden, Oneida: Utopian Com-
     munity to Modern Corporation (New York: Harper &
     Row, 1969), p. 58.

42. First Annual Report of the Oneida Association (Oneida:
     Leonard & Company, 1849), pp. 50-51.

43. William M. Kephart, "Experimental Family Organiza-
     tion: An Historico-Cultural Report on the Oneida
     Community," Marriage and Family Living 25 (August
     1963):262, 265.

44. Van De Warker, "A Gynecological Study," p. 789.

45. Anita Newcomb McGee, "Interviews August, 1891, at
     Kenwood, New York, with Herrick, Cragin and
     Hinds." Ms. at the Institute for Sex Research, In-
     diana University.

46. Carden, Oneida, p. 103.

47. January Thaw (New York: Times Change Press,
     1974), p. 140.

48. Ibid., p. 70.

49. See: Robert Houriet, Getting Back Together (New
     York: Coward, McCann & Geoghegan, 1971), p. 141;
     Lester Velie, "The Intimate Life of a Commune,"
     Reader's Digest, March 1973, p. 97.

50. Bill Wheeler, "Relationships," in Home Free! (Occi-
     dental, Cal.: Friends of Morningstar Publications,
     1978), p. 274.

51. Oneida: Record of Current Events, April 18, 1863.

52. Michael Weiss, Living Together: A Year in the Life
     of a City Commune (New York: McGraw-Hill, 1974),
     p. 157.

53. Laurence Veysey, The Communal Experience (Chicago: University of Chicago Press, 1973), pp. 199-200.

54. Bennett M. Berger, The Survival of a Counterculture (Berkeley: University of California Press, 1981), p. 131.

55. "Notes from Rainbow Farm," Ramparts 10 (September 1971):60.

56. Sara Davidson, "Open Land: Getting Back to the Communal Garden," Harper's Magazine 240 (June 1970):95.

57. Nick Stinnett and Craig Wayne Birdsong, The Family and Alternate Life Styles (Chicago: Nelson-Hall, 1978), p. 108.

58. Hal D. Sears, "Alcander Longley, Missouri Communist: A History of Reunion Community and a Study of the Constitutions of Reunion and Friendship," Bulletin of the Missouri Historical Society 25 (January 1969):130.

59. "Additional Facts Anent Ruskin Co-operative Association." Ms. in the Robert Carlton Brown Collection, Illinois Historical Survey Library, University of Illinois.

60. Isaac Broome, The Last Days of the Ruskin Co-operative Association (Chicago: Charles H. Kerr, 1902), pp. 107ff.

61. Ibid., p. 115.

62. Ibid., p. 131.

63. L. S. Everett, An Exposure of the Principles of the Free Enquirers (Boston: Benjamin B. Mussey, 1831), p. 31.

64. Hutchinson News Herald, August 21, 1950.

65. Garrett R. Carpenter, "Silkville: A Kansas Attempt in the History of Fourierist Utopias, 1869-1892," Emporia State Research Studies 3 (December 1954):26.

66. Jacob Beilhart, Very Personal (Ingleside, Ill. : Spirit Fruit Society, 1908), p. 13.

67. Jacob Beilhart, "Spirit's Voice Comes to You," Spirit's Voice 5 (April 1905).

68. Quoted in Robert S. Fogarty and H. Roger Grant, "Free Love in Ohio: Jacob Beilhart and the Spirit Fruit Colony," Ohio History 89 (Spring 1980):214.

69. Joyce Gardner, "Cold Mountain Farm," The Modern Utopian 2 (July/August, 1908):6.

Part III

Sexuality in Perspective

Why would an individual want to join a utopian community? There are many reasons, but the need for intimacy is certainly one of the more important reasons. Social psychologists have long known that one of the fundamental needs of all people is the need to establish intimate relationships. We are social creatures not only in the sense that we are formed by our social relationships, but also in the sense that we only find fulfillment as we engage in meaningful relationships with others. Isolated from other people, we tend to become something less than fulfilled humans. John Steinbeck once wrote that after living in the mountains alone for eight months, he noted that he had stopped whistling, stopped talking to his dogs, and stopped having any feelings other than simple pain and pleasure. The experience made him realize that we can only enjoy the full range of human emotions through interacting with other people.

How did the utopians manifest their need for intimacy? How did their need for intimacy relate to their sexual practices? What do their experiences contribute to our understanding of sexuality? These are some of the questions that we will explore in the final chapter.

8. SEXUALITY AND INTIMACY

In contrast to Freud, some social psychologists have argued that sex does not have biological primacy as a motivating factor for humans. Marlowe points out, for example, that the fact that there are healthy celibates shows that the sexual motive is learned behavior to a large extent. [1] Along somewhat different lines, Fromm has also asserted that Freud was in error. [2] Human love, Fromm argues, does not reflect the sexual instinct; rather, sexual desire reflects the human need for love and union. In other words, the need for union, for intimacy, has primacy over sex.

We agree that intimacy is a more fundamental need than the need for sex. The evidence from the utopian communities supports this argument, as we shall detail below. The evidence also suggests that humans have a need for erotic intimacy, though that intimacy can be gained in ways other than through sexual relationships.

THE THIRST FOR INTIMACY

Times of rapid social change are times of disruption of relationships. Our need for intimacy is intensified in such times. Since the utopian communities proliferated during times of rapid change, we would expect the need for intimacy to be not only a motivating factor but also a very salient aspect of the experience of members. The evidence supports this expectation. The utopian writings are filled with expressions of intimacy desired, sought and, frequently, found.

Expressions of Intimacy

There were a number of ways in which the utopians expressed the fact that they had sought and found intimate

214

relationships in their communities. One was their percep-
tion of the unity of their groups. As Cooley pointed out in
his discussion of intimate relationships, one of the characteristics of such relationships is a "certain fusion of indi-
vidualities in a common whole, so that one's very self, for
many purposes at least, is the common life and purpose of
the group. Perhaps the simplest way of describing this
wholeness is by saying that it is a 'we.'" [3] If intimate
relationships prevail in a group, there is a sense of oneness. It is natural to speak of "we" rather than of "I" and
"they."

Thus, a member of Brook Farm wrote to a friend
about the "inspiring" and "ennobling" experience which she
had at the community: "Whenever we meet, we breathe the
spirit of universal unity; we assemble, as it were, around
the altar of unity, and this gives a tone to all our commun-
ings." [4] Father Rapp wrote that his community was one
in which the members

> are so closely united by the endearing ties of
> friendship, confidence and love, that one heart
> beats in all, and their common industry provides
> for all. Here, the members kindly assist each
> other, in difficulty and danger, and share with
> each other, the enjoyments, and the misfortunes
> of life; one lives in the breast of another, and
> forgets himself; all their undertakings are influ-
> enced by a social spirit, glowing with noble energy,
> and generous feeling, and pressing forward to the
> haven of their mutual prosperity. [5]

And a Shaker wrote that although he had forsaken all for the
sake of the gospel, he had "received an hundred fold of heavenly blessings and gospel union, with parents and elders,
brethren and sisters, which I would not exchange for all the
glory, riches and honors of this world." [6]

Unity is necessary, but not sufficient for creating intimacy. Unity can result from coercion as well as be an
outgrowth of voluntary association. But as the above quotes
indicate, the unity created in the utopian communities
emerged in a context of strong and positive feelings. Thus,
a second expression of intimacy was the love and warmth
which members felt for each other, a point noted by visitors
as well as by the members themselves.

Members frequently wrote about the depth of their love and the tenderness of their feelings for each other. A woman who lived at Brook Farm when she was sixteen recalled the experience with a sense of deep gratification. She was sensitive to the fact that recollections can take on a very different cast from the original experience:

> Perhaps my recollections of Brook Farm are tinted by the rose-colored optimism of sixteen, but as I have grown old, and, looking back to the general standard of half a century ago, have compared the lives at Brook Farm with the most useful ones of these days, I am more and more convinced that my estimates are true, that there was very much "sweetness and light" there--a light too bright for most people at that time to bear. [7]

People at other communities also reported experiences of love and warmth and acceptance. William Pelham arrived in New Harmony when he was in his mid-sixties. He wrote his son that he intended to spend the rest of his life in that "abode of peace and quietness." He found nothing there to disappoint him, he said. On the contrary, he was accepted regardless of his opinions on various matters and had already become close friends with a number of men in the community. In fact, after being in the community for only three weeks, he was regarded as an "old inhabitant," with numerous friends and acquaintances. [8] A woman who joined the Brotherhood of the New Life wrote that she loved all of the others with a love that was "pure, and high, and holy," a love that was not like the "old way" of outsiders, but that was a "tender love" and a "nearness" unlike anything she had ever experienced before. [9] A man from Ruskin claimed that he and his wife suffered financial loss when the community dissolved. But the social loss was far greater than the financial, for never in their lives had the two of them experienced the "full and satisfying friendships" that they had known in the community. [10]

Many outsiders corroborated the reports of members. Visitors to the communities were frequently impressed by the obvious warmth and love that pervaded relationships. A visitor to Ephrata in the middle of the eighteenth century observed that the brethren lived "in great love" for each other, always calling each other by their proper name, kissing when they met, and washing each other's feet. [11] A man who visited the Shakers in 1829 pointed out that the members enlivened the "dullness" of celibacy by the "amenity of their intercourse with each other":

> And this intercourse is, indeed, much less re-stricted than is generally supposed. A stranger may not intermeddle with those affectionate friend-ships and pure platonic enjoyments that may spring up under what the world, perhaps falsely, calls an overwhelming obstacle to earthly happiness. The union of these people, their uniform kindness to each other, and the singularly benevolent and tender expression of their countenances, speak a stronger language than their professions. [12]

A visitor to the North American Phalanx was similarly im-pressed, more impressed than he expected to be as he ad-mits in a letter to the New York Tribune:

> There are fewer odd characters among them than I expected to see; generally there was much simplic-ity and self-containedness; they seem to care very little--too little--for appearances, or what the world outside thought of them, and greatly to love one another. They are, so far as I could learn, strongly attached to the Phalanx, feel confident it is the right way to live, have enjoyed it, and thus far have realized their hopes in joining it: "I wouldn't leave for worlds"--"couldn't live, it seems to me, in any other way;" "It is like the opening of heaven compared to what life was like before I came here," I heard from different indi-viduals. [13]

Finally, a visitor to Point Loma noted that the entire com-munity seemed to have an "atmosphere of loving kindness and gentleness." Even in the school room, he noted, there was a "wondrous bond of sweet sympathy between teacher and pupil as to impress itself upon the most casual observer." [14]

A third way that the utopians expressed their intimacy was through the use of familial imagery in describing their group. The family is one of the most intimate of all social groups. In the view of many of the utopians, the community itself had become a family to them. Familial imagery was used in the ideological writings and by members to describe their experiences in the communities.

Familial imagery was one of four kinds--family, home, parent-child relations, and brother-sister relations. Sometimes the utopians simply referred to their groups as a family. In the larger Shaker communities, the members were divided into distinct, largely self-sufficient subgroups. They called the subgroup a family. Thousands of our members, wrote one Shaker, live together as large families of thirty, forty, or sixty or more. And a number of those families "form societies, and live in peace and harmony, bound together by no other bond than that of love." [15] The Oneidans also stressed the fact that they formed a family. The tie that bound them, as Noyes put it, was "as permanent and sacred" as that of marriage. Moreover, he wrote, they would receive no members "who do not give heart and hand to the family interest for life and forever." [16] The community song of Oneida claimed that they formed "one family relation." This relation was a superior one, as one piece of literature pointed out. For in society at large, families have narrow boundaries and special interests. "We simply take away the limitations which instinct and ignorance set up for the inclosure of small families, and let the family sentiment and feeling out so as to extend over a large circle; and the result is a Community of fifty families, with the combined affection of them all dissolved in one." [17]

The family as a symbol of the community is also common in modern communes. In spite of the fact that some of them disavow permanent commitment in intimate relations, Zablocki found an intense need for intimacy in the 120 American communes he studied. That need, he noted, found expression in the use of the image of the family in their ideologies. A difference in modern communes from the earlier ones is that they have sought to gain the intimacy of family life without the restrictions of that life. That is, commune members have desired intimate relations but not the responsibilities of legal marriage. They have tried to use "voluntaristic structure to recreate family without nuclear dependence." [18] Their use of the image of the family, therefore, is different from that of previous utopians. But it still expresses the same need for intimacy.

Some members both in the nineteenth and twentieth century communes have used the family image to describe their experiences in the communities. For example, a member wrote of relationships in the Union Colony of Colorado in the following terms: "To a considerable extent people have that regard for each other that is found in the family, and

there is a tender concern for each other's welfare, while
there is charity for defects and short-comings ... bitterness
and slander are little known." [19] To the extent that the
family image was used in the ideology, we would expect
members to use it to describe their experiences. But members who wrote about their lives in the communities many
years after the communities had dissolved also used the
image. A former Brook Farmer recalled the relations of
the various residents: "We seem to have been one harmonious family. There may have been jealousies and misunder-
standings, but they were never allowed to appear on the surface and must have soon vanished in the cheerful, sunny atmosphere that prevailed." [20] A former member of Hopedale wrote that the "general kindly feeling" that prevailed in
the community made it "like one large family." [21]

Obviously, all these remarks about the family life of
the communities refer to the ideal family. Real families
are not as trouble-free and supportive and love-filled as the
utopians described their "families." As we shall see below,
the utopian communities were not as ideal as these remarks
indicate either. The point here is not that the utopians
actually achieved an ideal intimacy in their relationships
with each other, but that they did, for a time at least, find
satisfying intimate relationships. They expressed the extent
of their satisfaction, and undoubtedly at the same time the
extent of their dissatisfaction with relationships in the society
at large, by employing the image of the ideal family.

A second image employed was that of "home." At
Oneida, they sang about the community as their home. The
Shakers also sang about their communities as home, as well
illustrated by the hymn, Sweet Home, written in 1829:

> Midst a world fill'd with sorrow vice folly & crime
> And with mis'ry replete in each nation and clime
> How sweet to the soul that in sorrow did roam
> To find with believers a sweet tranquil home
>   Home, Home, Sweet, Sweet home
> The Heart broken wand'rer may find here a
>   home. [22]

Another line of the hymn states that "There's no place on
earth like a true Shaker home." Similarly, a member of
Brook Farm wrote to his father that he felt more at home
in the community than anyplace else. He had found, at least
for the moment, his "fit place." [23]

A third image, employed particularly by the Shakers, was that of parent and child. As Foster points out, Shaker hymns "speak, over and over again, of Mother (Ann Lee's) love for her loyal children and of her children's love for Mother and for each other." [24] As common "children" of Mother Ann Lee, the Shakers were bound together into one family and one home. The Shakers also referred to their early leaders as their "first spiritual parents." Those parents, as one sister said, were even better to their children than typical parents in the larger society:

> Their care and attention over all whom they accepted was constant, affectionate, and as much in advance of the selfish relations of the world that they were in truth parents in the Lord. Day and night they watched and prayed that the protection of our Heavenly Father might be upon the whole household of faith. As it was toward themselves, they anxiously sought that it might be to others: the way of life and salvation. [25]

The fourth image was that of brother and sister. For the Shakers, this image followed naturally from the above-- they were brothers and sisters because their common mother was Ann Lee. Consequently, they sang in their hymns of their brotherly and sisterly love for each other. Indeed, in one well-known hymn, they contrasted their love for their "gospel relations" with their disdain for their blood relations:

> My gospel relations are dearer to me
> Than all the flesh kindred that ever I see:
> So good and so pretty, so cleaver they feel;
> To see them & love them increases my zeal,
> O how pretty they look!
> How pretty they look!
> How cleaver they feel!
> My brethren & sisters, wherever they be
> I always can feel them a treasure to me;
> So good and so pretty, so cleaver they feel,
> To see them & love them increases my zeal.
> O how pretty they look!
> How pretty they look!
> How cleaver they feel!...
> Of all the relations that ever I see
> My old fleshly kindred are furthest from me,
> So bad and so ugly, so hateful they feel
> To see them and hate them increases my zeal.

O how ugly they look!
How ugly they look!
How nasty they feel! [26]

One brother, who had been a Shaker for nearly 44 years,
wrote about his experiences as though he had the hymn in
mind. He had found peace and "solid rest" in the gospel of
Ann Lee, he said. Moreover: "I have a spiritual relation
of Elders, Brethren and Sisters, who are dearer to me than
any of my natural kindred ever were." [27]

Members of other religious communities also found
the brother-sister image a natural one because of their common faith in a heavenly parent. For instance, in one of his
pastoral letters, Father Rapp pointed out that his followers
were brethren over whom "God constantly keeps his eye fixed,
so that he tests each member's works and actions, and
through the brotherly spirit he acts in a motherly manner,
while in the anxiety of conscience he acts as father." [28]
In some communities, including some modern communes, the
brother-sister image was reinforced by members calling
each other Brother and Sister.

Male-Female Intimacy

As the above suggests, the utopians were concerned
to establish intimacy between males and females, and not
merely between those of the same sex. The celibates as
well as the non-celibates recognized the need for intersexual
intimacy of some sort. As we noted in our discussion of the
ideologies of the celibates, they typically affirmed the male-
female nature of God, which meant that living creatures are
incomplete without both the male and the female element.
Neither a man nor a woman is complete within himself or
herself. Each needs the other in an intimate relationship.

Thus, in spite of their morbid view of sex, the Shakers fully admitted the need of male-female intimacy. As one
of the brothers expressed it to Fredrika Bremer, who visited
the Shakers in the mid-nineteenth century, the Shakers were
quite different from Catholic monks and nuns because the latter sought perfection through separation of the sexes, while
"we, on the contrary, maintain that it is only through this
spiritual union between man and woman that the perfected
human being can be produced." [29] Ms. Bremer asked him
if that meant a "spiritual marriage." He replied that the

Shakers did not call it marriage. They only asserted that
men and women cannot become perfect human beings except
through "reciprocal spiritual union and daily intercourse,
conformably with the intention of God, whereby they aid each
other in the attainment of a perfect life." [30] Another visit-
or to the Shakers was told that the relations between the
sexes was one of "the most intimate and delightful friend-
ship--friendship through all its grades and varieties of natural affinities; an experience unspeakably more sweet and
deep and satisfactory than any furnished by the married
state." [31] And a Shaker sister similarly praised the close
intersexual relationships achieved in the community:

> How beautiful is the social relation formed between
> the male and female among Believers, where the
> inferior passions are kept in subordination to high-
> er law! How true the manifestation of love in the
> sphere of daily duties, where the claims of both
> brethren and sisters are regarded with equal re-
> spect; and as co-workers in a noble cause, each
> unselfishly toils for the good of the whole. [32]

In none of the celibate communities was there a denial
of the importance of male-female intimacy. A Rappite book
told women to remember that they were made to be "man's
reasonable companion." Women were created not to satisfy
man's passion but "to assist him in the toils of life, to
soothe him with thy tenderness." [33] At Ephrata the brothers and sisters would invite each other to their respective
love-feasts to share the intimacy of the ritual. Thomas
Lake Harris urged his followers to find their heavenly counterparts of the opposite sex and enter into full, passionate
relationships with those counterparts.

Of course, the non-celibates also recognized the importance of male-female intimacy. Indeed, some of them
gloried in the fact that relations between the sexes were more
open in their communities than they were in the larger society. Robert Dale Owen, recalling his days at New Harmony,
said that his life there was happy and satisfying. [34] A
good part of the reason for that happiness, he wrote, was
the "free and simple" relationships that existed between
males and females. They called each other by their Christian names, strolled in the moonlight in groups and sometimes in pairs, and spoke and acted like brothers and sisters. Similarly, James Burrill responded to a letter from
his father expressing a measure of concern about the happen-

ings at Brook Farm that the young people there were all "innocent brothers and sisters" in the sight of God. They were able to join hands in a ring dance and hold hands in the moonlight. That was not shameful, he reassuringly told his father, as long as their spirits were pure. And he was grateful to God for the privilege of such experiences with the opposite sex. [35]

In the midst of a prudish society, the nineteenth-century non-celibates would find some of their practices misinterpreted and labeled as licentious. Nevertheless, they found their new patterns of male-female interaction too gratifying to conform to the norms of the larger society. At Oneida, for example, they said that they found working together an inspiration. They also felt aroused to

> new earnestness to favor the mingling of the sexes in labor. We find that the spirit of the world is deadly opposed to this innovation, and would make it very easy to slip back into the old routine of separate employments for men and women. But the leaven of heavenly principles about labor resists ... this backward tendency.... We believe that the great secret of securing enthusiasm in labor and producing a free, healthy, social equilibrium is contained in the proposition, "loving companionship and labor, and especially the mingling of the sexes, makes labor attractive." [36]

MECHANISMS OF INTIMACY

If both the celibates and non-celibates expressed a need for intimacy, including male-female intimacy, how did they go about achieving that intimacy? Clearly, intimacy does not automatically result merely from people interacting in a group. Even if the group is largely isolated from outsiders, the members, as we have seen, are often in a state of social disarray, suspicious and tense and fighting with each other rather than experiencing intimacy. But the utopians had a variety of mechanisms for creating intimacy. One is suggested by the above quote from Oneida--shared work experiences. We also noted earlier the statement by a member of a modern commune that shared tasks may be the best way to create unity in a group. In addition to shared experiences, such as work, the utopians attempted to create intimacy through shared ideologies and values and through an emphasis on the differences between the community and the outside world.

Shared Experiences

Not all of the utopians agreed that shared work is an appropriate way to create intimacy, at least intimacy between the sexes. The Shakers, for instance, had a sexual division of labor. Segregating the sexes for work was a way of minimizing the possibility of erotic interaction. But all groups provided some form of shared experiences, including shared experiences between the sexes. Many had communal meetings to discuss business affairs or ideological matters. The Shakers had union meetings at which rows of males would sit (at a respectable distance) across from rows of females. Each brother would converse with the sister directly across from him. Sometimes they would turn the meetings into communal singing rather than conversation. Many groups had worship services at which all members were expected to be present. We use "worship" here in the broadest sense; in some modern communes, the members gathered regularly in the early morning to chant and meditate.

One common experience in groups was the communal meal. The common meal includes both communal dining and the "love feasts" of some religious groups such as Amana and Ephrata. Love feasts were basically religious meals that were held at regular intervals. Communal dining occurred in some communities at every meal and in some only at the evening meal. A woman who had been a member of Brook Farm recalled the communal meals as the "most delightful times for talk, humor, wit, and the interchange of pleasant nonsense." [37] At Morning Star, a member reported, the communal meal was a "source of warmth and friendship that was, for most of us, our first experience in close communal living. We had the advantages of a big family and the privacy of our own shelters when needed." [38]

A number of the communities also practiced certain rituals designed to create intimacy. One was foot-washing, which a few of the religious groups practiced. A visitor to Ephrata in the mid-nineteenth century described the ritual, which took place in conjunction with the observance of the Lord's Supper. [39] Each sex, he noted, performed the ritual on others of the same sex. The ritual began when some members brought in tubs of lukewarm water. Members on the front bench then took off their shoes and stockings. A man on the men's side of the church and a woman on the women's side then washed the feet of each member in turn. The one who washed the feet was followed by another with a long towel, who dried the feet that had been washed. When all of the members' feet on the front benches had been washed, they got up and gave way to another group. During the time of foot-washing, the minister or another leader read portions of Scripture or spoke about the meaning of the ritual.

A second kind of ritual was holding hands. At Brook Farm, they worshipped in the woods and following the worship service the minister had them all hold hands and form a circle to symbolize their unity. At Morning Star, they held hands silently before their meal. As one member said, "some very nice things happened through this, a very warm feeling, becoming part." [40]

A third ritual was the kiss. Among some of the religious communities, a "brotherly" or "sisterly" kiss was observed between members of the same sex. A visitor to the Canterbury, New Hampshire Shaker community described one of the "symbolic games" used by the Shakers to teach the young girls to love each other, a game that included kissing. The game began with the girls placing themselves in a wide circle.

> They then began little verses, which, though I can not give literally accurate, were in substance as follows:
> Must I here alone be standing,
> Having none that I can love;
> Having none my friend to be,
> None who will grow fond of me?
> On this each little girl approached the one nearest to her, and, taking each other's hands, they laid them upon their hearts and sung
> Nay, my sister, come thou nearer,
> And I will to thee be dearer,
> Be to thee a faithful friend;
> I will share with thee thy sadness;
> Thou shalt share with me my gladness!
> With this the children all took hold of hands, and slowly moving round in a circle, repeated the while these last words, or something like them; and in so

doing, approaching nearer and nearer together, wove their arms round each other like a garland of flowers, then sunk upon their knees, singing the while a hymn, the first verse of which was

Heavenly Father, look down in mercy
On this little flock,
United in thy name!
Give us of thy Holy Spirit, etc.

While singing this hymn, and while still upon their knees, the children all kissed each other, after which they rose up and separated. [41]

The visitor was so moved by the scene, and the thought of the "difference in the spirit of this game to the bitter reality of many a solitary existence in the great community of the world," that she wept.

There were other practices in addition to those named. At Hopedale, for example, they communally celebrated each member's birthday. Whatever the practice, however, all had the same aim of generating a sense of intimacy, a loving unity like that of an ideal family.

Shared Ideologies and Values

We have discussed in detail the ideologies of the various groups. Ideally, each member was to subscribe fully to the ideology. For to the extent that members of a utopian community share an ideology, they share a set of values and are likely to develop intimate relationships (recall the problems that developed at some communities because of ideological differences). Wittingly or unwittingly the various groups appeared to recognize the importance of ideological conformity, for all used various means, from instruction to songs to group indoctrination sessions, to bring about ideological consensus.

Ideological consensus meant that the members realized that they shared certain interests and sentiments, as a number of them pointed out. A Shaker praised his group as one in which a new social order had been created, with people living together in love and comprising a "social unity of all interests." [42] Ralph Waldo Emerson wrote of Brook Farm (with which he was intimately acquainted, though not a member) that it was a "close union" bound together by a "sentiment which all shared, some of them hotly shared, of the honesty of a life of labor and of the beauty of a life of humanity. " [43] Shared beliefs helped create the intimacy that the utopians, like all of us, desired and needed.

Differences with Outsiders

The utopians were very conscious of their differences with outsiders, and frequently pointed out those differences, which helped them feel a stronger bond with each other. For example, at the New Age commune in New Mexico, Veysey found that the members distinguished sharply between their group and the "old civilization" and advocated as much detachment as possible. There was a "razor-sharp" sense of "we" and "they," and the boundary between the two was the edge of the ranch on which the commune was located. [44] Other than for business or necessary trips outside, members were expected to remain on the ranch, away from outsider influences.

Virtually all groups stressed their differences with outsiders, though they varied in the extent to which they tried to maintain detachment. In some cases, their detachment was a matter of desire rather than of rule. A member of Llano, for instance, pointed out that many people in the outside world lived in loneliness and isolation. But at Llano, there was a full social life. "Social intercourse is a constant joy. Everyone speaks to everyone else. There are no strangers. " [45] In other words, the differences with outsiders are such that members would hardly care to venture outside very often. A similar point was made by a woman who was at Brook Farm. In the larger society, she said, people refrained from expressing "fraternal good-will" towards each other because of the uncertainties of the future and the nature of competitive society. But at Brook Farm, "having common interests," the members could "afford to love our neighbor as ourselves. " [46] Such differences, she noted, were the basis for the lasting and happy impression left on all members at Brook Farm.

Intimacy--Achieved or Elusive?

The portrait we have painted so far is one of glorious achievement. Were the utopians really that successful? Did they achieve the intimacy they sought? Or was that intimacy elusive even in utopia? The answer must be that some

achieved it and some did not.   In some communities, the
bulk of the members appear to have established meaningful
intimate relationships with others.   In other communities,
the membership was fragmented from beginning to end.   And
in some, a good beginning gave way to disintegration and dissolution of the group.

The Shakers and Brook Farm illustrate the first type,
the communities where the bulk of members achieved intimacy.   But there were some members who never meshed
with the group, or who slowly dislodged for some reason or
other.   One Shaker writer acknowledged that, while his
Shaker home was the purest place on earth, it was not always what they wished it to be "in regard to our relations
and intercourse together."   Each member could live "in a
peaceful, Christian element, or in a state of discord and
inharmony." [47]   And in contrast to the glowing affirmations
of intimacy noted above, one observer of Brook Farm claimed
that it was not a community: "it is merely an aggregation
of persons, and lacks that oneness of spirit, which is probably needful to make it of deep and lasting value to mankind." [48]

Ora et Labora, a German Methodist utopian group in
Michigan, illustrates the second type, a community in which
conflict and fragmentation occurred from beginning to end.
Early problems deve. oped over the neglect of some original
subscribers to pay the first installment of their stock pur-
chase.   There was also conflict over private versus collective interests.   The founder noted, unhappily, that "Saturday
was devoted to the individual interest.   There was lively and
enthusiastic work done on that day." [49]   But on other days,
production was slack and the members spent a good deal of
time discussing community affairs rather than working for
the common good.   Finally, there was conflict between the
craftsmen and the farmers, between those already there and
newcomers who found frontier life hard to adjust to, and
among various members over policy.   The community lasted
about five years (1862-1868), all of which were marked by
conflict and bitterness of various kinds.

The third type of community, which began well but
disintegrated, is illustrated by New Harmony and by the modern commune, Cold Mountain Farm.   We have noted a number of reports of gratifying relationships at New Harmony.
But the community quickly deteriorated when Robert Owen
left for a period of time.   One man declared that the people
never had developed intimate relations:

> The people of this town continued strangers to each
> other in spite of all their meetings, their balls,
> their concerts, and their so frequent occasions of
> congregating in the Hall, and all their pretence of
> co-operation. From the time I first set my feet
> within this little town ... I think there is not with-
> in the range of my observations during my former
> travels, any other town in the United States where
> the same number of persons living together within
> such a compass ... were so perfectly strangers,
> and void of all personal intimacy with each other's
> feelings, views, situations, and (very generally)
> names. [50]

The author of the above statement was considered a trouble-
maker by most people in New Harmony. His statement is
undoubtedly an overstatement. Nonetheless, it is true that
the same community that some found deeply satisfying was
found by others to be deeply disturbing. Tension and conflict were rife in New Harmony after the initial honeymoon
period. Similarly, at Cold Mountain Farm, there was initially "an incredible feeling of warmth, of family." [51] But as
the group grew, the closeness somehow vanished and tensions
and disruptions set in and at times the group became "un-
bearable."

Visitors as well as members noted the lack of intimacy, the tension and conflict in many of the communities.
There were disputes about policy and ideology. There was
personality conflict. There were tensions from the difficulties of carving out a new community in lonely country. Many
of the communities ultimately collapsed from internal dissension more than from external pressures or challenges. One
group called their community Kaweah, an Indian name meaning "here we rest." For many of the utopians, their community turned out to be a place of rest, of peace, of meaningful relationships. For many others, the experience only
proved how elusive satisfying relationships can be. For
them, there was no rest.

THE SEARCH FOR EROTIC INTIMACY

One of the fascinating aspects of the utopian groups
was the obvious search for erotic intimacy that occurred in
the celibate as well as the noncelibate groups. The search
for erotic intimacy was manifested in the imagery used in the
groups as well as in certain practices.

Erotic Imagery

As pointed out in chapter 4, the nineteenth-century celibates were influenced by Jacob Boehme, who taught the bisexual nature of God and of God's first creation, Adam. Interestingly, the doctrine not only justified celibacy but also paved the way for erotic imagery. For on the one hand, if Adam was created as a bisexual being, he, like God, had no need of sexual relationships. He was complete within himself. But Adam sinned, and the result is that the human race is not bisexual. Humans cannot be the complete, male-female creatures they were meant to be until the resurrection.

However there is a way, according to Boehme, to approximate the ideal of bisexuality. Celibacy is part of the way. The other part is to enter into union with the heavenly Sophia. Sophia is the feminine Greek word for wisdom; it is sometimes personified in the New Testament to mean God or Christ. Thus, the imagery of marriage is frequently used to denote the relationship between humans and God (including Christ and Sophia). Accordingly, Beissel taught the Ephrataites that they could reunite their male and female natures through a relationship with the divine. He employed marital and erotic imagery along with his insistence on celibacy:

> Virgin Sophia will assume no male-property burning in the fire into her chaste embraces, and if you want to be called a consecrated favorite of her, you must first indispensably become a priest ... and if a virgin desired the title, to be the wife of the priest Jesus, she must first be a virgin in body and Spirit ... for the everlasting virginity doth disanull all separation whatsoever, in order that also might germinate the Godly union, which was lost by the apostasy. [52]

Thus, Beissel talked about women being married to Christ and men being married to Sophia.

The imagery of marriage was more than a simile for the relationship between God and humans. As one of his biographers notes, Beissel "revels in sexual imagery." [53] For example, he called Sophia the "constant lover of mankind" who "gives us the most endearing caresses" and engages us in "sweet intimacy." [54]

Similarly, the music of the Rappites expressed the ideal of wedlock with Sophia, a "noble bride" who generates ecstatic and erotic feelings:

> Sophia, from your glances rapture flows into my heart
> When a friendly love delights my soul;
> O the pure instincts your charm arouses in me;
> This flame feeds the blessed heavenly love.
>
> Beloved, let me experience the gentleness and faith if we were united,
> With your sweet caress many an anxious hour would flee,
> My wounds would be healed,
> Pure fire would be drawn to love.
>
> Your demeanor reveals that your heart treasures me;
> What joy, what rapture when you are close to me.
> If kings would offer me crowns instead of your love,
> I would cast them at their thrones,
> Since happiness is only when you are my own.
>
> Dip your brush into the rays of the sun to paint me your lovely picture.
> Your lips and cheeks scarlet,
> Should my mouth and heart be pressed thereon,
> My soul and spirit would be refreshed. [55]

In other writings, Sophia promised such things as a "kiss of love" to those who dedicated themselves to her through celibacy.

The imageries of marriage and of erotic behavior were also found in the writings of Thomas Lake Harris (see the detailed discussion in chapter 4) and of the prudish Shakers. The Shakers taught that they were married to Christ, but the relationship with the deceased founder, Ann Lee, was frequently couched in erotic terms. An old Shaker hymn tells of being "nourished from her breast." [56] In a revelation to one of her disciples, Mother Ann was said to have told her followers to come and enjoy her love, to "feast on this, my beloved." [57] Ann Lee herself, while she was alive, talked about "walking with Jesus as her Lord and Lover" and "described herself as his Bride." [58]

Thus, in the writings of the celibates, the sexual imagery is explicit. We could take a Freudian approach and find a great deal more imagery in the form of sexual symbolism. [59] We could, for instance, point out the sexual implications of the art and of the poetry of the celibates. At any rate, both implicitly and explicitly the celibates employed erotic imagery in their writings and their practices.

Erotic Experiences

As Victor points out, we can identify two aspects of sexual arousal. [60] There is a physiological sexual response that includes bodily changes such as male erection, female genital lubrication, and increased muscular tension. There is also a psychological erotic response, an emotional and attitudinal readiness for the physiological response. To what extent did the celibates have any experience of sexual arousal? There were, of course, the erotic experiences that were a violation of their codes of conduct, including masturbation, sexual intercourse, and such things as Beissel climbing into the room of one of the Ephrata sisters at night and caressing and "toying" with her body. [61] But such experiences were not typical. On the other hand, what of experiences generated by the imagery? That is, as they sang their hymns, read their literature, and contemplated their beliefs, did the erotic imagery result in any kind of erotic experience? There is not a great deal of evidence upon which to base an answer, but there are some indications that both physical and emotional sensations were experienced.

We have already pointed out the experiences of some of the leaders. Beissel, apart from his nocturnal visit to the sister, clearly reveled in his relationship with Sophia. Ann Lee spoke ardently of her life with Christ. Harris wrote passionately about his exquisite experiences with his heavenly counterpart, Lily, with whom he had two children. But ordinary members also had erotic experiences. A visitor to Ephrata discussed with an old monk the notion that the divine Sophia would ultimately descend into each Christian: "We wasted nearly two hours in listening to the idle prate of the old monk, who was happy to entertain us on this subject, and particularly enraptured at the idea, that the Sophia would descend into him." [62]

Similarly, a visitor to the Shakers told of speaking with one sister, Antoinette, who related to him the fact that "she had sweet and tender passages of love with many who were gone away out of sight--the beings whom we should call the dead." [63] The writer said that he knew of nothing other to call the experience than a wedlock of the soul. Another Shaker sister wrote a poem telling of her love for God and His works. But it was more than love that she felt: "I fill with ecstasy, and pant amid the palpitations of my heart." [64]

One of Harris' followers reported her experiences with her counterpart in considerable detail. [65] She felt strange sensations in her arms, as though the arms, previously empty, were being filled with something. When her counterpart would come to her, she said, there was a sensation of a hair on her hand; even thinking about her counterpart caused her to have chills all over her body. On one occasion, her experience with her counterpart was like having someone inside her and all over her, especially around her mouth and tongue. On another occasion, her counterpart came to her through the "generative organs." She thought that the experience was like sexual intercourse, "only infinitely more so," for every cell of her entire body had entered into total union with every cell of her counterpart.

Finally, we can assume that those who wrote the hymns and the literature were having some kind of erotic experience and not merely employing useful metaphors and similes. As Kring says of the many Rappite hymns written in honor of Sophia, they depict the heavenly Sophia as one who takes on "a warmth and ardor that becomes a lover." [66] We do not know how many of the celibates had erotic experiences with their divine lovers, but it is clear that some did and all could in view of the erotic imagery used.

Erotic Intimacy as a Basic Need

What are the implications of erotic imagery and erotic experiences among the celibates? First, we should note that we agree with the assertion that sexual motives are a form of learned behavior and that celibates can be healthy and content. As we have seen, some of the members of celibate communities left to pursue a sexual relationship, but turnover was not a serious problem and those who stayed in the communities wrote about their deep satisfaction with their lives. Second, we agree with Fromm that intimacy has primacy over sex. As Kieffer points out, "the quest for in-

timacy is one of the oldest themes of western civilization. " [67] Americans are, and always have been, engaged
in a serious search for intimate relationships. We all need
intimacy, which is a more fundamental need than a sexual
relationship. Intimate relationships enable us to develop and
to maintain a sense of our own identity and a feeling of
stability. [68] But there are different kinds of intimate relationships, including friends, lovers, spouses, and siblings:

> Friends are intimates insofar as they engage in all
> intimate behaviors except sexually related ones.
> Lovers are intimates insofar as they engage in
> sexually related intimate behaviors; they may be
> engaging in other intimate behaviors as well.
> Spouses are intimates insofar as they (by having
> become officially related) share a common future
> of potential intimate behaviors, though they may
> not be currently engaging in many intimate be-
> haviors. Siblings are intimates insofar as they
> (by having been officially related) share a common
> past of intimate behaviors, though they too may
> not be currently engaging in many intimate be-
> haviors. [69]

Thus, we can have both erotic and non-erotic intimate relationships.

Interestingly, the celibates as well as the non-celibates
had both kinds of intimate relationships. The celibates as
well as the non-celibates created communities in which they
experienced every kind of intimacy. Intimate relations between members were defined in terms of kinship and friendship. The relationship with the Divine (including Sophia) was
defined in erotic terms in the celibate communities. The
experiences of the celibates support the notion that intimacy
is a more basic need than is a sexual relationship. At the
same time, however, their experiences suggest that we have
a basic need for erotic as well as non-erotic intimacy.
There seems to be no other ready explanation for the fact
that the celibates were openly involved in eroticism. Of
course, erotic intimacy can be achieved through sexual relationships. Some members of modern communes have made
the point that they sought intimacy by the mechanism of free
sexual access among all members. But as the celibates
demonstrated, erotic intimacy can also be found in a relationship with the Divine or even with a non-living human
(Harris' counterparts and the Shakers' experiences with de-

ceased brethren and sisters). The celibates enjoyed their erotic as well as other kinds of intimacy. They managed to define the fulfillment of their erotic needs in terms other than that of sexual relationships. The experiences of the celibates lend support to the argument that we all have a need for erotic as well as non-erotic intimacy. Their experiences also demonstrate that erotic intimacy can be achieved without a sexual relationship.

Notes

1. Leigh Marlowe, Social Psychology (Boston: Holbrook, 1971), p. 151.

2. Erich Fromm, The Art of Loving (New York: Bantam Books, 1956), pp. 30ff.

3. Charles Horton Cooley, Social Organization (New York: Scribner's, 1915), p. 23.

4. Marianne Dwight, Letters from Brook Farm: 1844-1847, ed. Amy L. Reed (Poughkeepsie, N.Y.: Vassar College, 1928), p. 96.

5. George Rapp, Thoughts on the Destiny of Man (Harmony, Ind.: Harmony Society, 1824), p. 66.

6. "Testimony of Eliab Harlow," The Manifesto 15 (October 1885):220.

7. Ora Gannett Sedgwick, "A Girl of Sixteen at Brook Farm," Atlantic Monthly 85 (March 1900):398.

8. In Harlow Lindley, ed., Indiana as Seen by Early Travelers, Indiana Historical Collections, Vol. 3 (Indianapolis: Indian Historical Commission, 1916), pp. 373, 377.

9. In Herbert W. Schneider and George Lawton, A Prophet and a Pilgrim (New York: Columbia University Press, 1942), p. 521.

10. "Additional Facts Anent Ruskin Co-operative Association," ms. in the Robert Carlton Brown Collection, Illinois Historical Survey Library, University of Illinois.

11. In Felix Reichmann and Eugene E. Dollieds, "Ephrata as Seen by Contemporaries," The Pennsylvania German Folklore Society 17 (1952):72.

12. "The Shakers," Niles Register, September 19, 1829.

13. "Association," Letter to the Editor, New York Tribune, July 29, 1852.

14. John Hubert Greusel, " A Visit to Katherine Tingley," article published in the Detroit Free Press, reprinted by the Woman's Theosophical Propaganda League, 1907, p. 48.

15. John Dunlavy, Plain Evidence (Albany, N. Y.: Hoffman and White, 1834), p. 9.

16. Oneida Circular, February 6, 1865.

17. The Oneida Community: A Familiar Exposition of Its Ideas and Practical Life, in a Conversation with a Visitor (Wallingford, Conn.: n. p., 1865), p. 10.

18. Benjamin Zablocki, Alienation and Charisma (New York: Free Press, 1980), p. 352.

19. The Greeley Tribune, Nov. 16, 1871.

20. "A Girl's Recollections of Brook Farm School," Overland Monthly 72 (September 1918):239.

21. Hopedale Reminiscences (Hopedale: Hopedale School Press, n. d.), p. 31.

22. In Harold E. Cook, Shaker Music: A Manifestation of American Folk Culture (Lewisburg: Bucknell University Press, 1973), p. 48.

23. James Burrill Curtis, letter to his father, July 23, 1842, in the James Currill Curtis Letters collection, Illinois Historical Survey Library, University of Illinois.

24. Lawrence Foster, Religion and Sexuality (New York: Oxford University Press, 1981), p. 237.

25. Rachel Sampson, "In Remembrance of Our First Parents," The Manifesto 13 (February 1883):33.

26. In Edward Deming Andrews, The Gift to Be Simple: Dances and Rituals of the American Shakers (New York: Dover, 1940), p. 20.

27. "Testimony of Zipporah Oory," The Manifesto 17 (April 1887):93.

28. In Karl J. R. Arndt, A Documentary History of the Indiana Decade of the Harmony Society, 1814-1824, Vol. 1, 1814-1819 (Indianapolis: Indiana Historical Society, 1975), p. 98.

29. Fredrika Bremer, The Homes of the New World: Impressions of America, Vol. 1, trans. Mary Howitt (New York: Harper & Brothers, 1853), p. 563.

30. Ibid.

31. "The Shakers at New Lebanon," The Harbinger, August 21, 1847, p. 175.

32. Social Gathering: Dialogue Between Six Sisters of the North Family of Shakers, Mt. Lebanon, N.Y. (Albany: Weed, Parsons & Co., 1873), p. 14.

33. The Economy of Human Life (Allentaun, Penn.: J. Ehrenfried, 1814), p. 70.

34. Robert Dale Owen, Threading My Way: An Autobiography (New York: Augustus M. Kelley, 1967; 1st publ. 1874), p. 281.

35. James Burrill Curtis, letter to his father, August 1, 1842.

36. The Oneida Circular, October 8, 1853.

37. Sedgwick, "A Girl of Sixteen," p. 396.

38. Gay Leslie, "New Directions," in Home Free! (Occidental, Cal.: Friends of Morning Star Publications, 1978), p. 317.

39. Howard Pyle, "A Peculiar People," Harper's Magazine 74 (October 1859):777.

40. The Morning Star Scrapbook, 1973. Ms. in the collections of the University of California, Riverside, p. 80.

41. Bremer, Homes of the New World, Vol. 2, p. 575.

42. F. W. Evans, "Shakerism V. Owenism," Millennial Gazette, April 1, 1856, p. 8.

43. Ralph Waldo Emerson, "Historic Notes of Life and Letters in Massachusetts," Atlantic Monthly 52 (October 1883):543.

44. Laurence Veysey, The Communal Experience (New York: Harper & Row, 1973), p. 374.

45. Robert K. Williams, "Llano--A Social Success," The Western Comrade, February, 1917, p. 9.

46. Georgiana Bruce Kirby, Years of Experience: An Autobiographical Narrative (New York: G. P. Putnam's Sons, 1887), p. 175.

47. Odillon B. Elkins, "Our Home," The Manifesto 13 (April, 1883):84.

48. "Brook Farm," The Dial 4 (January 1844):354.

49. Carl Wittke, "Ora et Labora: A German Methodist Utopia," The Ohio Historical Quarterly 67 (April 1958):137.

50. Paul Brown, Twelve Months in New Harmony (Cincinnati, Ohio: Wm. Hill Woodward, 1827), p. 33.

51. Joyce Gardner, "Cold Mountain Farm," The Modern Utopian 2 (July/August 1968):4.

52. Johann Conrad Beissel, A Dissertation on Man's Fall (Ephrata, Penn.: n. p., 1765), p. 19.

53. Walter C. Klein, Johann Conrad Beissel: Mystic and Martinet (Philadelphia: University of Pennsylvania Press, 1942), p. 73.

54. Beissel, A Dissertation, p. 21.

55. In Hilda Adam Kring, The Harmonists (Metuchen, N. J.: Scarecrow Press, 1973), pp. 116-17.

56. Shaker Hymn Book (Westervelt, Ohio: n. p., 1833).

57. Marila Fairbanks, " A Bond of Love and Word of Comfort. " Ms. in the Shaker collection, Western Historical Society, 1842.

58. Foster, Religion and Sexuality, p. 28.

59. See Louis J. Kern, An Ordered Love (Chapel Hill: University of North Carolina Press, 1981), pp. 91-113.

60. Jeffrey S. Victor, Human Sexuality (Englewood Cliffs: Prentice-Hall, 1980), p. 125.

61. James E. Ernst, Ephrata: A History (Allentown, Penn. : The Pennsylvania German Folklore Society, 1963), p. 334.

62. Reichmann and Dollieds, Ephrata as Seen by Contemporaries, p. 154.

63. William Hepworth Dixon, New America (Philadelphia: J. B. Lippincott, 1867), p. 310.

64. L. S. Bowers, "Adoration," The Manifesto 24 (1894): 202-203.

65. Schneider and Lawton, A Prophet and a Pilgrim, pp. 523-32.

66. Kring, The Harmonists, p. 17.

67. C. Kieffer, "New Depths in Intimacy," in R. W. Libby and R. N. Whitehurst, eds. , Marriage and Alternatives (Glenview, Ill. : Scott, Foresman and Company, 1977), p. 267.

68. J. Askham, "Identity and Stability within the Marriage Relationship," Journal of Marriage and the Family 38 (1976):535-47.

69. Murray S. Davis, Intimate Relations (New York: The Free Press, 1973), p. xviii.

INDEX

Alcott, A. Bronson 64
Amana 33, 45, 57, 132, 158, 161, 163, 167-68, 170, 224
Ananda Cooperative Village 46
Anarchism 38-39, 43, 77-78, 130, 203-204
Arndt, Karl 171

Baumeler, Joseph 62, 63, 169
Beilhart, Jacob 125-26, 205
Beissel, Conrad 64, 101, 105, 108, 187, 189, 230, 232
Berger, Bennett 201
Bestor, Arthur 43
Bethel-Aurora 57-58, 157, 183
Birth control 113-14, 140
Bishop Hill 63-64, 183
Bliss, Nathaniel L. 50
Blue Mountain Ranch 78, 198-99
Boehme, Jacob 230
Bremer, Fredrika 221
Brisbane, Albert 42, 76
Brook Farm 70-71, 165, 191, 215, 216, 219, 223, 224, 225, 226, 227, 228
Brotherhood of the New Life 59, 216
Bruderhof 69, 169

Cabet, Etienne 36, 69, 169
Celibacy 18, 56-57, 74, 82, 125, 137, 150, 151, 153-54
Celibacy, and fulfillment 180-91
Celibacy, ideologies of 90-114, 162-63
Chapman, Eunice and James 186-87
Charisma see Leadership
Christ Communal Organization 67, 72, 167
Cold Mountain Farm 206, 228-29
Communia 174
Communism 34, 35, 36, 37, 42, 43, 44, 134-35
Complex Marriage 79-82, 193-98
Complex Marriage, ideology of

133-42
Confession 156-57
Conflict 24, 45, 74-75, 101, 186-87, 189-91, 197-206, 228-29
Cooley, Charles Horton 215
Coser, Lewis 56, 132

de Boissiere, Ernest V. 205
Dietsch, Andreas 128
Divorce 69
Doig, Ivan 43

Economy 32, 34, 38, 49
Education 163-64
Ellis, Havelock 196
Ellis, John B 193-94
Emerson, Ralph Waldo 226
Ephrata 33, 41, 62, 64, 66, 101, 105, 150, 151, 153-54, 158, 162, 182, 184, 187-90, 216, 222, 224, 232
Equality 36, 42, 47, 49, 113-14
Equality Colony 46

Family 24, 34, 35, 71-72, 112, 114, 131, 148, 217-21
Family, The 40
Farm, The 68, 123, 154
Father Divine 60, 103, 105, 114, 156, 161, 168
Foster, Lawrence 220
Fourier, Charles 37-38, 41, 76-77, 124, 127, 130-31, 149
Fourierism 37-38, 42, 43, 44, 46, 50, 70-71, 76-77, 149, 169, 217
Freehling, William H. 48
Free love 70, 71, 75-79, 122, 130, 203-206
Freud, Sigmund 4-5, 8, 9, 19, 214
Freud's theory of sexuality 22-24
Frey, William 45
Friendship Community 72-73, 159, 192
Fromm, Erich, 214, 233
Fruitlands 64